Praise for

Could It Really Be This Easy?

"*Could It Really Be This Easy?* is a must-read for every young person. This book, which is wonderfully written by Ted J. Peck, is based upon years of research and firsthand experience. It will help the reader identify a pathway for success that will bring a lifetime of joy, happiness, and prosperity. This inspiring book is a lasting gift or investment that will keep on giving throughout the entire life of the reader and will affect generations to come."
—Steven R. Shallenberger, CEO and
author of *Becoming Your Best*

"Great food for thought; straight from the heart!"
—Kevin Whitehead, CES educator

"Ted J. Peck has filled a void with *Could It Really Be This Easy?* It's like a needed talk with your grandpa that too often never happens. Ted presents the principles of happiness in a way that every teen can understand. Don't we all wish we would have learned these lessons in our youth? A great read to share with every teen."
—Lee Caldwell, executive director at Stillwater Academy

COULD
IT REALLY
BE THIS *EASY?*

COULD IT REALLY

BE THIS *EASY?*

THE ETERNAL EQUATION OF SUCCESS FOR TEENS

TED J. PECK

CFI
An imprint of Cedar Fort, Inc.
Springville, Utah

ISBN 13: 978-1-4621-1637-9

Published by CFI, an imprint of Cedar Fort, Inc.
2373 W. 700 S., Springville, UT 84663
Distributed by Cedar Fort, Inc., www.cedarfort.com

LIBRARY OF CONGRESS CATALOGING-IN-PUBLICATION DATA

Peck, Ted J., 1953- author.
Could it really be this easy? : the eternal equation of success for teens / Ted J. Peck.
    pages cm
ISBN 978-1-4621-1637-9 (alk. paper)
1. Mormon youth--Conduct of life. 2. Christian life--Mormon authors. 3. Church of Jesus Christ of Latter-day Saints--Doctrines. 4. Mormon Church--Doctrines. I. Title.

BX8643.Y6P43 2015
248.8'3088289332--dc23

                        2015006286

Cover design by Shawnda T. Craig
Cover design © 2015 Lyle Mortimer
Edited and typeset by Jessica B. Ellingson

Printed in the United States of America

10 9 8 7 6 5 4 3 2 1

Printed on acid-free paper

A conversation with my kids, grandkids, and all the other kids trying to figure out life.

$$\pi$$

This is for you: Madeline, Cameron, Carson, Alex, Zachary, Coleman, Lucas, Addison, Avery, Kendal, Caden, Caleb, and Taylor.

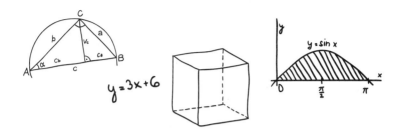

CONTENTS

CONTENTS

$$A = \begin{pmatrix} 2 & -1 \\ -3 & -2 \end{pmatrix} \qquad y = \sqrt{2x-1}$$

δ

INTRODUCTION

WHEN I FIRST started writing this book five years ago, I believed you could have a successful life here in America if you wanted it bad enough and were willing to work for it. After all, we're blessed to live in the greatest country in the world. But things have changed. I can hardly believe what's happened to America over the last few years—fewer jobs, higher education costs, and new laws about health care and marriage. I didn't see it coming, and I didn't believe it could happen so fast.

So in this changing world, is it still possible to get what you want from life? Yes. I believe it's possible because God is in charge. He wants you to have a successful life, and He's willing to help you get it. Being successful means you can create the life you want— but only if you want it bad enough and are willing to work for it.

Why do I believe God wants you to be successful? In the Book of Mormon, God repeatedly makes a simple promise: "Inasmuch as ye shall keep my commandments ye shall prosper in the land" (2 Nephi 1:20). The word *prosper* has many different meanings, but all those meanings have the word *better* in them—as in, when you prosper, your life is better. How much better is entirely up to you.

When I was young, I never took time to wonder how much better my life could be, and that was a big mistake. I don't want you making the same mistake, so let me show you what's possible.

Matthew 19:26 states, "With God all things are possible." Think about that. *All* means you can create the life you desire with God's help. This guarantee wasn't limited to people in Jesus's time. Even in difficult times like ours, all things really are possible—if you'll put your trust in God, follow His plan, and be careful and patient.

Economic conditions in our country may have changed, but God's promise hasn't. In this book I'll teach you how to create and enjoy a successful life. All you have to do is read it and use what's in it. How can I be so sure? I turned sixty-two this year. That may sound old to you, and it probably is, but all the experiences I've had during that time are a gold mine. I've learned a lot about life, and some of it I learned the hard way: by struggling in school, marrying young, doing different kinds of jobs, and making lots of decisions, both good and bad. Through it all, I was learning how to be successful in this life while preparing for the next one. I was learning how to trust God.

Over the past fifteen years, I've taught seminary for The Church of Jesus Christ of Latter-day Saints and served as bishop in my home ward and in a college campus singles ward. During this time, I've worked with many young people facing uncertain futures and struggling with important decisions. I've also watched my three children and thirteen grandchildren grow and face their own life choices. And being married to my childhood sweetheart for forty-four years has taught me things I never imagined I would learn.

Whew! It's been a wild ride. Now it's your turn.

In this book, I'll be drawing on the teachings of scripture, including the Bible, the Book of Mormon, the Doctrine and Covenants, and the Pearl of Great Price. If you don't already have copies of these scriptures, I encourage you to read or order them at www.lds.org/scriptures. All of them offer important teachings about how to be successful in this life and the next.

Let's get started. Your successful life is just waiting to be created.

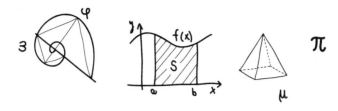

CHAPTER 1

WELCOME TO THE UNIVERSITY

WELCOME TO THE university here on Earth. Are you busy taking advantage of your once-in-a-lifetime experience? Each day represents a chance to learn, grow, and explore all the new and exciting opportunities life has to offer. I encourage you to enjoy each day during these years, because your excitement for life is a gift. As we age, the responsibilities of life often take over.

My wife and I married right out of high school and immediately started a family. Our new life together kept me busy, so I never took time to stop and think about life. I just got up, did what needed to be done, went to bed, got a little rest, and did it all over again the next day—and the next day, and the next.

This routine continued until one day I discovered that I had officially become old. I'm not sure how, because it happened so fast. But being old isn't all bad. Everything seems to slow down, and that gives you time to think. During one of those periods of thinking, I realized I finally understood what this life is really all about.

This new understanding made me happy and sad at the same time—happy because I realized I had more control over what I experienced in life, and sad because I'd realized it forty years too late. That's not important now because my early days are gone. But yours aren't. You still have most of your days ahead of you. If I can help you understand life now while you're young, you can use this understanding to control what you experience. When you have control, you can create a successful life.

But first I need to share a warning with you. I recently heard a popular radio personality say, "You can't let the younger generation know that you're trying to teach them something or they won't read your book." I won't trick you into reading my book. I want you to know that I'm trying to teach something important. So you have a choice: Do you want to learn how to be successful or not? You, and only you, get to make this choice.

Over time, I discovered that there are two ways to learn things in life. You can experience everything yourself, or you can learn from others' experiences. Learning from others is best because it's a lot less painful. But it can also take a long time. I'm offering you a quick way to learn by sharing what I've learned from sixty years of living. Can you imagine what you could do with my sixty years of knowledge and your lifetime to use it?

My sixty years of knowledge can help you see the end of your experiences from the beginning. How do you get knowledge? A few seem to be born with it, but most get it through experience. Experiences teach truths, and truths create knowledge. Here's a simple example of how you can use my experiences to gain knowledge.

A few years back, we took our family down to our cabin. It was during the winter, and back then we heated the cabin with a wood-burning stove. One day, I noticed my two-year-old grandson standing in front of the stove, staring at the glass on the door. It was like the flames behind the glass were saying, "Come and touch me so I can teach you what hot is." I could see his little mind trying to decide whether or not to touch the stove, but I knew he was going to do it. How did I know? I've seen those flames many times.

The family had warned him several times not to get near the stove, but before I could grab him, he touched the glass. And, of course, it burned his fingers. This experience taught him a simple, undeniable truth: if you touch a hot stove, you're going to get burned.

This is how experience creates knowledge, but my grandson could have acquired this same knowledge without touching the stove. He could have used my knowledge rather than experiencing it for himself.

This book contains the knowledge that I've gained from sixty years of experiences. If you read it and use it, you'll find it easier to make good choices. Making good choices now is important because what you do as a teen usually sets the course you'll travel for the rest of your life. It's normal for teens to think that this small period of time will have no effect on their lives, but nothing could be further from the truth.

If we don't understand why events happen here on earth, those events won't make sense and their purposes will remain a mystery. These mysteries can create confusion, which can cause us to make more mistakes, leading to unhappiness. I want to help you avoid as much pain and unhappiness as possible by explaining why things happen here on earth.

I'll be using reason and logic to pass on my knowledge. Teaching this way means starting with a few simple thoughts that are easy to understand, and then building on those thoughts with more thoughts until they reach a conclusion that makes sense. When you recognize how it makes sense, you'll have the knowledge I'm trying to give you. Since remembering knowledge can be difficult, I'll repeat some of the same thoughts several times.

Even though this method takes more time, it's the best way for you to learn new things for two reasons. First, by the time you reach a conclusion, there should be no doubt in your mind that it's true. Second, using reason and logic teaches you how to think so you can see the end of an experience from the beginning. This will help you find truth. Being able to find truth in this day and age is important because everybody has an agenda—even me.

Having an agenda just means I have a purpose for what I'm doing. My purpose is simple: I want to teach you to recognize truth so you can use it to create a successful life. But here's a warning. Just because I believe something is true doesn't mean you should believe it's true. I want you to think it through from beginning to end so you can decide for yourself if it really *is* true. You were sent to earth to learn, grow, and gain a sure knowledge of truth. The best way to do that is to learn how to think things through.

By the time you finish this book, you should understand how life really works. You can then use these truths to control much of what you experience in life. How? The truths you learn can be applied to produce the same consequences each time. How do I know these truths never change? I've had countless experiences that prove it.

Take your time while reading. I recommend that you read a page or two, and then use reason to see if those pages made sense. If they did, great! But if they didn't, *read them again.* If you'll honestly consider what I've written, I believe it will make sense in time. These truths will help you make better choices, and those choices will create better consequences.

I know that sounds too easy, but it really is that easy if—and I mean *if*—you're willing to learn the truth, believe it, and use it to guide your decisions.

π

YOUR TEEN YEARS are the most dangerous time of your life. During this time, you'll go through big changes that will make your feelings go crazy. But you still must use those feelings to make choices that will shape your life for decades to come.

Everybody has to go through these difficult years, so please don't let the "evil team"—God's opposition—make you feel self-conscious or bad. Avoiding the negative thoughts they send you will allow you to focus on dealing with the changes you're going through. That will make getting through your teen years much easier.

During your teens, your body must change to prepare you mentally and physically for adulthood. These changes may take years to complcte, but don't be surprised if you feel like you've become an adult shortly after they start. You may physically look like an adult, but you're not yet mentally ready for all the responsibilities

6

that come with adulthood. God gave this precious time of teen years to prepare you mentally for those responsibilities.

You may have heard the saying, "Don't put the cart before the horse." In this context, the cart is your physical body and the horse is your mind. Because I'm old, I understand that life always turns out better when you follow God's timetable instead of your own. Here's what happens when you become a teenager.

You're enjoying life as a kid, and all of a sudden you notice that older people are telling you what to do. For reasons you don't understand, you don't want to do it. At first it's just an annoyance, but after a while you feel frustrated or even angry. You feel like you're old enough to make your own choices, but adults won't let you. If that isn't bad enough, they even threaten you with consequences if you don't do what they say.

This time of life often causes friction between you and your parents or others who are older than you. These feelings are normal because God's plan requires you to start thinking for yourself so you can eventually separate from your parents. But it's right at this point when your life will get dangerous.

God's plan requires you to separate from your parents, but the evil team will encourage you to separate too fast. They do this by sending you negative feelings and thoughts, and then telling you that you're not normal for having them. They tell you that you're the only one who has ever felt this way, so no one could possibly understand what you're going through. These feelings and thoughts add fuel to an already hot fire, causing you to feel even more frustrated and angry. Separating from your parents because you're frustrated and angry isn't good, but there's another reason the evil team wants you to rebel.

Have you noticed that you never feel like rebelling against evil? The reason is that God will never tell you to rebel. The evil team encourages rebellion because they want to stop you from doing good things. They know when you do good things, God will bless you by helping you make good choices.

Now that you understand the connection between doing good things and receiving God's help, what is rebellion really all about? The evil team wants to separate you from God's help. Less help means more bad choices, which creates bad consequences and suffering. More suffering means more discouragement, which eventually causes you to lose hope. After you lose hope, you'll become depressed, and you'll quit trying. Then the evil team will have a much easier time destroying you.

This next thought is harsh, but I need to explain the evil team's goal. After you quit trying, your depression will deepen until you think there's only one way out. For a growing number of depressed teens, that way is suicide. Just writing that breaks my heart because there's always another way out. But the evil team will make sure that those who think about suicide never see it. If these special young sons and daughters of God choose to end their lives, they become another sad statistic in the game of life.

Have I oversimplified this problem? I don't think so. I realize that chemical and physical problems can contribute to suicidal feelings, but I'm confident that the odds of actually following through would decrease dramatically if those affected could understand the chain of events that lead to suicide. Did you notice that every single event in the chain was negative? Where do all negative thoughts, feelings, and emotions come from? That's right: the evil team.

The events that lead to suicide happen far too often to too many teens, but none of them need to happen. If teens will just try to obey God's commandments and repent quickly when they don't, God will lead, guide, protect, encourage, and prosper them. Does this mean teens won't have burdens, trials, and challenges if they obey? No. Life in this imperfect world creates more than enough opportunities for burdens, trials, and challenges. But if they'll choose to obey and repent when they don't, God will make these burdens easier to bear.

Matthew 11:28–30 explains this. In these verses, Jesus Christ asks you to yoke up with Him so that your burdens will be made light. Lighter burdens are easier to handle. How do you yoke up? By obeying His commandments—and repenting quickly when you don't. Repentance may seem difficult, but let's talk about it and see if it really is.

π

THE BASIC REPENTANCE process has just five steps. First you must *recognize the sin*. When was the last time you sinned? How long did it take you to recognize it? If you're like me, you recognized it before you even did it. Recognizing the sin before you even do it—that's not too hard.

The second step requires you to *feel remorse*. Few use the word *remorse* these days. What does it mean? Basically, you feel bad after you sin. Again, think back to the last time you sinned. How long did it take you to feel bad? Personally, I feel bad right after I sin, because I know I did something wrong. So that's not too hard either.

The third step requires you to *confess your sins to God or a priesthood authority*. The last time you sinned, what did you do right after you started to feel bad? Maybe you did what I do. I start apologizing in my mind to God or to anyone who will listen. In my mind, I say things like, "Why did I do that? That was so stupid! What's wrong with me? I wish I hadn't done that, and I'm sorry I did." This apologizing is the same as confessing. I usually start confessing right after I begin to feel bad.

This type of confession works for 99 percent of the sins you might commit, but there are two types of sin that require you to talk to your priesthood authority, the bishop. The two types of sin are immorality and any sin that involves banned substances or substance abuse. In our Church, if you use banned substances, you've broken the Word of Wisdom. Why must you talk to your bishop? I'll answer that question later when I teach you how to control the beast. For now, just understand that these two types of sins must be confessed to a bishop or a priesthood authority.

The fourth step requires you to *not commit the sin again*. Is that even possible? It might be for some sins but not for others. The evil team loves to make you believe that you won't do it again so they can beat you up when you do. We'll discuss this in detail later, but for now I would encourage you to not play the evil team's game. How? Just change the way you think. Instead of saying, "I won't do it again," say, "I'm going to try really hard not to sin anymore."

And then try hard not to sin. Don't give in every time the evil team tempts you. Fight hard to resist their temptations, and when it looks like you might sin, use the magic word: *No.* It's magic because it works every time you use it.

Step number five requires you to *reenter into the covenant.* When you sin, you break the covenant you made with God. You must reenter the covenant by taking the sacrament. Is taking the sacrament hard? No, because the priesthood brings it right to you. It happens every Sunday, and all you have to do is take it.

The evil team just told me that I oversimplified the repentance process. Maybe so, but I did it on purpose. I want you to see how easy the steps really are. Of the five steps, which ones are hard? I can see only one: step number four. Trying not to sin in a world filled with opportunities to sin is hard. All the other steps are simple because they're automatic. They happen without you having to do much of anything.

Even though the steps of repentance are easy, you still have to do them. They are extremely important. Why? God's kingdom is governed by laws. Two of these laws are the law of justice and the law of mercy. Father Lehi in the Book of Mormon taught us that God must honor both laws or He would cease to be God. He will not cease to be God, so you can bet He'll honor these laws.

What does *honor* mean? God sees everything as either black (sin) or white (not sin). There is no gray area (little sins that don't matter.) The law of justice demands full payment, or as I like to say, somebody has to pay the bill when a sin is committed. If it's your sin, you will pay it, or you can qualify for the law of mercy by accepting the Atonement of Jesus Christ. Either way, the bill must be paid.

$$\pi$$

IF YOU WANT to get the most benefit from this book, you must understand and be willing to use the repentance process as explained. If you do, God will bless you, and it's those blessings that will make your burdens light even though you live in an imperfect world. Life in this world will be difficult, but remember, all of your experiences—good, bad, or even terrible—are opportunities to learn. Each will give you knowledge that can't be gained in any other way, and gaining knowledge is one of the purposes of life.

Another purpose of life is to test you, but just living life will provide plenty of opportunities for you to be tested. Will you choose to be faithful, or will you choose to quit believing? That's the test, and you'll either pass or fail by the way you choose to live your life. I hope you'll choose to be faithful, because how and where you spend the rest of eternity will depend on that one choice.

Recently I had an opportunity to work with several hundred young single adults. It was an amazing experience, and I loved every minute of it. They were bright, beautiful, and extremely intelligent. But many of them seemed to have a common problem: they didn't understand life on earth, and that caused them to make some bad choices. These bad choices created bad consequences, which caused them to become sad and depressed. If they didn't get help, they eventually lost hope. They began to question the purpose of life, which led to more bad choices, more depression, and more lost hope.

You can't ever allow yourself to lose hope.

Hope is the opposite of depression. In fact, it can be used to eliminate depression. But it works both ways. Depression, left untreated, can also destroy hope. How can you make sure that you never lose hope? It's simple. *Choose to have hope each day.* Could it really be that easy? It can, if you're willing to make the choice.

Even though life can be difficult at times, you can still hope for a successful life. But just hoping for it won't make it happen. A successful life is a work in progress, and you're the one who gets to do all the work. Believe me, it's worth it, regardless of what it costs you in planning, sacrifice, and effort.

You only live once, so you might as well make the most of your once-in-a-lifetime experience. Read this book, find the truths contained in it, and use them to create the successful life you want. I'm excited to share what I've learned from my sixty years of experience so you can use my knowledge to make the most of your university experience.

REVIEW OF IMPORTANT POINTS

- Life is like a university, but you can control most of what you experience.
- Experiences teach truth, and truth creates knowledge.
- You can find and remember truth using reason, logic, and repetition.
- Your teen years are a time of change. Use that time to prepare for the responsibilities given to adults.
- Teen years prepare you to separate from your parents, but you don't control the timetable. Follow God's timetable.
- You will experience burdens, challenges, and trials. God will lighten them.
- You will make mistakes. Trust God and use the five-step repentance process.
- All experiences—good, bad, and terrible—have value. Think of them as opportunities to learn.
- Choose to have hope each day.

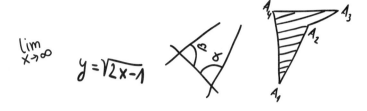

CHAPTER 2

SORTING OUT THE PIECES

OVER THE YEARS, I've noticed that life on earth is a lot like a puzzle. Most puzzles come in a box with a picture of the completed puzzle on the outside. But your life puzzle didn't. To make matters worse, some of the most important pieces are invisible.

So here you are on earth, trying to put your puzzle together, but you have no sure idea what it's going to look like. How will you put it together? In my case, I used my imagination and a lot of trial and error. My way wasn't bad because I learned a lot. But now that it's nearly complete, I've found an easier way.

Recently my wife and I were given a puzzle. It was a picture of the ten square miles surrounding our cabin in a topographical map, which means it was covered with lots of lines showing grades and elevations. It had five hundred small pieces. Every time I tried to put it together, I couldn't get much done. After trying and failing several times, I was ready to throw it away. What I finally realized was that the picture on the outside of the box was of a generic topographical map, not the one that was the actual puzzle. No wonder I wasn't getting very far!

Eventually I thought, "Why don't I sort out all the pieces into piles according to their shapes, sizes, and colors? Then I won't have to look at every single piece to find the one I need."

So I started sorting the pieces. My wife came over as I was finishing, and she laughed because she thought I was sorting them just for fun. I'll admit that I like things neat and orderly, and I probably have one of those alphabet-named conditions. But that's not why I was doing it. I let her have her laugh, and I then explained why I was sorting the pieces. Whether she believed me or not, sorting the pieces worked really well.

Afterward, I put the border pile together first so I could see the size and shape of the puzzle. That helped me understand how it would eventually look. Then I focused all my efforts inside the border and finished the puzzle.

Do people put puzzles together so they can become frustrated? No, they do it for fun. And what makes puzzles fun? Finding pieces that fit and accomplishing something. But in order to have fun, I had to sort all the pieces into smaller piles, put the border together, and focus on the smaller area inside the border.

Putting your life together is a lot like assembling a puzzle. If you want to have fun, you need to first sort out and identify all the pieces. Then you must use reason and logic to find where they fit into the puzzle. Why reason and logic? They allow you to see the end of a road before you travel it.

As you live your life, you will travel on countless roads. You start the day you're born, and you continue until you die. The roads you'll travel will be determined by the choices you make. When you need to make a choice, it's like you're sitting at an intersection. The choice you make determines the road you'll travel.

If that makes sense, answer this next question: If you could see the end of a road before you travel it, would that help you decide which road you should take? For me it would. In fact, I've learned that you shouldn't travel any road until you look to see where it's going.

For instance, let's say you want to be happy. What must you do before you choose a road to travel? You must decide what would make you happy. For example, you could say, "I'd be happy if I had lots of money," which isn't necessarily true, but let's have some fun and use that example anyway.

After deciding that money would make you happy, you need to look for roads that lead to money. To finds these roads, you need the right information. In this day and age, I can think of three honest ways to make a lot of money. I'm sure there are other ways, but let's not go there. The three honest ways are

- Inventing something that everybody wants
- Getting a good job and working hard for a long time
- Inheriting it by outliving your relatives

The first two ways are the best because you're in control, but most of us use the third way because it's easier.

Just for fun, let's say that you choose to invent something or work hard for the rest of your life. What do you need in order to travel either of these two roads? A good education. This doesn't always have to involve school, because you can get an education while working on the job. But here's the problem. In today's world, it's hard to get a good job without an education. I don't want to make this too complicated, so let's just say that you need to go to school before you can make a lot of money.

Look down the road, use reason and logic, and tell me what you must do to get a good education. You'll need to go to school, pay attention, and study hard. What would happen if you didn't do one or more of these necessary things? You wouldn't do well in school, and that would make it almost impossible to get your education. No education means no good job, and no good job means no good money. This is how you use information, reason, and logic to see the end of a road from the beginning.

What will happen if you want money but you don't travel on a road that leads to money? You won't get the money, and you'll waste a lot of time, effort, and money traveling on that dead-end road. Traveling dead-end roads isn't good because often when you reach the end, it's almost impossible to turn around. To emphasize this point, let me share an experience with you.

One day I decided to go snowmobiling. I thought it might be fun to go somewhere I hadn't been. I drove the truck and trailer to a place called Ephraim Canyon. As I drove up the canyon, I noticed that there weren't many places to turn around, but I wasn't worried because I was sure there had to be a parking lot at the top. I should say, I wasn't worried until I rounded a corner and saw that the plowed road dead-ended right in front of me. There I was, sitting on a narrow road with snow piled high on both sides and nowhere to turn around.

Since I'm here, you know I made it back. But it wasn't easy. I had to back down the road until I found a place to turn around. Backing down took a lot of time, so I never did go snowmobiling. Instead, I wasted the entire day and a full tank of gas and experienced a lot of frustration that could have been avoided. But I'm not complaining, because I feel lucky that things turned out as well as they did. Looking back, I can say without a doubt that if I'd known how that road ended, I would have never taken it.

Could I have known where the road ended without traveling on it? Actually, yes. I knew about Ephraim Canyon because I had talked to someone who had been there. If I had asked for more information, I could have avoided wasting all that time, effort, and money and simply turning around before I reached the end of the road. Was it better for me to go through the experience myself, or would it have been better to miss the experience by asking for more information? I should have asked, and then I could have spent my day snowmobiling instead of trying to find a place to turn around.

My experience shows why finding and using information is important. Before you make a choice, find others who have done it, ask them about their experience, and use that information to answer this question: What will the consequences be if I make this choice? Using information to determine the consequences before you make a choice will always lead you to better choices and better consequences. Every choice creates an action, and those actions have consequences that must be experienced whether you like them or not.

Determining the real consequences before you make your choice will require some work upfront, but it will be easier in the end because you won't need to spend time fixing the consequences of your wrong choices. I say "real consequences" because when I was young, I wasn't willing to recognize the real consequences of my choices. I thought I could do whatever I wanted whenever I wanted and everything would turn out the way I wanted because I wanted it to. As I've grown older, I've found that life doesn't work like that. If you want a consequence to happen, you must make the choice that leads to that consequence.

If you can find the real consequence before you make a choice, you'll find that identifying the right choice is actually pretty easy. But making yourself act on that choice isn't, because it requires planning, sacrifice, and work. When I was a teen, I had a hard time making myself want to work because work was, well, it was just work, and I thought work could never be fun. Again, that's not true.

Work can be fun, and I'm going to show you how to make it fun. But first I need to spend a little more time explaining why life is like a puzzle.

π

WHEN I PUT a puzzle together, I always put the border together first so I can see the area I have to work in. Finding this smaller area is important because that's where all the pieces of the puzzle fit. You can put pieces together outside of the borders, but the puzzle will never be correct until you put the pieces inside where they belong.

Life on earth works the same way. Life has borders that limit the area you have to work in. These limits define what you can and can't do and where and when you can do it. These borders exist to help you put your life together correctly. You can try to put your life together incorrectly, but that doesn't work because it's not right. Who determined which way was right? God did. You can choose to believe it or not, but your choice doesn't change the fact that God determines what's right.

God set the borders in life so you could focus your attention on the most important things—the things that matter when this life is over. Life is full of good things that rob you of the time that should be used to prepare for the next life. Preparing for the next life is the purpose of this life, so you must find the things that are important in the next life and do them now. Your time to prepare is limited, and unfortunately you won't know how much time you have. This is why you must focus on and pursue things that matter in the next life first.

Being willing to put your life together within the borders God has set eliminates a lot of confusion. Less confusion means fewer problems, and fewer problems make life easier. Just living in this imperfect world is going to be difficult, but you don't need to make it more difficult than it needs to be. If you want life to be easier, put it together inside the borders. It really is that simple. I'll help you identify the pieces, including the invisible ones, and then I'll show you how they fit together within the border God has set.

All the pieces in your life puzzle are important, but some are more important than others. These are the pieces you'll use to build your foundation in life. Everything you do must be supported by a strong foundation or it will never last.

What foundation is strong enough to support everything you do in life? I'll let you think about that while I share another experience with you.

π

OWNING A CABIN in the mountains has always been one of my goals. After about thirty years of wishing, hoping, and working, my wife and I were finally able to buy one. But my dream cabin had a defect—an unfinished deck that ran along the entire west side of the A-frame metal roof. It didn't look good because it wasn't finished, but the real problem was the way the previous owner had tried to support the deck. He'd installed several four-by-fours through the metal roof down to the foundation, so every time it rained or snowed, the water leaked into the cabin through the holes he'd cut in the roof. I tried to seal the holes several times, but the water always found a way inside. Since I couldn't stop the leaks, I finally decided to remove the deck and replace the metal roof panels.

Unsure how I should remove the deck, I used a saw to cut through the posts that supported it while I sat on it. At first my idea worked fine. I would cut a post, a section would fall, and then I'd move to the next section and cut the post that supported it. As each section fell away, my confidence in the process increased, so I began to cut away larger sections of the deck.

Midway through the process, I accidently cut the post that supported the section of deck I was sitting on. As the deck gave way beneath me, I knew I was in big trouble. There was a pile of broken boards full of rusty nails waiting for me below. I guess I was lucky—or blessed—because as I slid down the roof, my arm got wrapped around a post still attached to the foundation. This minor miracle stopped me from falling into the pile and allowed me to escape with a few small cuts and bruises, and a big blow to my ego.

I learned several valuable lessons. One was obvious: I needed to pay more attention to what I was doing. But the experience also showed why a strong foundation is so important.

When the deck was supported by a foundation, it was secure. When it was secure, it could be used. When it could be used, it had a purpose and value. After I separated the deck from its foundation, it became unstable. It could no longer be used and therefore had no purpose or value. Can you see why foundations are important? The deck's value was determined by the foundation that supported it. Let's now apply this reasoning to life.

Think of the deck as your life. When your life is attached to a foundation, it can be used. How you use your life will determine its purpose and value. But this is where it gets confusing. How many different ways are there to use a life? There are about as many as there are people using it. With all of these different ways, which way is the right way?

$$\pi$$

FINDING THE RIGHT way to use, or live, your life is important because you could end up using it the wrong way without even realizing it. If that happens, the life you've lived could have no value, but it will be too late to do anything about it. You and I both don't want that to happen.

If you want to find the right way to live life, you must understand its purpose—the reason you're here. If you know your purpose, you can use that purpose to guide you when you're making the choices that determine how your life will be used.

How can you know if what you think the purpose of your life is really is the right purpose?

Maybe you've heard the saying, "The only sure things in life are death and taxes." Of these two sure things, one of them should always be considered when you're searching for life's purpose. I'll give you a hint: it's not taxes, unless you get taxed to death. Either way, the thing to consider is death.

I'm sorry if my mentioning death bothers you. No one likes to think about death, but it doesn't change the fact that your life will eventually end. Death is part of God's plan, and we agreed to follow His plan or we wouldn't be here. But now let me give you some good news.

Even though life on earth ends, your life doesn't end when you die. There may be some who disagree, but that doesn't change what I believe. If you're one who believes life ends when you die, I have a question for you: Are you willing to gamble your eternity away? You know you can't defy death, so are you really willing to bet that life ends when you die? I'm not.

Since life doesn't end after death, the purpose of this life is to give you time to prepare for the next life by doing things that have eternal value. Sadly, I often forgot about those things and spent most of my time focusing on things that had no eternal value.

Here's an experience that helped me understand why I needed to focus more on things that have eternal value. About ten years ago, when I managed a retail store, my boss called and asked if he could come see me before the store opened Monday morning. When Monday arrived, he came in and after a short greeting said, "Ted, we don't need you anymore. You've got fifteen minutes. Clean out your desk."

I was shocked. That was the last thing I expected. I asked several times why I was being fired, but he wouldn't give me a reason.

Each time I asked, he just said that I had less time to clean out my desk. So I cleaned out my desk, and he escorted me out of the building. I'll never forget how that felt. For more than eight years, I had been trusted with the entire business operation, and now I couldn't be trusted to find my own way out the front door.

As I stood on the front sidewalk, an awful feeling came over me. I realized I had nothing to show for the work I had done over the past eight years. All the time, effort, and sacrifice I had put into that company now amounted to absolutely nothing—and when I say nothing, I mean nothing. I didn't even have a ride home because I'd driven the company truck to work.

As the reality of what had just happened hit me, another feeling came over me that was far worse than the first. The best way to describe it is to say that I experienced a mini version of Judgment Day—and it wasn't a good one. Not only did I have nothing of earthly value, but I also had little of eternal value. I had given all my time to the company, and that left no time for anything else.

If my experience leaves you thinking that you shouldn't get a job or you should quit working, you missed the point. Work is an important part of life, but there are only twenty-four hours in a day. If you use all of your hours doing things that have no eternal value, you won't have any time left to prepare for the next life.

As the news of me getting fired spread, I began to receive job offers from other companies in the area. I'd known most of the company owners for years and had even worked for some of them, so my choice should have been easy. But I couldn't decide which offer to take. This time of indecision went on for a couple of days. Then one night, something totally unexpected happened.

It was about 3:00 a.m., and I couldn't sleep because my mind was racing as I tried to decide what to do. That happens often when you get older—your body wants to go to sleep, but your mind keeps you wide awake.

There I was, wide awake, mulling over the employment offers. In my mind I could see all the offers lying side by side on a table, but I couldn't make a choice. Some of the confusion was my fault because I was trying to decide which of the companies had the best chance of putting my old company out of business. I know that's not the right way to think, but sometimes I can't help it—I'm kind of competitive. I was also mad, and that made me think it was okay for me to feel that way. But deep down inside, I knew it wasn't.

As I lay awake that night, I heard or felt a strong, distinct impression that simply said, "Ted, you've got enough. Go out and do something good." Because the impression was so strong, I lay there repeating the words over and over in my mind: *I've got enough. Go out and do something good.* What in the world did that mean? I didn't know, but I knew it didn't make any sense.

As I thought about what had just happened, my mind was suddenly flooded with negative thoughts: "Wait a minute, haven't I been doing something good? Isn't being honest, going to church, being true to my commitments, trying to obey the commandments, and just trying to be a nice guy doing something good?" I was trying to justify the type of life I'd been living. Was I perfect? Not even close, but I had lived long enough to know that I never would be. So what did the words "do something good" really mean? I was confused.

After what seemed like an eternity of negative thoughts, a more positive thought came, and I realized I had missed the point. I wasn't being condemned for the life I'd lived. I was being given a new opportunity to go and do something better, something that had eternal value—something that would really matter on Judgment Day.

That thought made me feel better, but it still didn't answer my question. What was I supposed to do? I was hoping that whoever had sent the first thought would tell me, but the answer never came. The choice was mine.

My thoughts went back and forth like a ball in a tennis match—serve and counter, back and forth—until I remembered that I had enough money because of my other job. For roughly five years, I'd been doing two jobs, one in retail and one managing commercial properties. My management job paid me enough to live comfortably, and it didn't take much time at all. All I had to do was occasionally pull a few weeds or fix a few lights and that was about it. It really was a great job.

The negative thoughts that flooded my mind caused me to feel like I immediately needed to find another job to replace my income so I could take care of my family. As fear and uncertainty filled my head, though, a new thought came. It said, "You really do have enough, and you know if you go back to work, you'll just spend all of your time working."

That hurt, because it was true. I'm a give-it-my-all type of person. With me it's always been all or nothing, but usually it ends up being all. The job I lost had taken all my time because I'd given it all I had to give, and that left little or no time for things that had eternal value.

You might be thinking, "Wait a minute. Isn't that the way you should be, totally committed to your job? Hard work and sacrifice—isn't that the way to get ahead in life?"

It may be for some, but not for me. I always ended up sacrificing the things that had eternal value for things that didn't. I knew if I went to work for another company, I would certainly have more money, but I also knew that I would have less time to do something good because I would always be at work. I try to look at myself honestly and recognize who I really am. What do people in self-help meetings say? "Hi, my name is Ted, and I'm a workaholic."

The experience I had that night encouraged me to look at life differently. Up to that point, my priorities in life were work, more work, and a little family time when I could find a few minutes. Then I was out of time, the day was over, and I needed to go to bed so I could get up and do it all over again the next day.

Even though I knew I was a workaholic, that didn't stop me from thinking, "Wait a minute. I can't just quit working. I'm only forty-five. Nobody is supposed to retire at forty-five. Wouldn't that be committing a sin?" Of course, I was probably sinning by spending all my time at work, but that didn't stop me from thinking that retiring so early couldn't be right.

While I was considering those thoughts, a new one appeared: "If you retire this early, people will think that you're being lazy and unproductive." Then another: "You can't quit now. You just got fired. If you quit now, you'll be a failure." I didn't want to be lazy, unproductive, or a failure, so what was I supposed to do?

All these negative thoughts kept coming, until another clear, distinct thought said, "You're not a failure. You're just being given an opportunity to do more good because you'll have more time. Do you want this opportunity or not?" After that, I knew what I should do. Did I want this opportunity? Yes, I did—so I quit looking for a new job and retired at age forty-five.

I say "retire," but I really didn't retire. I just quit looking for another job. I didn't know what I was going to do, but I knew what I needed to do, and it was going to change my life. I was able to make my choice because I understood the purpose of life. I had never really forgotten it; I'd just gotten so busy working that I didn't take time to think.

What is my purpose? It's best described by a scripture in the Book of Mormon. Alma 34:32 states, "For behold, this life is the time for men [me] to prepare to meet God; yea, behold the day of this life is the day for men [me] to perform their [my] labors." I decided that night that I needed to better prepare to meet God by using my time to do things that had eternal value instead of just going back to work and making more money. How was I able to make that choice? My purpose was securely attached to the foundation I had built my life on.

What is my foundation? I said it needed to be strong enough to support my purpose, but I haven't yet told you what it is. You may be able to guess, but before you do, let me tell you about someone I admire because he built his life on a strong foundation.

REVIEW OF IMPORTANT POINTS

- Life is like a puzzle. It will be easier to put together after you identify and sort the pieces.
- Use reason and logic to see where the pieces fit. If you look at the end or the consequences of your choices before you make them, you'll make better choices.

- Finding a road that leads to success is easy. Success today requires an education and information.
- God set borders. Use information to identify the borders. Borders limit the space you have to work in. They also help you eliminate confusion and identify what is most important.
- A strong, secure foundation gives life purpose and value.
- The next life gives this life purpose and value.

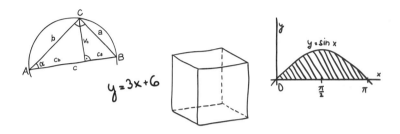

$y = 3x + 6$

$y = \sin x$

CHAPTER 3

CHARACTER MATTERS

HAVE YOU HEARD the saying "We're burnin' daylight"? John Wayne made that line famous. You may have heard of him, although he died many years before you were born. He was a movie star, but in today's world, stars come and go like taxi cabs in New York: they come out of nowhere, make an appearance, and are gone before you know it.

John Wayne is still an icon today because he played characters who fought fearlessly against the bad guys until they were begging for mercy or were taken care of. He usually let them choose, but when the job needed to be done, you could count on John Wayne to do it.

Why am I talking about John Wayne? He was a great example of a man who built his life on a strong foundation for good. Was he perfect? No. But in public he stood for something good, and that made him an American movie hero for about forty years.

Think about today's celebrities. Many are only popular for a short time when you compare them to John Wayne. Why is their time in the spotlight so short? I believe it's because they don't build their lives on a strong foundation for good. Today many achieve fame because they're incredibly talented, or they do bad or dumb things that help them get noticed. Regardless of how they become famous, it never lasts long because their foundations can't support their lives.

If you don't believe me, just look at all of the incredibly talented people who've come and gone too quickly. You can find them in movies, politics, music, business, sports, celebrity marriages, or almost any other pursuit. Examples are everywhere. If you'll honestly look, you'll see that there's a connection between doing good and how long someone is able to stay successful.

Did you notice the thoughts that filled your head when I tied doing good to lasting success? As I was writing that last paragraph, the evil team sent a thought that said, "This is baloney. There are all kinds of successful people in life who are bad." I'll admit that their thought was right, because lives aren't built, or lost, in a few days or years. You will see bad successful people in all walks of life. But will their success last? Judging from examples in history, it won't. I did find it interesting that the evil team admitted some people are bad. They usually tell me there's no such thing as bad. I think whoever sent that thought wasn't thinking.

If you want to succeed in life, *start doing good things*. How will you know that the things you're doing really are good? Before you make any choice, look at where your choice will take you. Earlier, I explained how you look at the end from the beginning. If the end is good, it's a good choice, and if it's not, it's a bad choice. Could it really be that easy? It can be, if you're willing to look before you make your choices.

The next step toward a successful life requires you to *define what a successful life looks like*. You may have heard the saying "How will you know when you get there if you don't know where you're going?" The answer is you can't. So what do you want your successful life to look like? I could only guess, so I'll keep it simple and tell you what my successful life looks like.

My vision of a successful life is having my family near, good health, the ability to continue learning, opportunities to do something good or things that have eternal value, and enough money to choose how I use my time later in life. As of today, I've been able to reach most of my goals, but who knows what tomorrow will bring? When you live in an imperfect world, the only certainty is that things are going to change—and they could change in an instant. I just hope whatever changes, changes for the better.

When you're trying to reach a goal, which is harder: setting a goal or reaching a goal? Obviously reaching a goal is a lot harder, but I'll let you in on a little secret. Reaching goals really isn't hard if you know how to do it. Let me show you how to set and reach goals. I'll use one of my goals—opportunities to do something good—in this example.

Since a goal isn't reached in a short amount of time, you must find a good reason for wanting it. Wanting creates excitement, and excitement is a great motivator. If you can't find a good reason for wanting, you won't be excited or motivated and you'll never reach your goal.

After I decided what I wanted, I needed to *define my goal* by deciding what "doing something good" actually meant. *Good* has many definitions, but the only one that really matters is God's definition. Where do we find God's definition of the word *good*? We find it the scriptures and in the words of His living prophets. After I made sure my definition was right, I made a list of the good things I wanted to do.

Next I needed to *list the resources I had available* to help me do the good things on my list. These resources were time, abilities, desires, and money that could be used to help me do things on my list. Then all I had left to do was decide how to use my resources to reach my goal. These simple steps make reaching a goal sound easy, don't they? But if it really was that easy, wouldn't everybody be doing it? I'm sure they would, so another step must still be missing.

The missing step is *working on your goal until you reach it*. This step requires planning, sacrifice, and hard work.

Did you just say, "Wait a minute, isn't this book called *Could It Really Be This Easy?* Having to plan, make sacrifices, and work hard doesn't sound easy. So what's easy?" The easy part is finding a way to reach your goal. Every goal you could hope to reach has probably already been reached by someone else many times over. Your life is a work in progress. You're the one who gets to do all the work, but inventing a plan to reach your goals won't require much work at all because hundreds, if not thousands, have already invented plans for you to use. All you have to do is find someone who reached the goal you want to reach and do what they did. How did they do it? They used their abilities and resources as they worked on it one day at a time. Any goal can be reached if you keep working on it one day at a time.

Are you wondering how you get the needed abilities? A few lucky people are born with abilities and natural talent, but the rest of us need to develop them. Developing abilities is never easy and requires time, but it can be done if you're willing to try because you have God on your side. He will help you as long as you continue trying.

But you do need to be careful for a couple of reasons. First, don't try to go beyond the mark. For example, if your goal is to learn to play the piano, you don't need to become a concert pianist; you just need to learn how to play the piano.

You also need to be careful because creating new abilities isn't easy. As you work toward your goal, you'll be tempted to give up and just accept the abilities you have rather than trying to learn new ones. If you give up, you'll end up in a rut. What's a rut? Back before roads were paved, tires would make deep tracks called ruts in the dirt roads. If it rained and your car or truck slid into a rut, it was almost impossible to get out of it. Not being willing to develop new abilities is an easy rut to fall into and a hard one to get out of.

Do you have to develop new abilities or talents? Yes. One of the purposes of life is to provide you with opportunities to learn and grow, and you do that by developing new abilities or talents. If you're still not convinced, read the parable of the talents in Matthew 25:14–28 or Luke 19:12–26. Either will answer any questions you may have about the need to develop new talents or abilities.

The next resource I needed to reach my goal was money. When I was young, I thought money grew on trees. I'd never seen the trees, but my mom knew where they were. All I had to do was ask her for some money, and she'd go out, pick a few bills off the tree, and give them to me. I wish I'd asked her where that tree was, because every time I need money now, I have to work for it.

Most of us will feel like we never have enough money regardless of how much we have, especially when we're thinking about spending it on something good. Recently I struggled with doing the right thing because I really didn't want to do it. Before you think I'm a bad person, answer this question: Would you rather have a brand-new beautiful Polaris Pro 800 RMK snowmobile or food storage? Of course I would rather have the snowmobile, but I bought food storage, and here's why.

For a few years, I'd been riding a Polaris 900 RMK that weighed close to 600 pounds. Then Polaris came out with a new 800 RMK that only weighed 435 pounds, and I knew I just had to have one. I asked my wife if I could, and she said no. But I knew if I kept asking, she would finally let me buy one. So I kept asking, and sure enough, she said, "Just go buy the stupid thing so we can quit talking about it." I said, "Thank you, I will," and headed for the snowmobile store.

As I stood there looking at the most beautiful machine I could imagine, the Spirit said, "Hey, Ted, how's your food storage?" I couldn't believe it would do that to me when I was buying a snowmobile, but I did what was right by walking out of the store without the new snowmobile. I spent the snowmobile money on food storage for my family. Later, I received a blessing for doing the right thing when Polaris took another seventeen pounds off the 2013 RMK 800 by giving it a new drive system. Guess what's parked in my shed today? And just for the record, that snowmobile really is incredible.

Choosing to buy the right thing instead of the thing you want is called *prioritizing* your purchases. Regardless of how much money you have, you'll always have enough to do something good if you prioritize your purchases. It's hard, but you can do it.

The last step in reaching my goal to do good things may seem like a no-brainer, but I still had to do it if I wanted the reward or blessing. I had to *learn to want to do good things*. Learning to want to do something good is hard because of the evil team, but as I've grown old, I've discovered an undeniable truth. If you want to feel good, you must do something good before you can receive the reward or blessing of feeling good. It's impossible to receive the reward or blessing unless you do something good. It really is that simple.

But here's another warning. The good feeling you get while you're having fun is not the same type of good feeling you'll get after you've done something good. The two may feel the same at first, but the one you feel while you're having fun always ends when the fun is over. In fact, depending on what you did to have fun, that good feeling could turn into a really bad feeling, so be careful.

What can you use to motivate you to want to do something good? It's easy when you get an immediate reward like a new snowmobile. But what will motivate you when there's no immediate reward—like buying food storage? The answer is *the foundation you build your life on*. My foundation is made up of my core beliefs, or what I really, truly believe. They are important to me in life. After I identified what's most important, those things became my purpose, and I used my purpose to motivate me.

Now pay close attention to this next question, because the answer is important. What, or who, could you believe in that will always be there to guide you when you're making choices?

I could walk you through all the possibilities, but that would use up a lot of valuable time, so I'll just give you the answer. Now that I'm old, I've found that there is only one person I can count on to be there when I make my choices, and that is God. I've learned through years of trial and error that God is the only one I can completely trust, so I've made my belief in Him my foundation in life. My belief in God is the only thing strong enough to always be there right when I need it most.

I can almost hear you saying, "What about all the bad things that happen? How can you trust God when all the bad stuff keeps happening?" Okay, I get it, but slow down and keep reading, because in the next chapter I'll explain why good and bad things happen. The answer to your questions is one of the gifts that I want to give you. But before I do, I need to give you another warning.

In order for you to use my gift, you must choose to believe in God and make Him your foundation. I hope you'll choose to believe, but I can't make you. The choice is yours and only yours.

If believing is too much for you to accept at first, just choose to believe that you might be able to accept it later and continue reading. I promise that my foundation won't be hard to accept after you've finished the book. So what is my foundation made of?

$$\pi$$

HERE ARE MY core beliefs, or the foundation that I've built my life on. First, I choose to believe that there is a God. I promise you there is, but you must choose to believe it. Why?

Everything you do on earth begins with a choice. I not only want you to choose to believe that there is a God, but I also want you to choose to believe that He loves you and has a plan for you. His plan is a perfect, eternal plan because He's God, and God doesn't make mistakes. This plan is the same plan that He uses in all His creations.

This plan was explained to you when you lived with Him before you came to earth in the premortal world. The premortal world is perfect in every way possible. You were raised there just like you're being raised here, and you lived in God's presence until you could no longer grow and gain knowledge. To gain additional knowledge, God sent you to earth to receive a body and experience mortality. In addition to gaining knowledge, this experience was designed to test you so you can prove that you're willing to obey God's commandments.

I also believe that you received your place on this earth based on the choices you made in the premortal life; and the place you'll receive in the next life, or the eternities, is based on the choices you make while living here on earth.

God understood that you would not always make correct choices, so He provided a Savior for you. Our Savior is Jesus Christ, and He has the power to fix the eternal consequences of the wrong choices you make while you're here on earth. Through His Atonement and your repentance, you will be forgiven and allowed to return to live in the presence of God.

But that's not all. You can also become like Him. That is truly God's greatest gift. This is why the choices you make in this life are so important, and that's why I've written this book. I want to help you understand life so you'll be able to make good choices and receive God's greatest gift.

How can I, an average, everyday person, get the answers to all the questions about life here on earth? The answers come from living, and sometimes not living, the commandments. Luckily for me, God is merciful in every way possible. I can't even begin to list the ways that He's been merciful, but I can show you one.

God was merciful when He sent us to earth, because He didn't say, "See you later, or sooner if you're not careful. Good luck. I hope you make it back." As part of the plan, He established His Church here on earth. You are, or can be, a member of His Church. Membership is open to all who wish to join, but it's forced upon no one. You get to choose, and this book was written to help you choose wisely.

His Church here on earth has a prophet who receives guidance and direction directly from God. I testify to you that the words and teachings of the prophet and Church leaders are true. I know this because I've seen and been involved in many life experiences that prove their words are true. I testify that our Church, The Church of Jesus Christ of Latter-day Saints, is true. If you choose to follow its teachings, your life will be easier and you'll eventually qualify to receive God's greatest gift.

This is what I firmly believe, and these beliefs make up the foundation that supports my purpose in life. I will continue to build on this foundation because it is the only foundation strong enough to support everything I do. Without this foundation, my life wouldn't have meaning or purpose.

One last thought before we move on. There is another scripture in the Book of Mormon that I really love. It's found in Mosiah 2:9. This verse is quite long, so I will paraphrase it, and I'll add a couple of words to help you better understand how it applies to my book. It reads, "All ye that have assembled [gathered] . . . can hear my words; . . . [don't] trifle [think these words have no value] with the words which I shall speak, but [listen to me because they are important], and open your ears that ye may hear, and your hearts that ye may understand, and your minds that the mysteries of God may be unfolded to your view."

What makes a mystery a mystery? A mystery is something you don't understand. Mosiah 2:9 teaches us that there are mysteries of God. Are they mysteries because God doesn't want you to understand, or are they mysteries because you haven't taken time to understand? I believe it's because you haven't taken time to understand.

In the next chapter, I'll help you gain a clear understanding of one of God's greatest mysteries: why good and bad things happen here on earth.

REVIEW OF IMPORTANT POINTS

- There is a connection between doing good things and lasting success.
- You must define your successful life so you can set goals.
- Inventory the resources (time, money, abilities) you can use to reach your goals.
- Doing what's right won't be easy, but you must do what's right if you want the blessings that come from it.
- The only foundation strong enough to support your life is your belief in God and Jesus Christ.
- Mysteries of God are only mysteries because we don't take time to figure them out.

$$A = \begin{pmatrix} 2 & -1 \\ -3 & -2 \end{pmatrix} \quad y = \sqrt{2x-1}$$

δ

CHAPTER 4

IT MUST MAKE SENSE

H AVE YOU NOTICED how the things that happen in life often make no sense whatsoever? Accidents happen to some but not others. Some enjoy good health, while others experience life-threatening illnesses. Some enjoy prosperity, while others work hard all their lives but remain poor. Some are beautiful and others aren't, and some are talented and others aren't. I could go on and on. The list of seemingly unfair things in life never ends.

Wanting to know why these things happen is normal, but it's also spiritually dangerous. I don't want you to be in spiritual danger, so I'm going to answer your *why* questions before you even ask them. I'll tell you what I think, and you can decide if it makes sense.

I found the answer to my *why* questions by choosing to look at life in a new way. I say "new" because it was new to me. There may be others who think this way, but I don't believe there are many. How many times have you heard someone say, "God gave me this trial," "This is God's will," or "God caused this to happen to me for a reason"? I've heard these or something like them said every time something happens, especially if it's something bad. I've chosen not to look at life this way, because it could make you think you're being punished for something you did or, in many cases, for something you didn't do. And that doesn't make sense.

The evil team just went nuts, so I want to make something perfectly clear. I'm not questioning God, His ways, or His abilities. Nor am I limiting His power. God is God, and that means there are no limits to what He can or can't do. I'm also not questioning anyone's beliefs, because people can choose to believe whatever they want. But in my view, the notion that God causes everything to happen doesn't make sense because it interferes with an important God-given right called *agency*.

I believe agency gives us not only the right to choose but also the right to experience the consequences of our choices, whether they're good, bad, or even terrible. If God gives you the right to choose and experience consequences but then makes things happen regardless of your choices, wouldn't that interfere with agency?

Hearing people say "God did this because . . ." caused a lot of confusion for me. After a lot of thought, study, and prayer, I've chosen to look at life this new way because it makes more sense. Even though God put us here on this earth, He doesn't personally cause everything to happen. I've also chosen to believe that agency gives me the ability to control a lot of what might happen. I know I can't control everything, but that shouldn't keep me from using my agency to control as much as I can. Agency gives you control by allowing you to make good choices that lead to good actions and good consequences—most of the time. Why only most of the time? I'll explain that a little later.

Why do good choices allow you to have control in life? In Doctrine and Covenants 82:10, the Lord makes this promise: "I, the Lord, am bound when ye do what I say [make good choices]; but when ye do not what I say [make bad choices], ye have no promise." God only makes a promise when He means it. Here, He's binding Himself to another promise: if you obey His commandments (make good choices), you will prosper. Since God doesn't lie, you can be sure He will keep His promise.

Throughout life, the evil team will continually try to make you doubt that God will keep His promise. Whatever you do, don't believe them. God will keep His promise if you're willing to make good choices. I know because I've experienced it many times. Let me show you how He does it.

$$\pi$$

REMEMBER WHEN I likened your life to traveling different roads? As you live your life or travel your road, you're going to pass through countless intersections where your road meets other roads. After you enter these intersections, you must make a choice, and that choice will determine the road you'll take from that point. Think about this as I explain how choices are made.

You come to an intersection where you must make a choice. As you're sitting at the intersection, a thought enters your mind that tells you to go one way; almost immediately, another thought tells you to go another way. You consider how you feel about each thought, and you choose the one that feels the best.

You have these different thoughts because there are two powerful opposing forces here on earth. One is good and the other is bad, or evil. If you choose to act on the good thought, God will bless you with better consequences. These better consequences help you prosper. If you choose to act on the bad or evil thought, God can't bless you. Your consequences won't be good, and you won't prosper.

The evil team again reminded me that there are many people who do bad and prosper, but remember, this life doesn't last forever. Sooner or later, their actions will catch up with them, and they'll no longer prosper for an eternity—unless, of course, they change their choices.

Now that you understand how good choices create good consequences, how many good consequences can one good choice create? Is it just one, or is it many? I believe each good choice opens the doors of heaven so God can bless you with many good consequences, or blessings. All of His blessings are good, but some are better than others. For example, one of His better blessings is an increased ability to hear or feel the thought God wants you to choose when you're making choices. Here's how that works.

You're again in the intersection and need to make a choice. Both powers send you their thoughts, and they both sound or feel good. All thoughts must sound or feel good or you would never consider them. As you consider the consequences of each thought, you notice the thought that leads to the real, good consequence will feel or sound slightly stronger or more intense than the other. Each time you choose the good thought, your relationship with God becomes stronger. That makes it easier for you to hear or feel His thought when you need to make your next choice.

Why would you want God helping you make choices? You want His help because He can see all the consequences before you even make your choices. This ability allows Him to know which choice you must make to receive His blessings. God loves you more than you could ever imagine and wants to bless you. You determine the blessings you'll receive by the choices you make.

When I was young, it was hard for me to understand how it was possible for God to see things before they happened. Now that I'm older, I think I might be able to understand one way that He does it. You see, God is perfect in every possible way, so He perfectly understands the consequences of every person's choices and how all the different consequences of those choices will interact with each other before people even make their choices. There may be other ways, and trying to figure out how God can see things before they happen might be fun, but it isn't really important. What's important is the fact that He can do it.

Can you even begin to imagine what you could do with God on your side, who can see things before they happen? I can, because I've experienced it.

Here's one example. Recently I found what looked like a new, small rubber basketball along the side of a country road, and I took it home. Then one of our grandsons came to visit. My wife thought he would like to play with the ball, so she asked me to clean it up and bring it into the house. Now watch what happened as I passed through several different intersections of choice.

After I wiped the dust off the ball, a thought told me to pump the ball up, so I took it to the air compressor and pumped it up nice and firm. Then a thought told me to bring the ball up to my face so I could check for leaks. As I did, another, stronger thought told me to get the ball away from my face, so I immediately did. After that, a thought told me to throw the ball away, so I took the ball to the garbage can, dropped it in, and closed the lid. As I stepped away, the ball exploded with enough force to raise the lid off the can. I guess I'd put a little too much air in the ball.

This experience was especially meaningful to me because I'm blind in one eye. Can you imagine what might have happened to my only good eye if the ball had exploded in my face? I'll never know for sure, but it makes me sick to think about it.

Can you see how both powers were sending me thoughts? One was trying to create a situation where I could have lost my good eye, and the other was helping me avoid that very situation. Can you also see how the choices I made created the consequences I received? If I hadn't listened and obeyed, heaven only knows what might have happened. But I did listen, and I received the better consequence or blessing.

This question is easy to answer, but I'll ask it anyway. Which team sent which thoughts? Obviously the one that tried to hurt me was the evil team, and the one that tried to help me avoid being hurt was the good team. But consider this: Why did I immediately act on the good team's thought? It felt or sounded stronger, and that helped me recognize it.

But remember, even though God is willing to help or warn you, He'll never interfere with your agency. He'll always let you make your choice, and He'll let you experience the consequence of your choice whether you like it or not.

If all that makes you feel uncomfortable, it shouldn't. When you continue to make good choices, your ability to feel or hear God's thoughts will increase until you're able to clearly recognize the choice He wants you to make. If you make that choice, you'll experience better consequences, and those consequences will strengthen your faith in the process. Stronger faith allows God to increase the intensity of His thoughts, making it even easier to recognize the choice He wants you to make. This positive cycle continues until God's thoughts are the only thoughts you feel or hear. Okay, maybe not the only thoughts. Life is an ongoing test, but they will become the only thoughts you'll want to listen to, because you'll know they're the only ones that always produce better consequences.

Does that make sense? Let's take these thoughts to the next step.

When I was going through my experience with the ball, what was God actually doing? He was leading me safely through a dangerous life experience. If you'll choose to let Him lead you through life, you'll have more control over the events you experience. If you're wondering how you gain more control by letting God lead you, you're not alone. One of the greatest challenges you'll face is choosing to believe that you have more control, not less control, when you let God lead you. Why? Blame it on the evil team. They're constantly telling you that He's trying to control you by making you do what He wants, but that's not what He's really doing.

While it's true that God is in control, He never tries to control you. That would interfere with your agency, and nobody—not even God—can interfere with your agency because it's against the rules. He's just trying to lead you to better consequences because He loves you. I know He loves us, because the consequences of my choices are always better when I let Him lead me. When He leads, I make fewer bad choices and experience fewer bad consequences, and that keeps me from losing hope.

I've already mentioned one reason that not losing hope is important, but here's another. If you ever lose hope, you'll live each day in fear, just waiting for the next bad thing to happen. After it happens, you'll wonder why God is doing that to you, and that question will always be followed by even more spiritually dangerous questions.

Here are some examples. After something bad happens, you wonder, "Why would God let this happen to me?" That thought will cause you to wonder, "Why doesn't God love me?" And that thought always leads to this even more dangerous thought: "There must not even be a God because no loving God would ever let this happen to someone He loved."

Can you see why I call these why questions dangerous? They're dangerous because they lead you away from God, and who wants to separate you from God? It's always the evil team. But the good news is you will never need to ask any of these dangerous, potentially life-changing questions once you understand why things really happen. Here's why things happen.

$$\pi$$

THINGS IN LIFE happen because everyone is making choices. All of these choices have consequences that come together to create events, and these events create our experiences here on earth. God doesn't need to make things happen because all the choices made by all the different people create plenty of opportunities for things to happen.

What is God doing while we're all making choices? Is He just standing idly by, watching? He isn't. He's constantly sending thoughts to encourage His children to make good choices so they can create the good consequences (most of the time) He wants us to enjoy. What is the evil team doing while God is trying to help you? They're trying to stop Him from helping you by sending you bad or dumb thoughts, which if chosen will create the bad consequences you experience here on earth. All of these different experiences give you the knowledge you need to prepare for the next life.

This is a simple explanation for why things happen in life, but I will give you a more detailed explanation as you continue reading. How can I be sure this is why things happen? Any other way would interfere with agency, and that can't happen because nobody can interfere with agency.

Are you wondering why I say that good choices bring good consequences *more often than not*, *most of the time*, or *almost always*? I use these qualifiers because there is always a chance your good choices will meet someone else's bad choices and create a bad outcome. In this imperfect world, about the best you can hope for is more control, not complete control. Sometimes life just doesn't treat you well, even when you're making good choices. I'll explain more about why this often happens in later chapters.

$$\pi$$

I ENCOURAGE YOU to believe what I've explained here about choice and consequence. Remember, how you look at life is a choice like any other. So are you ready to choose to believe? I hope so, because you'll never know what's waiting until you do. Here's why I've chosen to believe in this new, uncommon way of thinking.

As I've grown older, I've discovered that I'm a normal, mortal, imperfect-in-about-every-way dad, and yet the absolute last thing I would ever want to do is hurt my kids and grandkids. Instead, I spend every waking minute trying to keep them from harm. I try, without being too overprotective, to teach them, advise them, and lead them through life. I want them to be able to avoid as many bad things as they possibly can. In fact, I sometimes pray that if anything bad is going to happen to my family, then I could step in and take their place so it happens to me instead of them. I know it can't work that way, but that's the best way to describe how I feel about my family.

Stop and think about what I just said. I love my family enough to take their place if something bad is going to happen to them. This intense love for my family comes from a normal, imperfect guy who's just trying to be a good dad. But God is nothing like me. He's a perfected dad, meaning that He is everything I'm not and much more. If He's perfect, nothing is missing. Because He's perfect, He is the very best example of a perfect, loving, caring dad that you could ever imagine. Can you agree with that?

If what I believe is true and He is a perfect dad, why would He want to hurt His kids? I know He understands that we need challenges to grow in character, but I don't want to think of Him as a dad who would actually want or cause something bad to happen to me just so I could grow. Instead, I choose to believe, because it's evidenced on practically every page of the scriptures, that He loves me more than I could ever understand. How then could I make sense of these two complete opposites? On one hand, He loves me more than I'll ever be able to understand; on the other hand, He wants to hurt me. To me, the two thoughts are not at all compatible.

You may think that God wants to punish His kids after they do something wrong because He loves them, but I can't agree with that line of thought either. Look at it this way. If you're a parent and your child does something wrong, did you encourage them to do wrong so you could punish them, or did they just do wrong even though you told, begged, and even threatened them not to do it? In our house, the kids chose to do wrong even after we had done everything we could do to keep them from doing it.

Think about what you just read and answer this question: Would you purposely look for opportunities to make life hard on your kids, or would you allow them to find and experience challenges on their own while you teach them how to avoid them? Would you create life-changing or life-ending experiences and then force your kids to experience them just so they, or someone close to them, could develop character? Doesn't that sound silly? Of course it does. You would love your kids, and as a regular, normal, imperfect parent.

Can you see why it doesn't make sense to think that God, your perfect Dad, would want bad things to happen to you? Wouldn't it make more sense for Him to create a place where you can learn from your experiences while He tries to help you avoid problems? Makes sense to me. In fact, it's a lot like what I tried to do for my kids.

π

WHEN MY KIDS were young, my wife and I created a home where we could teach our kids how to avoid major problems in life. We put them through school, took them to church, and taught them to be good. To make a long story short, we did everything we could to prepare them for life.

What did your Heavenly Father and Mother do for you in the premortal world? They did the exact same thing—only They did it perfectly.

As our children grew, we realized that we couldn't, and shouldn't, make them do things like we did when they were young, so our child-raising strategy changed. We continued to teach them, but we started to allow them to make some choices and experience some consequences while we continued to beg, warn, threaten, and even bribe them to make good choices. Again, to make another long story short, we did what we could to prepare them for and protect them from life. We didn't want our kids making mistakes because mistakes hurt, and we didn't want them to hurt because we loved them. When they listened and obeyed, we rewarded them with good things. When they didn't obey, they didn't get rewarded, but we were always there to help them while they worked on fixing their mistakes.

Heavenly Father raises His kids here on earth the same way—but again, He does it perfectly. He raises them this way so that the consequences, not God, can be their teacher here on earth. The consequences teach truth, and truth helps them make better choices. Those better choices in turn allow God to reward them with blessings.

Why do His kids want blessings? Blessings help them avoid future challenges or trials in life, and they're the way God fulfills His promise. Remember His promise: if you obey, you will prosper.

Did you just say, "Wait a minute, I thought I was supposed to have challenges and trials so I could grow stronger and improve my character. Isn't that what this life is all about?"

Yes, that's exactly what this life is all about. You do need challenges and trials to grow stronger and improve your character, but my point is, your need for trials doesn't change who God really is. God is your perfect Dad, but He will allow trials if you refuse to listen to His warnings or obey His commandments.

Looking at God this new way probably goes against everything you've been taught, because you've been taught that God, either directly or indirectly, gives you the challenges or trials you experience in life so you can grow in character, understanding, and knowledge. I believe the same thing, but I believe He gives them to us in a different way.

God loves you, and because He loves you, He wants to help you avoid challenges or trials in life. But He also understands that you need them to grow in character. How then can He give you what He wants and allow you to receive what you need when these two things are complete opposites? The answer is, He can't—unless He first creates a place where these two opposites can coexist in perfect harmony in the same place at the same time.

There are a few other things this place would need to have or it couldn't work. The place must have a purpose, and it must have rules (commandments). He also must give us the freedom to make choices (agency), while He and His opposition (the evil team) send us thoughts. He or His opposition must not be seen because that would interfere with our agency. All of our choices must have good or bad consequences so we can learn; the good consequences would be blessings from God, and the bad consequences, our challenges or trials, would be from the evil team. He also must set a time limit for us to be in this place, and there needs to be a better reward for those who obey. Last, but certainly not least, He must also make a way for everyone to eventually be saved even when they choose to break the rules (sin). Everyone must have a chance to win, but no one can be forced to win.

Could the place I just described exist? A place where two complete opposites work together in perfect harmony? A place where all experiences, good, bad, and even terrible, have value because they teach truths? A place where these truths would help us obtain knowledge and understanding, which could then be used later to fulfill God's purposes? A place where God can be a perfect Dad but not interfere with agency?

The answer is yes. Such a place can exist, because you're living here right now.

Welcome to life in this imperfect world called earth, a place that God created so you could be tried, tested, and taught by your challenges and trials while He tries to help you avoid as many of them as possible; a place where both good and bad can happen without any help from God.

I'll bet the evil team just went crazy when I said "without any help from God," so I'd better explain what I meant.

Let's say God is watching you walk down the sidewalk. As you approach the curb, He says, "I wonder how he would react if I caused him to get run over by a garbage truck. Let's do it and see." He puts a garbage truck right where it needs to be, makes sure you don't see it, and then tells you to step off the curb at the exact right moment so you can get run over—just so He can see how you'll react and so you can learn not to step out in front of a moving garbage truck.

I hear you thinking, "That's stupid. Nobody would actually think God would do that." I hope they wouldn't, but haven't you heard someone say, "God made this happen for a reason"? My personal least favorite is, "God made this happen because I needed it." Yes, you may have needed it, but I don't believe God made it happen. I instead choose to believe that He allowed it to happen when you didn't listen to His warnings.

I'm sure people ask make these statements to help them try to make sense of things that happen. But do they really make any sense? I believe the answer is no. Making sense of things may help you find closure and put the event behind you, but closing it the wrong way could leave you with some really bad feelings about God. Closing the event and moving on is a necessary step that you must take in order to survive, but wouldn't it be better to close the event and still believe that God loves you and is on your side? I promise you it is better for at least a couple of reasons, which I'll discuss in the next chapter.

Right now I just hope you'll try to believe that God loves you and that He really is on your side. If you can do that, then you can begin to believe He's leading you through life. That will allow Him to help you avoid as many problems as possible. Remember, first comes faith, and then come blessings, and sometimes even a miracle.

$$\pi$$

THIS WOULD BE a great place to stop and think about what you've just read. This new way of looking at your relationship with God is really important. In fact, it's so important that I would liken it to crossing a bridge. If you come to a bridge but are unwilling to cross it, will you ever be able to see what's on the other side? You may get a glimpse of it, but to fully see, understand, and enjoy what's waiting on the other side, you must be willing to cross the bridge.

If what I've said makes sense, take the next step. Cross the bridge by starting to believe God is really on your side. Can you do that? I hope so, but if for any reason you can't, don't stop reading. In the next chapter I'll share a few experiences with you that will help you believe. After you start believing, some pretty amazing things can start happening in your life.

REVIEW OF IMPORTANT POINTS

- Some things that happen in life make no sense whatsoever.
- Agency is the right to make choices and experience consequences, whether we like them or not.
- After everyone makes choices, events happen that create consequences.
- God loves you and wants to help you avoid challenges and trials.
- You need challenges and trials to grow in character.
- God created this earth. It's an ingenious creation because it allows you to receive what you need while God tries to help you avoid bad experiences.
- Letting God lead you will give you more control over what happens in life.
- Understanding why things happen allows you to close an event correctly.
- First comes faith, and then come blessings, and sometimes miracles.
- You must choose to cross the bridge before you can see what's on the other side.

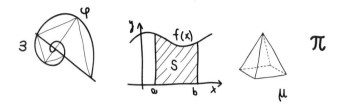

CHAPTER 5

DEPENDS ON HOW YOU LOOK AT IT

C AN YOU TELL me how two people can look at the same thing and see it two completely different ways? Recently I took my wife to the local Ford dealership to show her a brand-new cherry-red Shelby GT 500 Mustang. It wasn't a King of the Road or Super Snake, but it was still the most beautiful car I could imagine. Just looking at it made me think I'd died and gone to heaven.

After spending several minutes examining every square inch of that car, I turned and looked at my wife, hoping that she was enjoying the experience as much as I was. She wasn't even looking at the car. She was just staring at me, and when our eyes met, she didn't have to say a word. I knew exactly what she was thinking. But she said it anyway: "Why in the world would anybody pay that much for a Mustang?"

I was stunned, but I managed to say, "It's not just a Mustang—it's a Shelby GT 500 Mustang."

In an effort to convince her that the car was worth the price, I had her sit in the driver's seat. "Can you feel it?" I asked. Of course she said no.

I took her up front and opened the hood so I could show her how the motor filled almost every inch of space under that hood. I asked, "Can you feel it now?" She again said no.

I took her to the passenger side and told her how good she'd look riding in our car. That didn't work either. She said, "You're crazy if you think we're going to buy this Mustang. And if we did, what in the world would you do with it?"

I told her I'd probably just park it in the garage and polish it every single day, to which she replied, "Can we go now? I need to stop and get some groceries."

How can two people see the same thing in two completely different ways? The answer is—drumroll please—it depends on how they choose to look at it. This experience and countless others have taught me that the way you look at anything, including life, depends entirely upon how you choose to look at it.

As you live your life in this imperfect world, good and bad things are going to happen to you and to those around you. All of these events will have to be dealt with, but whether you're able to deal with them may depend entirely upon on how you choose to look at each event. Will you join the "things happen because" group, or the "because things happen" group? If you choose the "things happen because" group, you'll believe God causes everything to happen. This way of thinking doesn't mix well with agency, so I've chosen to join the "because things happen" group. Here's why you should also join this group.

How you choose to look at events will either have a positive or negative effect on your relationship with God. If you'll join the "because things happen" group, all good things that happen will be looked at as blessings from God. Looking at these events as blessings will strengthen your faith in God. This strengthening will continue until you're confident that God is on your side.

When bad things happen, you'll recognize that they are nothing more than bad consequences created by bad choices. Because you believe God is on your side, you'll go to Him with faith and ask Him to help you get through the experience. Your desire, coupled with faith, will allow Him to help you. Then as things do eventually get better, your relationship with God will be strengthened even more.

Up to this point, your relationship with God has been strengthened almost daily, but then something terrible happens. Even though it's terrible, you still believe that it happened because of choices—not because God wanted it to happen. This belief allows you to go to God in the depths of sorrow and humility and with a firm belief that He will help you get through this difficult time. Eventually, one way or another, you will get through it. That creates an even deeper appreciation for God, and your relationship is strengthened even more.

Can you see how everything that happens strengthens your relationship with God when you join the "because things happen" group? Now let's look at what happens if you join the "things happen because" group.

π

IF YOU'RE IN the "things happen because" group, when something good happens, you won't even think to ask why it happened. The evil team will tell you that you're just lucky or you deserve it, or they may even make sure that you don't think about it at all. If you don't think about it, you won't make a connection between those good things and blessings. If you don't recognize the experience as a blessing, you won't be prompted to thank God, and that weakens your relationship with Him.

When something bad happens, you'll immediately find yourself wondering, "Why did this happen?" No answer will make any sense, so you'll believe the evil team when they tell you that it happened because God wanted it to happen. That causes lots of confusion, because you've been told that God loves you. To rid yourself of this confusion, you look back at your life to see if you've done anything bad, and of course you find something. This allows the evil team to tell you that it's your fault and now God is punishing you.

Why would the evil team want you to think God is punishing you? It's so you won't feel you can ask Him to help you. But if you don't ask, He can't help you. If He can't help you, you'll end up suffering more, and that creates an even greater divide between you and God. This greater divide damages the relationship you once had even more, which keeps you from seeing God as your loving, caring Father in Heaven. You instead see Him as a vengeful God who wants to punish you when you do something bad.

Looking at God this way isn't good, but something else can happen too. If you can't find anything bad enough to justify His punishment, what will that do to your relationship with God? Will you ever be able to see Him as your loving, caring Father, or will you see Him as someone who wants to hurt you for no reason at all? Can you see how the evil team could—and I promise you they do—use this strategy to destroy your relationship with God? This is why you should want to join the "because things happen" group.

But I need to ask you a question. Why does the evil team want to damage or even destroy the relationship you have with God? You might think the answer is obvious, but let me show you something you may have missed.

$$\pi$$

THE EVIL TEAM wants to destroy your relationship with God so you'll no longer believe in right and wrong. If there's no right and no wrong, then you'll think that the choices you make don't matter. If your choices don't matter, why wouldn't you want what the evil team offers? Nothing is right and nothing is wrong, and everything they offer makes you feel good, so why wouldn't you want it? The only reason you wouldn't want it is that it's wrong. If they can convince you there is no right or wrong, they'll have a much easier time destroying you.

Remember, your relationship with God is always changing. Usually the changes aren't big, but you're always moving a little closer or drifting a little farther away. The best way to help you understand your relationship might be to liken it to a boat sailing on the ocean toward its home port. The port is God, the ocean is the world, the boat is your life, and you're the captain of the boat.

As captain, you must constantly steer your boat toward the port as the currents of life try to pull you away from it. It's a battle every day, but it must be fought and won or you'll eventually end up being lost at sea. Here's another thought to consider.

How would you feel if you really loved someone and tried in every way all the time to help him, then he chose to blame you every time something happened? The word *blame* may sound harsh, but isn't that what we're saying when we say God causes everything to happen? I know I'd feel bad if I were blamed for everything.

A person I respect had an interesting thought after reading this chapter. She asked, "If the experiences we have in life are just random, wouldn't that be cruel and unfair?" I used to ask myself the same question, but now that I'm old, my answer is no—because no experience is random. See if this makes sense.

We're all God's children, but we're not at the same place in growth or character development because this life is not the beginning of our existence. Prior to this life, you lived in God's presence until it was your time to come to earth. God created this earth as a place which not only has everything you need to sustain life, but it also provides, by its nature, every opportunity you need for character growth and development.

This opportunity to grow is based entirely upon what you need. For example, if you need to learn to be honest, this life will teach you to be honest by experiencing the consequences of not being honest. If you need to learn to be nice, this life will teach you to be nice when you experience the consequences of not being nice. If you're already honest and nice, this life teaches you the importance of being honest and nice when you enjoy the blessings you receive as a result.

The way it all works is the absolute genius of God's plan. Nothing about this life is random. God gives you commandments to follow, and then He allows you to choose whether or not you'll follow them. After you make your choice, you experience the consequences of each choice, which teach you the things you need to learn.

Who, then, determines what you need to learn? You do. God already knows which character traits you need to develop. To put it as simply as I can, many of the things you need to learn are determined by which commandments you're not willing to obey. It really is that simple, and it provides more evidence that the things we experience are not random. They're all catered to our own personal needs.

Did you notice that I said *many* of the things you need to learn? What about all the other things you experience? For instance, you're choosing to drive carefully, but you're still involved in an accident that wasn't your fault. Or you try to eat right, exercise, and take care of yourself, but you still get a life-threatening disease. There are more of these unfair experiences than you could ever count, but the answer for why they all happen is exactly the same.

Unfair, undesirable, or unwanted experiences happen here on earth for several different reasons. First, the evil team is sending thoughts to people that encourage them to make bad choices. These bad choices create bad consequences that can involve you if you happen to be in the wrong place at the right time. You also have an imperfect, defective telestial-model body that is designed to self-destruct over time because of age, illness, or disease. Other challenges are created because the earth is constantly changing as it prepares to fill the measure of its creation.

This earth really is an ingenious creation, because it gives you every possible opportunity to learn. If you choose to join the "because things happen" group, you'll be able to look at all these different experiences as opportunities to learn, grow, and receive additional blessings. Learning is never easy, but it can be made easier if you choose to join this group.

$$\pi$$

NOW THAT YOU understand why things happen, you're probably wondering if God wants bad things to happen to you. My answer is yes and no.

I say yes because He put you here on this earth, but that's as far as I'm willing to go. I choose to believe that even though He put you here, He really doesn't want you to experience bad things. If He did, why did He give you commandments to help you avoid them? And why does He send His Spirit to warn, lead, guide, and try to protect you? God loves you. He also knows you need experiences to gain knowledge, so He created this imperfect world. Is it unfair or cruel because bad things don't happen to everyone equally? Again, my answer is no.

The Church of Jesus Christ of Latter-day Saints teaches that all who came to earth attended a council in heaven where the plan, or this earth life, was explained. I've often wondered if there was just one or if there were more than one council. That really doesn't matter. All that matters is that the plan was explained and we accepted it. But here's the problem. Even though we accepted the plan, we had no idea what they were talking about because we lived in a perfect world. I like to say, "I shouted for joy after hearing the plan because I had no idea what I was getting myself into."

Some people believe that they knew or even chose what challenge they would face before they came to earth. I can believe that they knew, even though they didn't understand, but I see two problems with the choice part. First, we don't believe in predestination (things happen because), and second, it doesn't mix well with agency. I instead choose to believe that I attended a council in heaven prior to coming to earth. In this council, the plan with all of the possible problems was discussed, and I then agreed to the possibility that I might experience these problems—even though I didn't fully understand the problems.

Now that you understand why events happen, I hope you're ready to join the "because things happen" group. Joining this group will allow you to choose how you're going to deal with events that happen here on earth. Will you choose to believe that God is willing to help you, or will you choose to believe God is working against you? I've chosen to believe He is willing to help me, and He has more times than I can count. These experiences have convinced me without doubt that God loves me and wants to help me make it through life safely and successfully.

This same blessing is also available to you if you're willing to join my group. Once you choose to believe, God will start helping you make good choices. Good choices create good consequences, and these consequences create most of the events you experience in life.

$$\pi$$

DID YOU JUST hear the evil team scream? In my head they said, "Choices don't make earthquakes happen. God makes earthquakes happen, so choices don't create the events you experience in life." That's interesting, but it's not a valid point. God created the earth, so you could say that He causes everything to happen. But again, that's as far as I'm willing to go.

This earth, like all His creations, has a purpose, and it's working on fulfilling its purpose by continually evolving and changing. All these changes have consequences. Some bring beautiful days, gentle rains, and times when everything is almost perfect. There are also times when you could experience droughts, floods, big waves, earthquakes, and hurricanes. With today's technology, all of these events can be explained, and some can even be predicted. But we don't know what eternal purpose they fulfill because all of God's purposes aren't known to man. So now you're right back where you started: you must choose how you're going to look at all these different events.

This is how I choose to look it. God created the earth, and it's continually changing as it fulfills the purposes for which it was created. God, through His prophets, has told me how to prepare for the natural consequences of these changes. The prophets said I should buy extra food, clothing, and medical supplies, and store some water. If God told me through His prophets to prepare, which side is He on? I believe He's on my side, but He still must honor my agency by allowing me to choose whether or not I'll obey His counsel. After my choice is made, I then get to enjoy, or not enjoy, the consequences of my choice. God knows some of my choices will be good and some will be bad, but He still allows me to experience the different consequences because they all teach me something if I'm willing to learn.

Here's a real-life example of how this works. For some reason, someone decided to build New Orleans below sea level. I'm not questioning their judgment, but building a city below sea level doesn't make a lot of sense. Because the city is located below sea level, they also had to build dykes and dams and install pumps to keep the area from flooding. These protections worked well until Hurricane Katrina hit the area. This storm gave them more water than the dykes, dams, and pumps could handle, and New Orleans flooded. This flooding caused the people living there to suffer, which probably made many wonder why God did that to them. Let's see if looking at it that way makes sense.

If you believe God did that to them, then you must believe they did something wrong and God is punishing them. Or you must believe God wanted it to happen just so He could see how they'd react. If either of these is correct, then God must have intentionally created a huge hurricane and guided it to New Orleans so the area would flood and the people would suffer. This suffering would let them know they were being punished, or it would allow Him to see how they'd react to that bad situation.

What do you think? Did either of those reasons make any sense? They don't to me. They sound totally out of character for a God who loves His kids more than they could ever understand.

Let's look at the flooding from the "because things happen" point of view. Having New Orleans built below sea level worked pretty well for a time, but eventually their luck ran out when an unexpected, uncommonly big hurricane hit the area. The people who planned the city hadn't seen anything like it, so they weren't prepared for it, and the city flooded. The people living there were given an opportunity to show they learned something from the experience by doing one or two really obvious things: First, they don't rebuild the city below sea level. Second, because they live in a city that's built below sea level, they should choose to move to higher ground as quickly as possible.

Did those who live in New Orleans learn something from the experience? I'm sure some did, and because they did, they won't be there the next time it floods. What about the other people who just waited for the water to be pumped out and for the dykes and dams to be fixed so they could move right back into a city built below sea level? Did they learn anything?

Which one of these points of view left you with good feelings about God? Can you see how your relationship with God is either strengthened or weakened by how you choose to look at life's events?

$$\pi$$

SO WHAT MUST you do to receive God's help? You must be willing to choose and act on His thoughts instead of the evil team's thoughts. I'm currently at the point where His thoughts are easily recognized, but I'm still trying to make myself consistently choose to follow them.

Want an example? Recently I was trying to open a product that came in a bubble pack. I couldn't get it open, so I took out a razor knife to cut the plastic. Just as I put the knife to the plastic, the Spirit said, "Don't do it. You're going to cut yourself." Did I listen? No, and guess what happened. I cut my hand. Why didn't I just listen? Because life is an ongoing test, and sometimes my test is to not do dumb things. But I'm not giving up. I'll just keep trying to do better each day. Did I learn something? I did. But will I remember it?

This example shows why you'll still have problems when you have God on your side. Just living in this imperfect world creates many opportunities for problems, but with God's help, you'll experience fewer of them because God will warn you before bad things happen to you. I've experienced this several times. Those experiences have convinced me that God wants to help me avoid problems, but the consequences can't change unless I change my choices.

The evil team just said, "If God warns you about problems, doesn't that change the consequences?" It does if you change your choices. Choices change actions, and different actions create different consequences. So who is really changing the consequences?

It's you. God will help you, but it's up to you to change your choices so the consequence can change.

Some would say that being able to avoid problems is nothing more than luck, and others may call it receiving blessings. What it's called doesn't matter. I usually say that I was just really lucky to be blessed right when I needed it the most, but that's not the only benefit you receive after you've chosen to believe God's on your side. The list of benefits is long, so I'll just mention a few.

With God on your side, you'll be able to get more done in life. Sure, you can get more done as you get smarter with age, but answer this question: Can you get more done by yourself, or can you get more done with God's help? I've learned that you can get more done with God's help because you make fewer mistakes, and that means you'll spend less time fixing the consequences of your mistakes. Less time fixing gives you more time to get things done.

Another benefit you'll enjoy is the ability to do things that you could never do by yourself. For example, I was able to write a book. What will you be able to do? You'll never know until you choose to believe and then go to work. When I look back at my life, I can clearly see how God has helped me do many things I couldn't have done by myself. That gives me the faith, courage, and confidence I need to keep going even when things that happen don't make a lot of sense. I want to make sure you understand why you can keep going, so I'll explain.

After I chose to believe God was on my side, I received a benefit or a blessing I didn't expect, and it has helped me more than I could have ever imagined. This blessing was the ability to clearly understand why I'm here on earth. Understanding why is absolutely critical, because many of life's experiences are going to be confusing, depressing, and, quite often, pretty darn scary. I don't want these types of experiences, but now that I understand them, I don't fear them. Instead, I look at them as opportunities for growth. Has life been easy because I've made this choice? No, but it's been easier. God loves you, and His blessings are real, but you have to choose to believe before you can enjoy them.

So what's it going to be? Will you join the "things happen because" group or will you join the "because things happen" group? I promise you that life will be easier if you join my group, because God will help you avoid many—or perhaps even most—of the typical problems you could experience while living in this imperfect world. It's your choice. I hope you choose wisely.

REVIEW OF IMPORTANT POINTS

- How you view events that happen in life will depend entirely upon how you choose to look at them.
- Choose to join the "because things happen" group, not the "things happen because" group.
- Each experience provides you with an opportunity to learn.
- God wants you to be safe as you learn, so He gave you commandments.
- Events in life are not random, because you determine what you'll experience. This world was designed to teach you what you need to learn.
- Understanding why things happen will keep you from becoming depressed and discouraged.

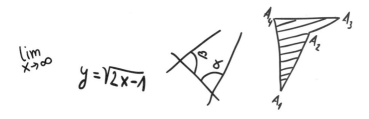

CHAPTER 6

PLAYING THE GAME AND WINNING

IN THIS CHAPTER I'm going to compare life on earth to the game of football, because life really is just like football. Do you like football? I hope so, but even if you don't, life is still a lot like football.

When I was young, I played a lot of football. If I remember right, my football career started when I was in seventh or eighth grade. I was excited because our town was going to sponsor Little League football for the first time.

There were just two teams: the Packers and the Giants. I joined the Packers, and I'm glad I did because we never lost a single game. Always being on the winning team was probably the reason I loved playing football. Life is a lot more fun when you're winning, and you win by creating a successful life.

In football there are only two teams on the field—your team and the opposing team. Once you join a team, the other team automatically becomes your opposition. Your team has only one purpose: defeat the other team. When I played, my coaches weren't content with just defeating the other team. They wanted us to destroy them.

This same feeling exists between the two teams here on earth—the good team and the evil team. Saying that these two teams merely have a heated rivalry would be like calling the ocean a pond. There are no words to adequately describe how the evil team feels about you, nor is there any limit to what they will try to get you to do so they can destroy you. Read that again: there's no limit to what they will try to *get you to do*. They can't do anything *to* you. You must do it to yourself.

In the Bible, there's a story about a man named Job. It's a great story because it helps you clearly understand the rules that the evil team must follow. As you may recall, Satan told God that Job would hate Him if God took away His protection and Job's possessions. Listen to what God said to Satan in Job 1:12: "All that he hath is in thy power; only upon himself, put not forth thine hand." That may be a little hard to understand, so let me put it the way we'd say it today: "Go ahead, Satan. Do what you want to his stuff, but you can't touch him."

Satan and the evil team can't force you to do anything. All they can do is send you thoughts that encourage you to do things to yourself. Remember this when you try to excuse what you've done by saying, "The devil made me do it." The devil can't make you do anything, but he can talk you into just about everything, so be careful.

In the football game of life, there are no spectators in the stands. Everyone must play in the games. If you decide not to play and stand idly by, you automatically become a member of the evil team. If you want to be on the good team, you must work with the team as they try to win the games. This is how games are won.

Members of the good team win games by scoring points. Members of the evil team can't win any games, because points can only be scored when a player does something that has eternal value. Since evil things have no eternal value, the evil team can't score any points. They're not in the game to win; they're only in the game to stop you from winning. I believe this is one reason they're so miserable.

You would think not being able to win would cause them to want to give up, but they never will because envy and hate are great motivators. They'll never quit until you quit or defect to their side. They know if you quit playing, you won't score any points. They also encourage you to defect by offering you all kinds of worldly possessions and pleasures that keep you on their team while they use you to stop members of the good team from scoring points.

In the football game of life, there are two types of rules. The first type tells you what you must do to score points and win, and the second type helps you stay in the game. Rules that allow you to score points are called commandments. When you obey commandments, you score points. If you don't obey, you can't score points. It's just that simple.

The rules that help you stay in the game are called common-sense truths. Here's an example: if you step in front of a moving garbage truck, you will get run over and probably be knocked out of the game. Here's another: if you touch something hot, you will get burned. There are more of these common-sense truths than you can count, and you learn them by living your life or by watching others live theirs.

The evil team will tell you that there are no rules, because they want you to think you can do whatever you want whenever you want. Life doesn't work that way. All actions have consequences that teach the players there really are rules. But by the time they figure it out, it's usually too late to do anything about it other than suffer the consequences. So why does the football game of life have rules? Let's talk about that.

$$\pi$$

WHAT IS A game, and how is it created? A game is just the sum total of the rules for that game, and it's created by someone smarter than me. Rules are important because they teach players when the game begins, when it ends, and what they must do to win. Knowing these three things helps the players understand the purpose of the game.

Look at it this way. If a game has no rules, it has no purpose and there's no reason to play the game. The evil team wants you to believe there are no rules. No rules mean no one created the game. If no one created it, it has no purpose and nothing you do really matters. If nothing matters, you can do whatever you want. Just for fun, make a mental list of what you'd like to do in life. I could never know what's on your list, but I can tell why it's on your list. You put things on your list because they make you feel good, or you think they will.

The evil team knows that the desire to feel good is the reason behind everything you do in life, so they'll tell you to "eat, drink, and be merry, for tomorrow we die" (2 Nephi 28:7). Eating, drinking, and being merry will make you feel good, and that's okay—until you break the rules by going beyond the bounds the Lord has set. If you break the rules, you can't score points. If you can't score points, you'll lose the game. And if you lose the game, the evil team will have successfully destroyed you.

The evil team also wants you to believe the football game of life has no rules so you'll think you can't win or lose the game. If that's the case, then this life must be it, meaning after you die, that's the end of you. There's a problem with that way of thinking. You don't end when you die; you just move into your eternal life.

What you do in this life matters because it determines your place in eternity—just as what you did in the premortal world determined your place in this life. This world and the football game of life were created by God to help you gain the knowledge you need to continue your eternal progression.

How do I know God created this life? I know it for two reasons. First, a while back I decided that I wanted to know, so I asked God and He answered me. The second reason I know is that the evil team spends every minute of every day trying to convince me that nothing I do really matters—which is their way of saying that there isn't a God who will hold me accountable. If nothing really matters, why do they even bother talking to me? Have you ever wondered about that?

Here's how they try to convince me that nothing really matters. See if this sounds familiar.

You're living life and all of a sudden you have a thought that makes you feel like you want something. As soon as you recognize that thought, another thought tells you that you shouldn't want it because it would be breaking the commandments. After that, another thought tells you that one time won't matter, you deserve it, or it's okay to want it. This debate continues in your head until you make your choice.

In my example, did you notice that two opposite powers were sending you thoughts? These two powers are the good team and the evil team. The good team tells you to do good things, and the evil team tells you to not do good things. This constant battle between good and evil is all the evidence I need to believe God really exists.

Next you must understand that since God created the game and the rules, He is the head official over the game. In every football game there is a head official sitting high up in the stands so he can see the whole field of play. This head official has undisputed authority over the game, which means he decides what the rules of the game actually mean. If you watch a football game closely, you will see the officials on the field call him whenever they need clarification or a final ruling during the game. The officials on the field make sure the players follow the rules so that the game can proceed according to what the creator or lead official intended. If the game is played by the rules, then the game will be fair to all the players.

When I used the word *fair*, I could almost hear you say, "What are you talking about? Nothing in the football game of life is fair." You know what? You're right. Thinking that this game is fair really would confuse the players. Why? They think *fair* means *equal*, but that's not what *fair* means. *Fair* simply means the rules of the game are the same for every player and they're applied equally to all the players.

Since God created the game and wants it to be fair, the evil team is going to tell the players to cheat. Cheating gives players a temporary unfair advantage, but the advantage is just that—temporary. Sooner or later, the officials on the field or the head official will catch them, and they will be punished for their cheating. Because you live in an imperfect world, there will be times when cheaters seem to get away with it, but they won't forever. The evil team will tell you that if they can cheat, you can cheat. Don't believe them. Eventually we all must stand before the Creator of the game and account for our actions. I guess that's why they say cheaters never (really) win.

π

SINCE GOD IS the head official, some choose to believe that no other officials are needed. It's true that God doesn't need any help because He is God, but that's not the way He designed the game.

God sent His Son, Jesus Christ, to earth to teach us how to set the game up. Jesus Christ called and ordained the Twelve Apostles and other priesthood authorities to be officials over the game. Right before He left, He set apart one of His apostles to be His chief, or lead, apostle. We call this lead apostle a prophet today because he talks with God and God talks back to him. The other priesthood authorities today are the various groups of General Authorities.

The next level of authority is the coaching staff. They have authority over the players but not over the games. The members of the coaching staff include parents, grandparents, local Church leaders, teachers, friends, and anyone else who tries to influence you while you play. In the football game of life, you must pay close attention to what a coach is teaching so you can know which team he belongs to. Now let's take a look at the games and the season.

π

GAMES REPRESENT THE days of your life, and a season represents your lifetime. Because you live in an imperfect world, everyone is not promised the same number of games or length of season. You play in the games every day, and there are no days off or days that don't count. The evil team will tell you that there are days that don't count, and they'll even say the season will never end, but don't be fooled. Every game day counts, and the season will eventually end.

The games start on the day you're born, and they continue until you die. You play two different types of games during your season: practice games and regular season games.

Practice games are a real blessing because they give some coaches—your parents—time to prepare you for the regular season games. During practice games, they teach you the skills you'll need to score points so you can win the regular season games. Practicing isn't too difficult at first, but as the regular season games get closer, it becomes intense. The coaches are right there with you every day to watch, encourage, and push you physically and mentally beyond what you think is possible. The coaches will tell you that they're trying to get you in shape, but it will feel more like they're trying to kill you.

Day after miserable day, the coaches will make you do the same thing over and over until you do it the way they want it done. Then they'll continue until you do it without even thinking about it. Practicing will seem to drag on forever, and you'll find yourself wondering, "Why do I have to keep practicing? Why can't I just play in the games?" That question will be answered in the regular season, when you recognize that the other team's players are really good. The coaches push you hard so you can become the best player possible. They know that the best team wins the games, and the best team is made up of the best players.

The coaches know you'll need every skill you can develop to win the games, but skill alone isn't enough. You'll also have to want to win more than the other team wants you to lose. The coaches know what you need because they've played in games, and that gives them experience you don't yet have.

Practice games are also a real blessing because they allow you to play without being held completely responsible or accountable for your wins and losses. But you need to be careful. Not being held accountable can make you think that actions don't have consequences. Somebody is always held accountable for your wins and losses, so you need to play the best you can.

When you're young and don't play well, your parents usually step in and cover for your mistakes. They accept your responsibility because they know you haven't yet developed all the skills you need to play the games correctly. During this time, it's normal for you not to appreciate your parents, but that doesn't make it right. You should love, appreciate, and thank your parents every day because they really do go through a lot for you.

I would encourage you to enjoy the practice games while you can. Like everything else in life, they will eventually end, and the regular season games will begin. Then the responsibility for your actions will be given to you. If you make good choices, you'll enjoy life. But if you don't, life will not treat you well. How can you know you're making good choices? Use the commandments to guide you.

Answer this question: At what age do the practice games become more difficult? It's when you become a teen. Why? I'll give you a hint: What usually starts at about age eighteen? The regular season games—college, jobs, missions, and so on. So naturally the practice games would get more difficult right before the real games begin.

I hope this helps you better understand why your parents (coaches) push you so hard when you're a teen. I hope you'll be smart and listen to them, because they love you. Try not to resist their efforts, ignore their advice, or rebel against them. This time of life can be difficult, but I encourage you to try to learn what you can before the regular season games begin.

Your teen years are an important part of God's plan. This is the time when you begin to separate from your parents so you can find a spouse, marry, and start the game over again by having children of your own. The evil team knows this, so they're also going to try to help you separate from your parents. Before you start thanking them, let me tell you why they're doing it. They know teens typically think they don't need their parents anymore, which may be true, but they do need their parents' experience to help them make good choices so they can score points. The evil team doesn't want teens scoring points, so they're more than willing to help them separate from their parents and anyone else who tries to help them.

Teens need to use their parents' experience because they don't yet understand the consequences of their actions. Consequences can only be understood after they're experienced by you or someone else. But here's the problem. After you act, the consequences are set into motion, and you get to experience them whether you like them or not. This time period is difficult for teens, but again, it's not going to last forever. Life will be much easier for you if you'll use this short amount of time to learn as much as you can from your parents while you still have them.

This difficult time of life gradually ends when your parents start letting you make your own choices and experience your own consequences. This is a dangerous period for teens because they know just enough to get themselves into real trouble. After you start making your own choices, it will be normal for your parents to be less involved in your life, but you can still use their experience to help you make good choices by talking to them about everything.

During this critical time, the evil team will send you thoughts that will make you not want to talk to your parents. Don't fall for that evil team trap. I would encourage you to take advantage of this once-in-a-lifetime opportunity to learn as much as you can from your parents.

Can I share a closely guarded secret with you? If you're willing to talk to your parents and let them help you make good choices, they'll let you separate from them more quickly. Why? When teens make good choices, their parents feel safe. This time of separation is an important part of God's plan. It must happen, or teens will end up living with their parents for the rest of their lives. That is not the way the game was designed to be played.

$$\pi$$

WHEN YOU'RE YOUNG, it will seem like your football game of life will never end. I promise you it will—but you won't know when until it ends. Most will enjoy a long season, but some will not. The football game of life is a rough-and-tumble game. You could get injured and be out for a few games, or there is a possibility that you could be knocked out for the entire season. Not knowing how many days you have should motivate you to make each day count by scoring as many points as you can. Never forget that once the games are over, the ability to score points is also over. Making each day count by scoring points is the road to a successful life.

You must also remember that somewhere high up in the stands, an official scorekeeper is watching you play. His score is the only score that counts, but it's a good idea for you to keep score by taking a few minutes each day to look back on how well you played. While you're looking back, don't be surprised when the evil team points out things that you could have done better. They'll even try to discourage you by telling you things that aren't true just to make you feel bad. They know if they can make you feel bad long enough, you'll give up, and that's exactly what they want you to do.

Don't get discouraged; just know you're going to have some good days and some bad days. It's all part of the game.

It also helps to recognize that while you're on the field, you can only see the small part of the field that's right in front of you. This is important to remember. There are things happening all around you that you can't see that affect how well you play. These events can cause you to make choices that you would never make if you could see the whole field.

I would also encourage you to not push yourself too hard or allow yourself to become content. Doctrine and Covenants 10:4 teaches, "Do not run faster or labor more than you have strength and means."

Other scriptures warn about being content. My favorite is in Revelation 3:15–16: "I know thy works, that thou art neither cold nor hot: I would thou wert [were] cold or hot. So then because thou art lukewarm [content], . . . I will spue [spit] thee out of my [the Lord's] mouth."

These verses clearly teach that the Lord doesn't want you pushing yourself too hard, and He doesn't want you to become lukewarm. He wants you out on the field, playing in the games to the best of your ability and scoring points.

After I wrote that last paragraph, the evil team said, "What do you mean you can't be content? Isn't it okay to just chill? Are you saying you have to have laser-like focus all the time? Can't you take a break and relax for a while?" If you heard any thoughts that sounded like these, let me make sure you understand what I meant.

You should never allow yourself to become content, but you can be at peace. Being at peace means you accept who you are while trying to improve. It's impossible to become perfect, but the good news is you don't have to. You just need to continually work on improving. A little here and there is all God expects, as long as you keep moving forward.

Remember, the direction you're heading is every bit as important as actually getting there. If you're willing to do your part, the Savior is willing to do the rest.

Being at peace while you're trying to improve will keep you from becoming content, and it will also keep you from burning out. A burnout can happen when you try to do too much or when you push yourself too hard, so be careful. How will you know if you're headed for a burnout? Your body will tell you. If you're always tired, frustrated, irritable, having problems sleeping, not feeling well, constantly getting sick, or any similar symptom, you could be burned out.

Now I'll explain how the game ends.

$$\pi$$

YOU'LL BE PLAYING the games day after day, and then all of a sudden, sometimes without even a warning, the games end and the season is over. Your season was never meant to last forever, and that means someday you're going to die. I know that sounds harsh, but it isn't—if you choose to believe that death is nothing more than the final experience in the football game of life.

While you're young and full of energy, optimism, and good health, death looks like a bad thing. Something I've learned from getting old is that sometimes it's not such a bad thing. But I'm still trying to find a way to avoid it. I haven't found one yet, but I'll keep working on it and let you know if I find something.

On a brighter note, death may not be something you have to worry about, because I believe the Second Coming is close. If it gets here before your season ends, you'll miss out on the death experience because in the Millennium, you change from mortality to immortality in the twinkling of an eye. I don't know how that works, but it sounds a lot better than dying and rotting in the grave. I don't know what you did in the premortal life to deserve that blessing, but you must have done something.

Either way, whether it be death or twinkling, you do need to prepare for the time when your opportunity to score points will come to an end. Right now, it may seem like that day will never come, but it will, and you need to be constantly preparing for it.

When I was young, the evil team told me that my day to die would never come because they wanted me to think I'd have plenty of time to score points. They said, "Today doesn't matter. Go ahead, have some fun. You'll have lots of time to score points later." Don't listen to them. Your season is going to end, and it may end when you least expect it. Make every day count.

$$\pi$$

DID MY COMPARISON of life to the game of football help you better understand life? Can you see how it really is a lot like football? If you answer yes, you're ready to learn how to control a lot of the events you'll experience in life.

Controlling events isn't hard if you'll choose to believe God can help you make good things happen. What God-given right allows you to make that choice? It's agency. I've briefly mentioned agency, but in the next chapter I'll discuss it in detail. If you can understand what agency is and how to use it correctly, you can control a lot of what you experience in life. Gaining control is the key to creating your successful life.

REVIEW OF IMPORTANT POINTS

- Life is like the game of football.
- God is the lead official over the games. He sits high above the field where He can't be seen.

- There are other officials on the field: prophets, apostles, and other General Authorities. These officials ensure the game is played fairly.
- There are coaches that have authority over the players but not over the games. These coaches are parents, grandparents, teachers, friends, local church authorities, and any other person or thing that tries to influence you while you play. If you look at what they're influencing you to do, you can know which team they're coaching for.
- There are two types of games—practice games and regular season games.
- No one is guaranteed the same number of games or length of season, so it's important to make every game day count.
- The season was never meant to last forever. It's important to use the time you have to prepare for the end of your season by doing things that are most important.
- Your life does not end at death; you just change from mortality to immortality. What you do in this life determines your place in the next life.

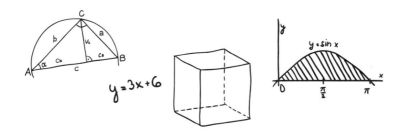

CHAPTER 7

YOU MUST CHOOSE

WHAT IS AGENCY? It's the God-given right to make choices and experience the consequences of your choices, but guess what? Agency also gives you the right to experience consequences even when you don't make a choice.

Let's say a choice needs to be made, but you decide to make no choice. What just happened? You used your agency to choose to do nothing. Choosing to do nothing might make you feel safe, but you aren't. You're just allowing someone else to make the choice for you. If you let them make the choice, they'll determine the consequence you'll experience, because it's the choice, not the person making the choice, that determines the consequence. Once a choice is made, you will have to experience the consequence whether you like it or not, unless you make a different choice.

When you make a choice, you control the consequences you'll experience. When you control the consequences, you control your life, and when you control your life, you can make it whatever you want it to be. Your ability to make choices is a gift from God, but you must use this gift correctly before you can receive His blessings. Let me show you how to use agency correctly.

$$\pi$$

I'LL BEGIN WITH a question. Is being able to use agency a bless-ing or a curse? If you think like me, it's a great blessing—until you actually have to use it and experience the consequences. The evil team also knows agency can be a blessing, so they're going to try to make you believe anything good is a blessing, which is not true. Let me show you what I mean.

A blessing is something good, but *good* has several different meanings. For instance, chocolate donuts and sodas are good, but they're not good *for* you. How then can you know if you're really receiving a blessing? You can know it's a blessing if it has eternal value.

If a blessing has eternal value, then what is a curse? A curse is the opposite. It's something that has no eternal value. I want to make sure you understand the difference, because the evil team will try to make you think you're being blessed when you're really not.

Here's an example. You're prospering in life, but you're not obeying the commandments. Since you're prospering and pros-pering is good, the evil team will tell you that you're being blessed. Why would the evil team want you to think you're being blessed? The Book of Mormon answers that question in 2 Nephi 28:21: "And others will he [the devil] pacify, and lull them away into carnal security, that they will say: All is well in Zion; yea, Zion prospereth, all is well." *Carnal security* means you think you're okay because you're prospering, but you're not because you're not obeying the commandments.

This can happen even when you're not prospering. For exam-ple: Life may not treat you well, even though you're trying hard to obey the commandments. You're working hard, hoping God will bless you with prosperity, but nothing in your life changes. Day after day, week after week, year after year, you continue to struggle to make ends meet, but nothing ever changes. When this hap-pens, the evil team will tell you that obeying the commandments doesn't matter because nothing ever changes.

Can you see how these two life situations could confuse you?

Take a look at this example. Over the past few months, an acquaintance has been struggling with an aggressive disease. I don't know him well, but he seems like a great guy who has tried to obey the commandments. Recently I was in a meeting where a report was given about his condition. This isn't exactly what was said, but it's what I heard: "The treatments aren't working, and he's dying. But, oh, how he wished we could experience what he's experienced—without the dying part—because he's been blessed so much and grown so close to God through this experience."

Even though this type of experience is not what I'd call good in any way, shape, or form, it did have eternal value because he used his agency correctly. Instead of choosing to become bitter and resentful, he chose to remain faithful. That choice allowed God to bless him during his difficult time, and it allowed him to score some eternal points. Those who do good things, or score points, are those who receive the greatest reward in the next life.

Now let me show you how to use your agency to score a lot of points. There's an unlimited number of points available, and you can never score too many.

When I say the word *agency*, what word comes to your mind? The word that comes to my mind is *free*. I used to say, "I have free agency," putting the emphasis on *free*. The word *free* means whatever you're getting costs you nothing, so it didn't take long for the evil team to have me believing that I could use agency any way I wanted and it wouldn't cost me anything.

Maybe you've heard people say, "It's my life, and I can do what I want." When I was young, I used to say the same thing, but I'd say it a little bit different: "It's my life and I have free agency, so I can do what I want." I used to think that I was free to use agency any way I wanted without having to experience the consequences of my actions, because I hadn't yet experienced those consequences. I thought *free* meant that there was no consequence.

Regardless of what I thought, it never worked out that way. I had to learn the hard way that my actions always had consequences and somebody had to accept them. The first people to experience the consequences of my actions were my parents, but it didn't take them long to pass those consequences down to me. That helped me understand what free agency actually meant.

Agency is a gift that costs you nothing, so this is the correct way to say it: "You were given the free gift of agency." Looking at it this way is the first step toward being able to use it correctly. God gave you agency, and it should only be used in a way that qualifies you for His blessings.

If you want to qualify for His blessings, you must also choose to believe there are rules in the game of life. The evil team will tell you there are no rules, and sadly a lot of people believe it. They believe they can do whatever they want and everything will work out. It usually does, but not in a good way. When you break the rules, the consequences are always bad, because the evil team is the only team that tells you to break the rules. If you don't believe me, consider what you're thinking about doing when you're tempted to break the rules. If you're honest, you'll see it isn't something you should be doing.

Rules are given to protect our spirits and our bodies, and they help us live life correctly so we can be happy. Here's an example of a rule that protects our bodies.

You're in a store and you see the junk food aisle. If you like junk food, a thought will say, "There's some junk food. Buy some. It'll taste really good." Almost immediately, another thought will say, "Don't buy it. It's not good for you." Do you see the rule? Junk food isn't good for your body.

This debate will continue until you make your choice. Wasn't it Shakespeare who said, "To buy or not to buy? That is the question"? Okay, that's not what he said, but you still have to make a choice.

That was a simplified version of what happens every time you make a choice. After you make your choice, you eventually receive the consequences that come with the choice you made. A little junk food now and then isn't a big deal, but what happens when you eat too much? You won't know until you visit the doctor or dentist, or until you look in the mirror and notice that you're bigger than you used to be.

Think about this: Did you have to wait for the consequences to know you shouldn't eat too much junk food? No. You knew what would eventually happen before even buying it. Why? You heard the feeling or voice tell you it isn't good for you. So is eating lots of junk food something you should be doing? The answer is no.

Did you see the qualifier in that example? It was the word *eventually*. The rule is simple: good choices have good consequences, and bad choices have bad consequences. They may or may not come immediately, but they come eventually—and that's what causes the confusion. Consequences that aren't immediate may cause you to think breaking the rules doesn't matter.

π

THE RULES IN the game of life were created by God to protect you. If you'll make good choices and use agency correctly, you'll experience good consequences—most of the time. There is one unfortunate exception to this rule. This exception happens when your good choices meet someone else's different or bad choices and causes your consequences to be bad. Let me share with you an example of how this works from when I played football.

When I was a junior in high school, several schools across the country thought I had the potential to play college-level football, so they sent me a letter of intent. If I signed it and mailed it back to them, it meant that I intended or at least was interested in trying out for their football team. It was quite an honor to have big-name schools believe I had the ability to play on their team.

Looking back now, I doubt I would have ever played for any of those schools, but none of that matters because my opportunity to play came to an unexpected end partway through my senior season. My life-changing event happened during a game with a school twice as big as mine; you could liken the game to the story of David and Goliath, but this time, David didn't win.

I remember thinking we were in big trouble the minute I saw their team get off the bus. They were physically bigger, had twice as many players, and were all dressed in what appeared to be brand-new uniforms. They looked just plain scary.

After the game started, I could see I wasn't the only one on our team who was intimidated. We all played like we had already given up. In fact, we had to punt the ball on almost every series of downs.

When we punted, I was one of three players who stood back a few yards behind the front line, and it was my job to keep the opposing players from blocking the punt. On one of the plays, the other team sent every player to block the punt. The front line held fairly well, but two or three of their players made it around the front line and were coming right for us, running at full speed.

As I prepared to extend into my block, I saw the guy next to me step back instead of stepping into his block, and that left the entire right side of my leg exposed to the rushing players. As luck would have it, a player dove to block the punt, but instead of hitting the ball, he hit me right in the knee. The force of the impact broke a bone in my knee, and my season, along with any opportunity to play college-level ball, was over in an instant.

Some might think this is just another example of why life isn't fair. For me it is an example of agency in action. Why? First, all the coaches and players made many choices during that game. All of those different choices could have had many different consequences, especially if some had changed their choices.

I also made choices years before the game was even played. For instance, I chose to play football five or six years before I actually got hurt. So did I get hurt because I chose to play football many years earlier? You could say yes. If I'd never played football, I wouldn't have gotten hurt. But the correct answer is no. All my choices leading up to that game only made it *possible* for me to get hurt.

So was I supposed to get hurt? Were all the players involved told by a higher power at that exact moment in time to do what they did, just to make sure I got hurt? Again the answer is no. That would interfere with our agency, and that's against the rules.

Why then did I get hurt? Believe it or not, I found the answer when I was watching an old movie called *Heaven Can Wait* (directed by Ernst Lubitsch [1943; 20th Century Fox], video). There are a couple of things I loved about that movie. First, there was the way the lead characters, a guy and a gal, looked at each other, eventually fell in love, and got together in the end. It almost gives me chills just thinking about it. Most of you are probably rolling your eyes as you wonder what kind of guy I really am. Trust me, someday you'll understand. But let's get back to the movie so I can tell you why I got hurt.

I found my answer in a scene when an angel tried to explain why things happen on earth to the lead character. The angel said, "It all happens because of probability and outcome."

When I heard those words, I was stunned. I had just received the answer to all of life's *why* questions, and it was given to me in a movie. I thought, "Now that makes sense, because that's the only way things can happen without interfering with agency." Let's take another look at my football experience using probability and outcome. Then you can decide if it makes sense.

My very first choice to play football didn't cause me to get hurt; it merely increased the probability of a good or bad outcome. All of my choices leading up to that game simply increased the probability that something could happen, but it didn't *make* it happen. It also didn't dictate a particular outcome, because breaking my bone wasn't the outcome until it actually happened. That only became the outcome when all the choices made by all the different players and coaches came together on that one day in that one game, and the consequence was me getting hurt.

Just for fun, let's review some of the different choices made that eventually resulted in the outcome. First, there were all my choices made over several years to play football that led me to that one single play, in that one single game, on that one single day.

Then there was the choice made by the guy next to me, probably for some valid reason, to step back instead of stepping into his block like he had been taught. That choice left my knee unprotected, and that increased the probability that an outcome might happen. But it didn't make it happen.

Next there was the choice made by the other team's coach or the team captain to have their team try to block the punt. Then there was the choice the other player made to dive for the ball just as it was about to be punted.

When you consider all the choices that were made by everyone involved, wouldn't it be safe to say that had any one those choices been different, the outcome may have also been different? That makes sense to me.

That's agency in action. You make choices, everyone else makes choices, and then all the consequences of those choices come together to create the outcome. Change any one of the choices, and it's possible that the outcome will also change.

My experience was a great example of an unfortunate exception to the rule. Normally the rule is good choices (using agency correctly) creates good consequences, but sometimes there are exceptions because we live in an imperfect world.

These types of rare exceptions are just part of the mortal test. Will we choose to remain faithful, or will we become discouraged and give up? Now that you better understand agency and the law of probability and outcome, I hope you'll choose to remain faithful.

There's still more that I need to teach you about agency, but let's take a short break before we continue.

REVIEW OF IMPORTANT POINTS

- Agency is a free gift from God. There's no such thing as free agency.
- Agency requires you to make choices. A choice to make no choice is still a choice.
- Everything good isn't a blessing. Blessings come after agency is used correctly.
- Things happen in life because of probability and outcome.
- Changing your choices will change the outcomes.
- The rule is good choices create good outcomes.
- There are unfortunate exceptions to the rule because we live in an imperfect world.

$$A = \begin{pmatrix} 2 & -1 \\ -3 & -2 \end{pmatrix} \qquad y = \sqrt{2x-1}$$

δ

CHAPTER 8

ASK WHAT, NOT WHY

*D*ID MY FOOTBALL experience help you understand why things happen here on earth? Everyone is using agency to make choices, choices have consequences, and consequences create your experiences here on earth. Most experiences will be good, a few will be bad, and some may even be terrible if you happen to be in the wrong place at the wrong time. All this happens when you live on an imperfect world.

If you can understand this one point, you will never have to ask any of the dangerous *why* questions—questions like, *Why did this happen? Why would God do this to me? Why doesn't He love me?*

Asking any of these *why* questions will always lead to more questions, because there are rarely any answers that make sense. When you can't make sense of what happened, the evil team will prompt you to think even more spiritually dangerous *if-then* statements and *but* questions. These you definitely want to avoid. Here are some examples to help you understand why they're so dangerous.

When something bad happens, the evil team will send you these thoughts: *If God loved me, or if He were really there, He wouldn't have done this to me.* Here's one more. Watch where this reasoning leads. *If God did this to me, then I must have deserved it.*

But what could I have ever done to deserve this? If you can't find anything to justify the experience, the evil team will then send you these thoughts: *There must not be a God. No God would ever do this to someone He loves.*

All *why*, *if-then*, and *but* questions and statements cause uncertainty about your relationship with God. That uncertainty leads to doubt, doubt leads to fear, and fear destroys faith. If you choose to believe that things happen because of probability and outcome, you'll never need to ask any of these questions.

Speaking of questions, I bet you have a lot of other questions about how you should live your life. I also bet you think getting answers to all your questions is impossible, but it's not. The answer for all your questions is the same, and it's simple. I've already mentioned it several times. The answer is three words that start with the letters O–T–C. Can you guess the answer? If not, I'll help you figure it out.

This may sound crazy, but in the game of life, it's the rules that create all the questions, and it's those same rules that answer them. If that caused your head to spin, I'll explain what I mean. It's going to sound way too simple, but listen to this.

The rules that create all your questions are called *commandments*, and the rules that answer all your questions are those very same *commandments*. The answer to every question you have about how you should live your life is "**o**bey **t**he **c**ommandments."

Don't believe me? You're not alone. In this day and age, many people choose to break the commandments and think nothing of it. How did they get to that point? Did they start out thinking that obeying the commandments wasn't important, or did they change their minds along the way? I believe most changed. When did they change? I can't say for sure because it was probably different for everyone, but I'll bet it started when they were in their teens. Now you know why this book was written for teens.

After someone quits obeying the commandments, what do they usually do? They try to get others to join them. Why? Some might say it's because misery loves company, but I believe it's because they know what they're doing is wrong. If they know it's wrong but sin anyway, what happened? They quit believing God.

Did you notice that they quit believing God, not quit believing *in* God? Doctrine and Covenants 1:16 states, "Every man walketh in his own way, and after the image of his own god." A person who believes in God but doesn't obey His commandments is remaking God into the image of his own god.

This may surprise you, but you can remake God into someone He is not by making Him more strict or less strict than He really is. More strict will cause you to fear Him. Less strict will cause you to think that He doesn't mean what He says.

π

THE EVIL TEAM just reminded me of all the scriptures that tell you to fear God. I should say thanks—but I won't. Their complaint reminded me of a point I would have otherwise passed right over.

The Bible was translated from one language to another until it was eventually translated into English. We owe a great debt of gratitude to those who worked tirelessly to bring this book of scripture to us, but I believe one important point didn't make it through this translation process clearly. This missing point is the true nature and character of God. The consequence of this misunderstanding is that we end up fearing God instead of respecting Him.

The evil team went nuts, so I better explain why you shouldn't fear God. Then you can decide if I'm right.

Most of us have feared something in life. It could have been the dark, monsters, or the boogey man under the bed. We got over our fear when the dark always turned to light, and no monsters or boogey man came to get us. Since *nothing ever happened,* you quit believing. When we fear God, the same thing can happen.

God will not show Himself to us for many reasons, but one is rather important. If we were able to see God and then turned away from Him, we would become sons or daughters of perdition, and we'd be cast out of His presence for the rest of eternity like Satan. He loves us too much let that happen.

This inability to see Him and not immediately seeing the consequences of breaking His commandments makes it easy to not believe Him. Here's why.

God gave you a list of commandments, and each one has a penalty attached that must be paid if you refuse to obey it. He then gave you agency, which gives you the right to choose to obey or not obey. If you choose to obey, life continues on. If you choose not to obey, nothing usually happens and life continues on. Can you see the problem this creates? Life continues on whether you obey or not. And honestly, sometimes life gets even easier when you choose not to obey. Here's an example that actually happened.

A member of our Church decided to quit believing. I asked why, and he said, "After I quit believing, I felt a sense of peace I hadn't felt in years." I replied, "Of course you did. The war being fought for your soul between good and evil has ended, and you lost. What is there left to fight over?"

I then listed all of the things that he no longer had to do: "You don't have to help your family get ready and go to church. You won't have a calling, be a home teacher, pay tithes and offerings, or have to find time to go to the temple. You can just do whatever you want whenever you want. Why wouldn't you feel a sense of peace?"

$$\pi$$

LET'S BE HONEST. When you break most commandments, nothing much immediately happens. You may experience the feeling of guilt, but that's about it.

The evil team will then tell you that obeying the commandments must not be important because nothing happened. If you believe them, they'll tell you God really didn't mean it when He commanded you to obey the commandments, again because nothing happened.

If you feared God in the beginning, why would you fear Him now? Nothing much happens when you don't obey, and that allows you to temporarily overcome your fear of Him like you overcame all your other fears. I say temporarily, because most find their fear again right before they die.

When death is close, the evil team withdraws its spirit and leaves you all alone so you can clearly see the mess you've made of your life. Seeing the mess robs you of hope, and once hope is gone, misery sets in because you'll know you wasted your opportunity to prepare to meet God. I know this happens, because I've seen it. In fact, there's even a name for it. It's called *deathbed repentance*—and it doesn't work. The good news is that none of it needs to happen if you'll learn to respect God, not fear Him.

When you choose to respect God, you believe He is real, so there will be consequences when you don't obey His commandments.

These real consequences will motivate you to believe in and believe the Savior. Believing in Him makes Him real; believing Him helps you believe He really will save you.

If He saves you, He must have paid for all of your sins, and that makes His Atonement real. Since His Atonement is real, you recognize His suffering for you, and that helps you understand the true nature and character of God.

He is no longer the angry, vengeful God often portrayed in the Bible. He is your merciful, loving, caring Father in Heaven who willingly gave up His Only Begotten Son so you could be given the gift of eternal life.

God gave you commandments so you could qualify for the gift of eternal life. Commandments also make living life on this imperfect world easier. Again, if you'll choose to obey, the consequences will be good, or better than they would have otherwise been. If you choose not to obey, the consequences are going to be bad, or not as good as they could have been.

π

I'D LIKE TO share some thoughts about a couple of other things that may be troubling you. Let's first look at why bad things happen to good people who are trying to obey the commandments.

We live on an imperfect world, so there are going to be diseases, birth defects, and other hard-to-understand physical experiences that you can't control. These unfortunate experiences might be caused by the environment you live in, the food you eat, or even the genes you received from your ancestors. All of these bad experiences are part of the mortal experience, and they should be looked at as additional opportunities to gain knowledge.

I believe God allows these experiences so you can gain knowledge, but He doesn't *want* them to happen. If you still don't believe me, look at the scriptural account of the life of Jesus Christ. He spent His entire ministry teaching, helping, healing, and showing His love and concern for those around Him. Can you think of a single example from the scriptures when He refused to help anyone who asked for it, anyone who really wanted and was willing to accept His help? Or can you find a scripture where He caused personal suffering and pain?

That question just opened a floodgate of objections from the evil team. As I asked it, they filled my mind with stories from the Bible where it appears that God caused pain and suffering. But did He do it, or did He just warn the people about the pain and suffering coming. If they didn't heed His warning, He honored their agency by allowing them to experience the consequences.

Again, I realize that He controls everything, so in that sense He is responsible for everything, but my question is: Did He do it, or did something or someone else do it? He got credit, but did He personally do it? He didn't, did He? It was the forces of nature or other people that caused the suffering.

I point this out because the destruction is what we focus on, but it's not what we *should* focus on. We should look at what happened before the destruction to see the true nature and character of God.

What did God always do before any destruction happened? He warned, begged, and pleaded with those who would be affected to bring their lives into line with the commandments so He could bless them by providing a way for them to escape. I can't think of a single instance where He didn't warn them and try to provide a way of escape. If He wanted everyone to experience pain and suffering, why did He warn them before it happened? Wouldn't it have been better to surprise them? That way He could make sure no one missed the lessons He wanted them to learn by experiencing the pain and suffering.

Wanting everyone to experience pain and suffering goes against the nature and character of God. He is your Eternal Father, and He loves you more than you'll ever understand. This intense love motivates Him to help you whenever you'll let Him.

Here's an experience that shows what you can expect when you firmly believe God is willing to help you when you need it. I experienced this event a couple years ago, but I'll never forget it.

We decided to go ride four-wheelers about fifteen miles west of where we live. We were only going a short distance from home, so I decided to put everything and everybody in one vehicle. I put two extra four-wheelers in the trailer and two extra grandkids in the truck. The extra four-wheelers caused the trailer to be overloaded, and the two extra grandkids meant that one had to ride in the front and two had to double up in the seat belts in the back.

I'll quickly admit this wasn't one of my better choices, but I thought, "We're only going fifteen miles. What could possibly happen in fifteen miles?" Nothing happened on the way out, and we did receive one big blessing while we were riding.

Before we were to head home, the grandkids found a place on top of a tailings pile where they could spin around in circles and create all kinds of dust. They looked like they were having fun, so I parked up on a hill, away from the dust. After a few minutes, I noticed they had all gotten off their machines and were standing at the edge of the pile.

I wasn't too worried, but I thought I'd better go down and see what was going on. I drove down, parked the four-wheeler, and started to walk up behind them. As I got close, an ice-cold chill shot through my body when I saw that all six of them were standing on the edge of a cliff. I was about to scream at them to get away from the cliff, but that voice or feeling I know so well said, "Don't scream; just call to them and have them come over to you."

I calmly said, "Hey, guys, come over here. I want to talk to you." Because they all knew my voice, they turned around and came away from the cliff right over to me. I gathered them in a circle, put my arms around them, and said, "You idiots, don't you know you should never stand on the edge of a cliff? Don't you understand probability and outcome?"

I didn't actually say "idiots," but that's what I was thinking. I'd forgotten they hadn't fallen or seen someone fall off a cliff so they didn't understand how dangerous it was to be there. But the evil team knew exactly how dangerous it was, and they knew that my grandkids did not yet understand anything about probability and outcome. They told the kids to stand on the edge of the cliff so the probability of a bad outcome would increase. We were certainly blessed on that day, because it turned out to be a probability and not an outcome. All I could do at the time was say, "Thank you, Father." But I didn't know that I'd be thanking Him a whole lot more a little later.

We managed to stay out of trouble for the rest of the ride until after we loaded up and headed home. About halfway home, there was a hill that went down into a small town. At the bottom of the hill were a few homes and a small gas station with a convenience store attached. As I was coming down the hill toward the convenience store, a pickup pulling a horse trailer was coming the other way. As we came closer, the truck suddenly turned across the lane right in front of me into the convenience store parking lot. I was far enough away that we would have been okay had he gotten off the road. But for some reason, instead of pulling completely off the road, he stopped with the trailer sitting broadside across my lane.

I slammed on the brakes, lay on the horn, and looked for somewhere to go, because I knew I wouldn't be able to stop in time. Remember how I overloaded the trailer? I realized within a split second we were in big trouble. I looked at the convenience store parking lot, but I couldn't go there because people were standing in it. I also couldn't go into the other lane because two other pickups were coming.

I don't remember what I said as I realized I was going to have to hit the horse trailer, but whatever it was, it caused the grandkids to tell their dad and mom that Grandpa wasn't going to heaven anymore!

This all happened within a few seconds. I will never forget how sick I felt as I realized my wife and young grandson, who were sitting in the front seat, were probably going to get the worst of the impact when I hit the trailer.

Then a small miracle occurred. Just before we hit the trailer, right when I needed it most, the two pickups coming in the other lane drove right off the road into the weeds and cleared a way for me to escape, like the Israelites passing through the Red Sea. The escape I experienced right when I needed it most was no less of a miracle to me!

Some would say that I was lucky, and I would agree. But here's my point: I promise you that this is what you can expect if you'll choose to obey God's commandments. You don't have to obey all of them; you just have to do the best you can. The reason I can make this promise is that I am by no means perfect, but I do try hard to make good choices and to obey the commandments. Because I do, God has been merciful to me, even when I do dumb things.

I need to make an additional point here because the evil team pointed out something I hadn't considered: "You said God rarely, if ever, steps in and changes a consequence. Isn't that what happened when He helped you avoid the collision with the horse trailer?"

Of course the answer is yes, but how did He change the consequence? I believe He sent thoughts to the pickup drivers coming the other way, which told them to get off the road. They made the good choice to listen, and that allowed me to change my consequence. What would have happened if they hadn't chosen to listen? We probably would have had a different outcome.

Throughout history and in the future, there are and will be examples of those who choose not to obey His commandments. They instead remake God into something He is not by choosing not to believe Him. After their choice is made, His Spirit must withdraw, and that makes it impossible for God's thoughts to reach them. After that, they're on their own, but they're never alone. The evil team will always be there to help them make bad choices that create bad actions and consequences.

I believe that God doesn't want you to suffer any type of bad consequences because He loves you as a perfect dad would love you—because He is a perfect Dad! Remember, even though He loves you that much, He must allow you to use your agency. He too must obey the rules, and the rules state that agency must be used correctly before He can bless you. Most of the time these blessings come in the form of thoughts that help you make good choices. However, there will also be a few times when they come to you in the form of miracles to help you when you need them most.

I hope this chapter made sense to you. For the record, it's the only thing that makes sense to me, because any other way of looking at life conflicts with agency, and no one can interfere with agency.

Now that you've learned how to use agency correctly, you're *almost* ready to start controlling events you'll experience in life. Why only almost? You still have a few more steps to learn. The next step is important because it's the one that makes all the other steps work. This next step teaches you how to use the power of faith.

REVIEW OF IMPORTANT POINTS

- Having to obey the commandments creates all of life's questions.
- "Obey the commandments" is the answer to all of life's questions.
- God is merciful. He will bless you if you'll try to obey the commandments.
- You cannot remake God into someone He is not. You must believe in Him and believe Him.
- God's blessings come in the form of thoughts that help you make right choices.

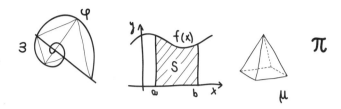

CHAPTER 9

FAITH MAKES THINGS HAPPEN

WHAT DOES WINNING the game of life really mean? If you think it just means you'll be able to create a successful life, you don't understand what winning means. Let me show you what it means by likening it to a birthday cake.

It's your birthday, and you have a great big perfect cake sitting on the table in front of you. You can't wait to eat it, and because it's your birthday, you think you should get all of it. Then you watch as your mom cuts you a tiny piece and divides the rest of the cake into big pieces for everyone else. You get a tiny piece while everyone else gets a big piece. Would you call that winning? You did get a small piece of the cake, but I wouldn't call that winning.

In my example, the cake represents the prize being offered to all the players in the game of life. This prize is being able to be successful in this life—and in the next life. Since this life is only a small part of your total existence, just winning in this life would be like getting a tiny piece of a great big cake.

You're now a player in the game of life, so you have to decide how much of the cake you want. The reason I said you have to decide is that no one else can do it for you. You and only you must decide if you want it all or if you are going to be content to play for a tiny piece of it. I'll bet you want it all, so let me show you how you can get it by using the power of faith.

I'm really excited to share what I've learned about the power of faith. Faith is an important piece of the success puzzle because it's the key that unlocks the door between you and help from God. If you're willing to use this key and open the door, God is willing to lead, guide, protect, and prosper you. All of these blessings are possible because of the power of faith.

With God's help, I believe you can have anything you want in life by following four simple steps. I promise you it's true, but I won't feel bad if you don't believe me. Just four simple steps. And when I say anything, I mean *anything*. It doesn't matter if you want a car, a house, a boyfriend, a girlfriend, a husband, a wife, or a great job—it could even be straight As in school so you can get a scholarship and go to college for free. Use these four simple steps and you can have it. No one explained these steps to me, but that didn't stop me from using them. You've also used them; otherwise, you wouldn't get anything done.

Here's an example of how you've used the steps without even realizing it. Do you remember when someone taught you two plus two equals four? When you first heard it, you probably didn't understand it equaled four, but you decided you wanted to find out. Does two plus two really equal four? It does, and that's why I know you wanted find out. How did you find out? If you're like me, you asked someone how two plus two equals four and they probably said, "Hold up two fingers on each hand and count them."

When you were told to count your fingers, did you doubt it could equal four, or did you choose to believe it could? You chose to believe. At that moment, you were using faith. You didn't yet know; you just believed it could, and that allowed you to continue until you could find out if it was true. If you had allowed fear, doubt, or uncertainty to stop you from using faith, would you have ever been able to know that two plus two equals four? You wouldn't because you would have given up. Faith is the bridge between not knowing and knowing, and you must cross it before you can know anything.

You now know that two plus two really does equal four, but can you remember what happened when you learned this simple truth? At that moment, something clicked in your brain. A split second before the click, you didn't know that two plus two equals four, and then a split second after the click, you knew and understood it so well that I could never convince you that two plus two really equals five. Why? It's not true. So what happened during that split second?

Doctrine and Covenants 88:7–12 explains what happened during the split second between knowing and not knowing. Let's begin with verse 11: "The light which shineth . . . is through him who enlighteneth your eyes [or minds], which is the same light that quickeneth your understandings." Verse 12 states, "Which light proceedeth forth from the presence of God to fill the immensity of space." Verse 7 identifies the light as the Light of Christ, and it ties the light to truth: "Which truth shineth. This is the light of Christ." His light is truth, and that's why I can't make you believe two plus two equals anything but four. The moment you learned that simple truth, you were being taught by the Light of Christ, or the light of truth, which enlightened your mind and quickened your understanding of a truth. This is why you now know without any doubt that two plus two equals four.

Here are the steps you used without even realizing it. Could we have a drumroll, please?

- You have to want it.
- You have to ask for it.
- You have to believe it will happen before it happens.
- You have to go to work and make it happen.

These are the four simple steps you must use to get anything you want in this life and everything you want in the next life.

Can you see how you already use the steps without even realizing it? If you didn't, you wouldn't have or know anything. But think about this. If you're already using them and not realizing it, can you imagine how much more you could know if you started using them on purpose? I hope you have a good imagination, because the list is endless.

Being able to use the steps to get things sounds pretty good, but there's another really good reason to learn about the steps. They are also the same four steps you would use to get something bad, and it happens more often than you might think. Now that you know the steps are used for good and bad, I hope you want good things, or I'd rather not teach them to you.

If you were to choose, which of the four steps would be the hardest to complete? I bet you would choose step four, the one that requires you to go to work and make it happen. That's the one I would have chosen when I was young. But now that I'm older, I believe the hardest step is number three, the one that requires you to believe it will happen until it happens.

The reason is that even though working is hard, I've found that believing something will happen before it happens is actually harder. If you don't believe me, answer this next question: What always happens right after you quit believing?

You quit working.

Even though step three is the hardest, it doesn't make step four any easier. You're still not sure? Okay, look at this. Step three requires you to believe it will happen, but you must complete step four before you can *see* it happen. Step four requires you to work until it happens, but you have to keep believing it will happen until it happens. See how either step can't happen without the other?

I believe the difficulty of steps three and four is the reason few people are able to reach their goals in life. What percentage of the total population keeps working until they reach their main goal in life? Many reach smaller goals along the way, but how many reach their main goal? Could it be 10 or 20 percent? I could never know for sure, but I doubt it would even be 10 percent of the total population, because most give up long before they reach their main goal. Why? They quit believing it can happen.

Are you wondering how the same four steps can be used for both good and bad when they're complete opposites? It's because you have to use the steps before God or the evil team can help you. Why? Both teams must respect your agency. Here's how this works.

π

AGENCY REQUIRES YOU to decide what you want and make a choice. The choice then determines which power can help you. If you decide you want something good, God will help you. If you decide you want something bad, the evil team will help you. Did you notice that both powers can help you, but they haven't yet started to help you? Before they can start helping you, you must choose to believe they will help you. When you choose to believe, you're using faith. But remember, faith is neutral, which means it can't do anything until you use it. And you use it by choosing to believe that either God or the evil team will help you. This choice to believe becomes the key that unlocks the door between you and the power of God, or you and the power of the evil team. Yes, the evil team also has power, but it's not the same, nor is it as great, as God's power.

Now that you understand how faith unlocks the door between you and help from God or the evil team, I hope you'll only use it to receive help from God. Here's how you do it.

First, make sure you're only using faith to get things that have eternal value. You can know what things have eternal value by looking into the future. If the life you see is good according to God's definition of good, then use your faith and go to work until you get it. If it's not, don't use faith to try and get it.

You'd think seeing good things in the future would be all the motivation you need, but unfortunately it isn't quite that easy. The evil team also knows you're going to want good things, so they're going to make their bad things look good. You must always be willing to look at your future honestly, and then you'll be able to see if the evil team is trying to deceive you. Here's an example of how they make bad things look good.

The evil team tells you to goof off in school because it's more fun than doing schoolwork. Goofing off really is more fun, but what will your future look like if you don't do well in school? One probability is that you won't be able to find a good job and enjoy a prosperous lifestyle. Why then do kids goof off in school? The evil team is deceiving them.

The next step requires you to understand what faith really is, how it works, and how you use it. So what is faith? Faith is choosing to believe in something you can't yet see. That sounds easy enough, right? It may sound easy, but if it really was that easy, wouldn't everyone be using it? They would—so what makes using faith hard?

When I think of faith, I always think of religion. Does that happen to you? Thinking about faith and religion together isn't bad, but I believe there's a reason the evil team wants you to think about faith and religion together. Faith and religion are connected because religion can't exist without faith. But that's not why the evil team wants you to think about faith and religion together.

They want you to think faith is only used in religion so you won't try to use faith outside of religion. That brings up a couple of interesting questions. First, why doesn't the evil team want you using faith, and second, what are they so afraid of? The answer to both questions is the same. The evil team knows that when faith is used it has incredible power, and that power could be used for something good. They don't want you doing anything good, so they're going to do everything they can to keep you from using the power of faith.

When I said faith has incredible power, did a tiny bit of doubt enter your mind? If you felt any degree of doubt, it's because the evil team sent a thought to make you doubt that faith really could have power. You probably didn't recognize their thought as anything special, because they send thoughts to you all the time. Why do they want you to doubt? Doubt is the opposite of faith. Let me show you why you felt some degree of doubt.

In religion, everything works on faith because you have to believe in things before you see them. This requirement to believe before you see can be difficult because you rarely see any immediate results when you use faith. So it's perfectly normal for you to have a few doubts. But the evil team isn't content with you having a few doubts, because doubts can be overcome with a little bit of effort. So what are they really trying to do? They're filling your head with doubts, hoping you'll eventually quit believing in God.

Can you see why they cause you to think about faith and religion together? They know when you use faith in religion you'll be using it to try to believe in things you may never see, like moving mountains, healing the sick, raising the dead, or God Himself. Never seeing these things can easily cause you to have doubts. These doubts, if they're not dealt with, will eventually cause you to quit believing in anything you can't see, including God. It usually doesn't happen overnight, but it does happen.

Why am I so sure? Take a look at the world you live in. You can see that the evil team's plan is working pretty well, because so many people have decided to quit believing in the one and only true God. They instead choose to believe in the image of God they've created.

$$\pi$$

REMEMBER WHEN I asked if having and using faith was hard? Believing faith only applies to religion is what makes faith hard. I know this because I've done some real-life research. Here's what I found.

Whenever I have an opportunity to work with young people, I always find a way to ask them if they think having and using faith is hard. The answer I get, almost every single time, is yes. In fact, they don't think it's merely hard; they think it's *really* hard. When I ask them why they think it's so hard, their answers are different, but all of them have something to do with religion.

As I said, believing that faith and religion are connected isn't bad, unless you don't understand that faith can also be used outside of religion. Thinking faith only applies to religion will cause you to become trapped in the cycle of uncertainty. Have you heard about the cycle of uncertainty? It happens when you never get to see any results after you use your faith. Even if you haven't heard about it, I bet you've already spent some time in it. See if this sounds familiar.

You try to use your faith, but you don't see any immediate results, so you begin to doubt the power of faith. Once you doubt, your faith becomes weak, and that keeps your desired outcome from happening. Not seeing it happen creates even more doubts, and that further weakens your faith, until it completely vanishes. When faith is gone, what you hoped for will never happen, and that naturally creates even stronger doubts. Can you see how each step in the cycle of uncertainty feeds on the previous step? The evil team loves to use the cycle of uncertainty because it will eventually cause you to quit believing in the power of faith and God. Deciding not to believe isn't the only consequence of not seeing any results after using faith. See if this also sounds familiar.

When you use your faith and nothing immediately happens, you'll be tempted to think God didn't want it to happen. Believing He didn't want it to happen makes it easy to believe that God is doing this for a reason, or because you need it.

I'm not trying to limit God's power, question His ways, or tell Him what He can and can't do. He is God, and He can do anything He wants. I'm just saying it makes more sense to choose to believe He isn't doing it because that allows me to keep seeing God as my loving, caring Heavenly Father and not as some all-powerful being who's mad at me or who's intentionally using some form of pain and suffering to teach me something. Watch what happens to the cycle of uncertainty when you look at God from this more positive perspective.

Because you believe God's not doing it, you can choose to believe He really wants to help you. This choice increases your faith, and that allows God to help even more. But don't stop now, because you're on a roll. When you get more help, you gain confidence. More confidence creates more belief, or more faith, and that allows God to help you even more. Why? The amount of faith you have and use determines the amount of help you receive.

Can you see how each of these steps also feeds on the previous step? While they're feeding, they're creating a cycle of certainty. Notice that I said *certainty*, not uncertainty. These two cycles are exact opposites, one being bad because it creates negative feelings and beliefs, and the other being good because it creates positive feelings and beliefs. Let me share a verse from the Bible that clearly explains what can happen if you'll use your faith to create a cycle of certainty.

In Matthew 17:20, Jesus explains that the amount of faith needed to move a mountain is only about the size of a tiny mustard seed. When you read that, did you notice a little doubt pass through your mind? If you did, I want to point that out so you can see how the evil team works. That little bit of doubt almost felt natural, didn't it? You have to give the evil team credit, because they are good at what they do. Let's take a look at why you felt doubt.

If you're young, you may have felt doubt because you don't understand how a small amount of faith could ever move a great big mountain. If you're older, you may have felt doubt because you've tried to use faith before and it didn't work too well, so that caused you to think it probably wouldn't work now. Once again, even though the reasons that cause you to doubt will definitely affect the power of your faith, those reasons are not what you should focus on.

When you focus on the reasons faith won't work, it makes it impossible for faith to work, because faith and doubt are complete opposites. Having doubts is a normal consequence of rarely or never getting to see any immediate results when you use faith. So why are you focusing on results? You can blame it on the evil team. They want you to focus on results because you usually don't see any, and that makes it easier for them to get you to quit believing.

When I use faith, I focus all my efforts on choosing to believe it's going to happen instead of wasting my efforts waiting for it to happen. In the scriptures, there's an oft-quoted verse that may help you understand why you shouldn't focus on results. The same basic scripture is found in several places, but I'll use Matthew 7:7 because it's probably the one most widely recognized. It states, "Ask, and it shall be given you; seek, and ye shall find; knock, and it shall be opened unto you."

I'm sure you've heard this many times before, but did you notice that one really important word is missing? I'm not saying the scripture is wrong. I'm saying there's one word left out that you need to recognize before this scripture will work for you. Do you know which word it is?

I'll give you a hint. It starts with W, and it has an H, an E, and an N in it. The word that's missing is *when*.

Can you see why you shouldn't focus on results? You don't control the timetable; God does. If you ask, seek, and knock with faith, sooner or later you'll receive, find, or have the door opened to you. But it can only happen if you continue to use your faith. So make sure you don't give up too quickly, because you may never know what is, or isn't, God's will.

π

NOW THAT YOU understand how to use faith, are you happy or sad? I hope you at least feel happy, but feeling happy isn't good enough. You should be excited because you now know how to control most of your experiences in life. Did you feel any fear or uncertainty when I said you could only control *most* of your experiences? If you did, don't worry about it, because when you live in an imperfect world, controlling most of your experiences is really good. In fact, that's what turns an ordinary life into a successful life.

Are you ready to start using the power of faith? I hope you'll choose to believe, because faith won't work until you do. Choosing to believe sounds easy, but that's what creates a big stumbling block for most of us. It's not easy to believe in something you can't see. And when you add in all the unfortunate things that happen in life, it's no surprise why some find it difficult to believe that God is willing to help, or that He is even there.

All the reasons and questions about God are valid, but they're not what you should focus on. You must focus all your efforts on choosing to believe so faith can work for you. If you choose not to believe, everything stops the second you make that choice. Faith is like a bridge between you and what you want. All you have to do is step onto the bridge and keep walking until you get to what you want. Could it really be this easy? It can.

Have you heard the saying, "Seeing isn't believing. Believing is seeing"? It's in the movie *The Santa Clause 2* (*The Santa Clause 2: The Mrs. Clause*, directed by Michael Lembeck [2002; Buena

Vista Pictures], DVD). When I first heard it, I had one of those aha moments. I've heard it said the same way for most of my life, but for some reason, when I heard it in that movie, it really sank in. "Seeing isn't believing. Believing is seeing." That's what faith is all about.

I'm sure the evil team is telling you it's hard to believe before you can see. But guess what? You're already doing it every single day without even realizing it. Here are some real-life examples.

A person tries hard to do what's right because he believes doing so will make a difference in his life. He can't yet see any real difference, but he keeps trying because he believes it will make a difference, and it eventually does.

Another person is not trying to do what's right. He's just having fun because he thinks fun is happiness. He can't yet see any difference, so he keeps having fun. He can't yet see where his actions are taking him, but he'll eventually get there. When he does, he'll realize it's not where he wanted to go, but it will be too late to do anything about it.

The people in both these examples used faith to get what they wanted. Neither could immediately see the end, but both kept going because he believed it would take him to where he wanted to go. And it eventually did.

In either example, was having and using faith hard? No, because both were simply living the life they chose without realizing they were using faith.

Here's another example that shows why using faith is a lot easier than you might think. When you went to bed last night, did you think, "I won't wake up in the morning"? I bet you didn't. If you're young, you probably got into bed and went to sleep, excited that you were going to be able to wake up in the morning and experience another new day.

If you're older like me, you were just excited to get into bed. Either way, you never would have gotten into bed and gone to sleep unless you believed to the point of knowing that you were going to wake up the next morning. In fact, you may have even believed you were going to wake up at a certain time in the morning without an alarm clock—and you did!

When you believed you were going to wake up, you were exercising or using your faith. When you got into bed, did you think about making that choice, or did you simply believe you would wake up without thinking about it? I'll bet you didn't even think about it. Using faith last night wasn't hard, was it?

Here's another example. You're sitting in school waiting for the bell to ring so you can go home. The bell finally rings, but you sit there, paralyzed, because you don't know if you can actually make it home. In fact, you're so uncertain that you sit there in your classroom until the next morning, waiting for school to start again. Is that what you do? I know it isn't because I've taught school. The students I taught would jump to their feet the second the bell rang and make their way out the door toward the bus they knew would take them home. How did they know the bus would take them home? They knew it because they chose to believe it. This is another example that shows how you use faith without even thinking about it. Want more examples?

You use faith when you cross the street; ride a bike; go to the store, to church, or to a movie; or when you go out to get a treat with the family. You use faith to build things, go on vacations, fly in an airplane—the list never ends because you have to use faith to do everything in life. This is an easy question, but I'll ask it anyway. Because you must use faith to do everything in life, what will you accomplish if you decide not to use faith? The answer is nothing.

Does this help you see why the evil team doesn't want you to use faith? Faith is what helps you get things done, and the evil team doesn't want you getting anything done, especially anything good. God wants you to get things done, so He's always going to be right there, ready, willing, and able to help you when you use your faith. The scriptures teach this principle clearly: "With God all things are possible" (Matthew 19:26). Does this help you see why having and then using faith is so important? I hope so.

NOW THAT YOU'VE seen why having and using faith is important, let me show you how to put your faith to work so you can start making things happen.

Do you remember when I said there are two ways to get things done? The first way is to do it all by yourself. The other, better way is for you to do it with help from God. Either way, it's up to you to get it done, but it's a lot easier with God's help. How do you get God's help? First, you must qualify by obeying His commandments the best you can and repenting quickly when you don't. The next step is actually four steps. Remember, you have to want it, ask for it, believe it's going to happen before it happens, and then go to work and make it happen. Following these four simple steps will bring down the powers of heaven so God can help you get what you want—as long as it's good. I know it sounds too easy, but that's all you need to do to receive help from God.

Here's how I used this formula to get something done that first seemed impossible—writing this book. One of my favorite Book of Mormon prophets is Nephi, the son of Lehi, because he could explain things so I could understand them. My absolute favorite chapters are the last few he wrote before his death, where he explained everything I needed to know about life in words "as plain as word could be" (2 Nephi 32:7).

One day when I was reading those last few chapters in 2 Nephi, a thought popped into my head: "Why don't you write a book about things you've learned before you die and take it all with you?" After thinking about it for a while, I decided to start. I'm not planning on going anywhere soon, but I thought if I'm going to get a book done, I better get going. I was chasing after my fifty-seventh birthday, and it looked like it wouldn't be too long before I caught it.

I'm sure you're thinking I'm old, but I don't feel any different than I did when I was twenty-five—unless I actually try to do something. Then I'm quickly reminded of what being old really means. It means I'm going to hurt whenever I try to do anything. It also means that when I open the newspaper, I get to see pictures of people I went to school with staring back at me from the obituary page. These experiences helped me realize that if I wanted the book to actually happen, I'd better get started before I run out of time.

What do you think happened as soon as I decided to write the book? The evil team filled my head with all kinds of negative thoughts, telling me I couldn't and shouldn't write a book. "What in the world are you thinking?" they said. "You can't do this. You're not qualified. You don't have the skills. People are going to laugh at you. You didn't go to college. You slept through English in high school. There is no way you can write a book."

What's sad about those thoughts is that some of them are true, like the one about not going to college and sleeping through English in high school. But why did I have all those negative thoughts? If I really couldn't write, why didn't the evil team let me try and fail? Wouldn't that be better than trying to talk me out of it? Of course, but that's not why the thoughts flooded my mind. I believe it's because the evil team knew I was trying to do something good, and they didn't want me to try.

After hearing all those negative thoughts, I knew I had to make a choice. Should I give up, or should I use the four steps and write the book? As you can see, I used the four steps, and now a little over five years later, you have my book in your hands. But guess what? Finishing the book wasn't the only good thing that came from my choice to write. I also discovered a way to make all the steps, including steps three and four, a lot easier. Here's what I discovered. For most of my life, I've tried hard to obey the commandments. I'm not close to being perfect, but I know the Savior promised to save me. That belief made me confident His Spirit would help me write this book. I then sat down and started thinking about what I wanted to write. This caused countless thoughts to come to mind, which I used to create sentences on the pages. I couldn't yet see the finished product, but I kept writing until I finished the book.

Did you see how I made the steps easier? I did it by not trying to write the whole book all at once. I just focused on writing one line at a time and that kept me from giving up and becoming overwhelmed and depressed. This is the way you accomplish things that seem almost impossible. Follow the steps and work on your goal one day at a time, and eventually you will reach it, regardless of what it happens to be.

$$\pi$$

BEFORE WE MOVE on to the next chapter, I have a final question: How was I able to write this book one line at a time? I gave you the answer. Did you catch it? All of the words you see on these pages came to me in the form of thoughts, but where did all those thoughts come from? They had to come from somewhere. If you said they came from me, I'd thank you for the compliment, but I'm really not that smart.

When I wrote that last line, the one about me not being smart, the evil team threw a thought into my mind that sounded like this: "Why would you think this book would cause anyone to think you're smart?" You've got to love—or not love—those guys. They never miss an opportunity to discourage you when you're trying to do something good. I'll ignore them and ask the question again. Where did all those thoughts come from? I know where they came from, but I'm not going to tell you until you read the next chapter.

Could it really be this easy to do things that may seem impossible at first? Yes, it is—if you're willing to first qualify for God's help and then use the four steps to get it. Before I could finish this book, I had to want to write it. Next I had to ask for God's help, because I needed it. Then I had to believe it would happen before it happened. Finally, I had to go to work one day at a time until it happened. This is how you accomplish things that seem impossible. Why do the four steps work? They work because you have God on your side, and He wants you to be successful.

REVIEW OF IMPORTANT POINTS

- Winning means being successful in this life and the next life.
- Use faith and the four steps to reach your goals in life.

- You're already using the steps every day. Start using them on purpose.
- Faith unlocks the door between you and help from God.
- Will you use the cycle of certainty, or the cycle of uncertainty?
- "Seeing isn't believing. Believing is seeing."
- Work on your goals one line and one day at a time.
- You can do the impossible.

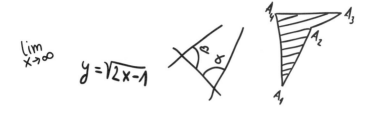

CHAPTER 10

NOTHING IS IMPOSSIBLE

WHERE DID ALL the thoughts for my book come from? I'm sure you know the answer, but I'll say it anyway. They didn't come from me; they came from God through His Spirit because I was trying to do something good. Some may laugh, but that doesn't change what I believe. From the moment I started writing until I finished, I experienced something unbelievable.

As I thought about what to write, different thoughts popped into my mind. Some came as a single word, and others as sentences. Some came quietly, and others were strong enough to hear. These thoughts would tell me what to write, or they'd tell me to erase what I'd written and write it another way. After I erased it, a new thought would appear, and I'd write it down. If I wrote it wrong, another thought would tell me to change what I'd written. I'd then make the suggested change, reread the sentence, and, if no other changes were needed, move to the next line.

The evil team went nuts when I said "the thoughts would tell me," so I'd better explain what I mean. Thoughts always come with a feeling attached. When the feeling is strong, it's almost like you can hear it. Whether you call this a strong feeling or a voice really doesn't matter. I've learned not to ignore these feelings because they've proven to be valuable. In fact, they've proven to be so valuable, I've started asking for them to come more often.

I believe God sends these thoughts through His Spirit because He loves me and wants me to succeed in every good thing. This is what Alma teaches in Alma 5:40: "Whatsoever is good cometh from God."

Why did I write this book? I want to help you. Why do I want to help you? I love you. If you're not one of my grandkids, you might think I couldn't possibly love you because I don't know you, but that's not true. One of the greatest blessings in life is to be able to have Christlike love for those you meet and those you haven't yet met. This Christlike love makes me want to help you as much as I want to help my own kids and grandkids. This book will help you if you'll use what I've learned to make better choices.

This desire to help everyone made me want to write. In fact, I wanted to write so much that I would look for, and even create, opportunities to write because I loved what I was doing. That's why, even though the book was hard to write, it was never work because I loved writing it.

One thing I've learned over the years is that work, even physically hard work, is never work when you love what you're doing. If you're looking for another way to make steps three and four easier, find a way to love what you're doing and it will never be work. Remember this advice when you're getting your education or choosing you're occupation.

I point this out because every time I've had opportunities to work with young adults, I've noticed that many of them were becoming discouraged by the challenges they were facing each day. They didn't yet understand this one simple truth: yesterday is gone, and tomorrow isn't here, so today is the only day you have to work on anything. They were getting discouraged because they tried to focus on everything that needed to be done instead of focusing only on what needed to be done *that day*. Here's something else I've learned: If you focus on doing your best today, yesterday will be nothing more than a pleasant memory and tomorrow will take care of itself. I can't remember where I first heard that, but it helped me make completing steps three and four a lot easier.

Even though I've showed you how to make the steps easier to complete, they'll still be difficult because you have to make yourself do them. You can plan, talk, and intend to get them done, but nothing will ever happen until you actually do them. Doing the steps will require a lot of effort, effort requires determination, and determination is an easy thing to lose when you have to continually put forth effort. That's why you must train yourself to only work on your goals one day at a time. If you can make yourself work on a goal for one day, every day, you'll eventually be able to reach it—and that's how you become successful.

$$\pi$$

IN THIS DAY and age, a good education must be one of your most important goals. It will require a lot of work, so how can you stay motivated? The best way is to compare what your future will look like with and without an education.

At this point in your life, you're being fed, clothed, and entertained at your parents' expense. That's going to change since your parents can't take care of you forever. Living life requires money, and getting money will be a lot easier if you have a good education. An education creates job opportunities and makes you much more valuable to a future employer. A company will value, or pay, you more when it really *wants* to hire you because of your excellent qualifications.

Getting a good education probably means little or nothing to you now, but later, when you're looking for a job, you'll quickly see how important it is. I know how important it is because I'm old, and I can see things you can't yet. So once again, you're going to have to trust me.

There are ways to make getting a good education easier. Remember, the first two steps toward getting anything you want in life are want it and ask for it. Wanting a good education is a choice only you can make. I could encourage you, beg you, or even try to bribe you, but none of that will work unless you decide you want it. Please take a moment and think about what your life will be like if you choose not to get an education. If you look at your probable future, you will have all the motivation you need. So how do you get it?

First, you must choose to believe you have God on your side and He is willing to help you if you're willing to ask for His help. I'm sure you could get an education without His help, but why would you want to? It will be a lot easier, and you won't waste as much time, effort, and money if you let Him help you. But remember, you're just asking for help; you're not asking Him to give you the education. It would be easier if He gave it to you, but that's not the way He designed this game to be played. This game requires you to ask as if everything depended on Him and then go to work as if everything depended on you. He will help you, but you have to keep working on it day after day, week after week, month after month, and year after year until you finally get it.

How will you keep working on it that long? You'll need a lot of determination, which you can access through faith and hope. Accessing it is a choice. If you'll make that choice and use it to motivate you to bring you closer to your goal of getting a good education each day, you'll eventually get it.

Because getting a good education will take some time, the evil team is going to try to discourage and depress you along the way. They'll tell you it's going to be too hard, that you aren't smart enough, or that getting it will be impossible. Nothing is impossible when you have God on your side, so don't believe them.

The next step requires you to learn how to use your time wisely. You start by recognizing there are only twenty-four hours in each day. Then you break those hours into three groups. The first eight hours pass while you sleep, so subtract those. That leaves you with sixteen hours. Next you'll subtract the six hours you spend in school, because those are already being used to reach your goal. Subtracting roughly an hour to get ready for and get to school and home, that leaves you with about nine hours to use any way you want. Some of these hours will be used for things you need to do, so those hours will also need to be subtracted.

Did you notice that I said "need to do" not "want to do"? I said "need" because the evil team is going to tell you the only things that matter are the things you want to do. Confusing wants with needs is the main reason many people never reach their goals.

After you subtract all of the used hours, you should have four or five hours each day you can use any way you want. If you'll use one, two, or maybe three of the hours on homework while you're in school, you can create a successful life. One or two hours is a small price to pay for success—and you still have a few hours left to do whatever you want.

What is a successful life? You'll have to decide that for yourself, but it should include getting good grades, graduating from high school with a scholarship, and going to college for free. Then while you're in college, if you'll use that time wisely, you can graduate with an advanced degree, get a great job, make lots of money, pay your tithes and offerings, take your spouse and kids on trips, travel the world, build a cabin in the mountains, retire early, and enjoy life with your grandkids. I'd call that successful, wouldn't you? This life can be yours by learning to use your time wisely.

The evil team brought up another interesting point. When I mentioned college, they said, "That's not true, because a college degree will require you to spend a lot more than two or three hours each day doing homework." Normally I would ignore their objection, but this time I want to use it to warn you one of their traps.

One day I was visiting with a stressed-out student who said in passing that he was taking eighteen credits. I didn't know what that meant, so I asked, "How many credits is a full schedule?" He answered that a full schedule consisted of twelve credits, credits being assigned based on how many hours it would take to complete a course of study.

Can you see why the student was stressed out? He was taking six extra credits that required extra study time. Where did he find the time? He only had a few hours that weren't being used during the day, so he took it out of his sleep time. At first he was able to handle it, but as time went on, missing those few hours of sleep began to really wear on him. And that's why he was in my office looking for help.

If you want college to be a fun and exciting time of life, make your studies your first priority, but don't overload your schedule by trying to do more than you can do. You also need to make sure you obey the commandments, especially those listed in Doctrine and Covenants 88:124: "Cease to be idle; cease to be unclean; cease to find fault one with another; cease to sleep longer than is needful; retire to thy bed early, that ye may not be weary; arise early, that your bodies and your minds may be invigorated." That verse was written for all of us, but I think it can apply especially to college kids. Most problems I dealt with could have been avoided if that verse was strictly obeyed. My experiences have shown that if you choose to go against any part of that verse, the odds are good that you'll end up in an office looking for help.

Let's review what you need to do to reach your education goal. First, decide you want a good education. Then commit to your goal, ask God for help, learn to use your time wisely, do something every day that brings you closer to your goal, don't overload your schedule, and go to work. If you'll do these simple steps, you'll learn to love school, and that will make reaching your education goal a lot easier.

$$\pi$$

TO FURTHER UNDERSTAND why a good education is important let's take a look at those who don't do well in school. Are they excited about being there and committed to their education? They may look happy while they're goofing around, but they really aren't, because they're not doing well. Here's how this often happens.

It usually starts years before when they couldn't keep up with their schoolwork and fell behind. To hide their embarrassment, they started goofing off. If you're behind in your schoolwork, get some help now before you fall any further behind. Need some motivation? Here's where the not-doing-well-in-school road leads.

When people aren't doing well in school, they're usually unhappy, depressed, discouraged, and sometimes even angry. These negative feelings cause them to goof off and skip classes.

This causes them to get into more and more trouble until they quit or get kicked out of school. As a result, they won't get a good education.

Without an education, they won't have a lot of job opportunities, so they'll have to take whatever job they can get—if they can get one at all. How much do those types of jobs pay? It's not enough, and that leaves them stuck in a low-income lifestyle. Once they're stuck, the only choice they have is to live their lives with regret. Regret means they look back at the things they wished they hadn't done.

This negative behavior isn't good, but what else can they do? They have no way to change their lifestyle—at least, that's what the evil team will tell them. If they choose to believe the evil team, their regrets will eventually consume them. Regret is a dangerous emotion because it's the first step toward discouragement, depression, and anger.

Did you say, "Wait a minute. Doesn't everyone have a few regrets?" Yes, but regrets have to be dealt with correctly or they'll eventually destroy you. Here's how you deal with regrets.

Spending any time wishing you could change the past isn't productive. No matter what you do or how hard you try, you can't change the past. All you can do is learn from your experiences, move on, and quit worrying about it. Of course, that's easier said than done. I recently heard a saying that really helped me deal with my regrets: "I don't think about the past, because there is nothing I can do about it. I also don't think much about the future, because there is nothing I can do about it. The only day I think about is today because that's the only day I can do anything about." If you'll choose to look at life this way, regrets will never consume you. But again, that's easier said than done.

So how do you let the past go?

You start by answering this simple question. What would make you happier—doing something that makes your day better, or doing something that makes your day worse? If you're living with regrets, try focusing on making today better than yesterday, and then focus on making tomorrow better than today.

Will this be easy? No. It's always easier to fall into the hole than it is to climb out, but you can do it because God wants to help you climb out. The evil team doesn't want you to be happy, so they're going to tempt you to focus only on the past. They want you depressed, discouraged, angry, and just plain miserable.

Can you see now why the evil team doesn't want you to get a good education? They're looking for every opportunity to make you miserable, and it can happen if you don't prepare for your future by getting a good education. Now is the time to prepare, while you're in school. An education gives you freedom, and freedom allows you to control things you'll experience in life. If you lose control, then you become subject to those who have control, and you do not want to live your entire life under someone else's control.

π

THE EVIL TEAM just said, "That's baloney. Everyone works for other people who control them to some extent, so why should they bother getting a good education?"

Okay, I'll bite. Let's talk about it.

If you get an education, companies will have to compete against each other to get you to work for them. If they have to compete, you become more valuable to them, and that will make them appreciate you more, treat you better, pay you more, and give you more freedom. None of that can happen without an education. Let's compare this lifestyle with the one you'll live if you choose not to get an education.

If you go to work for a company that just *lets* you come to work for them, they won't appreciate you. They'll pay you practically nothing, offer you no benefits, tell you what to do and when to do it, and after all that, they'll lay you off if there's even a ripple in the economy.

Which type of lifestyle do you want? I'll bet it's the one that comes with a good education. Do you want it bad enough to work for it?

I hope you won't let the evil team stop you from getting your much-needed education. Getting it will be hard, but you must have it to be successful. Regardless of the time you live in, God wants you to be successful. All you have to do is decide you want it, ask for it, believe it's going to happen before it happens, and go to work and make it happen. It's your choice. I hope you choose wisely.

REVIEW OF IMPORTANT POINTS

- Work is never work when you love what you're doing.
- Reaching a goal is easy if you use the four steps to success.
- An education is an important goal. Your future depends on it.
- Use the four steps each day and you'll get your education.
- Education makes you more valuable to your future employer.
- Value allows you to earn more money and gives you more freedom.
- All things really are possible with God's help.

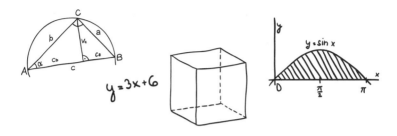

CHAPTER 11

YOU ALREADY USE THE STEPS

WHEN YOU'RE BEING taught something you don't yet understand, how do you feel? I feel dark and confused. How do you feel right after something in your brain clicks and you understand what is being taught? I feel enlightened as the darkness of not knowing is replaced by the light of knowing. When I'm enlightened, I feel good. That good feeling comes from God.

The "two plus two equals four" example I used earlier was simple, and that's why I used it. I wanted you to clearly see how God teaches simple truths and uses these simple truths to teach you good things so you can be successful. So how can my "two plus two" example help you become successful?

Merely learning that two plus two equals four isn't all that important, but understanding how you learned it is. It's the same way you learn every good thing—and every bad thing—in life. God uses His light to teach you good things, and the evil team uses their dark thoughts to teach you bad things. The evil team can't use light because they have no light, but they have plenty of dark thoughts. Think about the last time you received thoughts from the evil team. Did those thoughts make you feel enlightened or darkened? When I say "darkened," I mean ashamed, confused, or any other type of negative or bad feeling. Even if their thought made you feel good in the beginning, you probably felt darkened after you acted on that thought. When you act on dark thoughts, you'll always feel bad sooner or later.

Now that you understand how God teaches you good things and how you can learn those good things by using the four steps, can you imagine how much more you can learn if you'll start using this new learning process on purpose?

I said "can learn" because I'm confident you can learn a lot, but how much you learn is entirely up to you. The amount you learn is determined by your willingness to learn. Doctrine and Covenants 88:32 teaches us this principle plainly. The first few times I read this verse, I thought it only applied to the previous verses. But on one special day, it took on a whole different meaning that answered a lot of questions I had about life.

The first part of Doctrine and Covenants section 88 teaches you how you learn. Then, in the last half of verse 32, it explains why souls are assigned to the various kingdoms of glory in the next life: "They shall return again to their own place, to enjoy that which they are willing to receive, because they were not willing to enjoy that which they might have received." I believe that within this simple statement rests one of the most misunderstood mysteries of God, because it applies to not only the next life but also everything in this life.

Here's why understanding this verse is so important. I'll again use school in this example. Why do some students get good grades and others don't? The answer could be (and I'm sure it's the answer the evil team wants you to believe) that even though we were all born with the same standard equipment, some are born with greater abilities than others.

It is true that some really are born with more abilities. The Book of Abraham in the Pearl of Great Price teaches this idea clearly, but that's not why the evil team wants you to think you have fewer abilities. They want you to think you have fewer so they can depress you and you won't try to get any more abilities. If you weren't born with more abilities, does that mean you can never have more abilities? The answer is again no, but let's go back to verse 32 and see if I'm right.

In verse 32 there are a couple important words you need to recognize. The first word is *might*. If it *might* be possible, then it *could* be possible, and if it could be possible, then there are no limits to what is possible. If there are no limits to what is possible, then there are no limits on what you can receive. If verse 32 said, "You receive what you receive because that's all you get," then that would be all you get. Lucky for us, it doesn't say that, so the possibilities are left wide open.

So what determines what you will receive? The answer is in three other important words: *they*, *not*, and *willing*. These words are the qualifiers, or the words that determine what you can actually receive. Let me help you understand the qualifiers, and then you can better understand what is possible.

The word *they* means *you*. You will determine what you can receive by being either willing or not willing to receive what is being offered. If you're willing to receive what is being offered, then there is no limit to what you can receive because there is no limit on what's being offered. God is willing to let you receive whatever you're willing to receive because that's what He said in verse 32. This can be confusing, so let me show you how this works in real life.

This life is not your beginning. Your spirit lived in the premortal world before you were sent here to receive a physical body. In the premortal world you had experiences and learned abilities that came with you when you came to earth. After you were born, you continued to learn more, and that created more intelligence and abilities. Some abilities also came from your ancestors, and some from the way you were raised. For instance, if you're athletic, your ancestors were probably athletic. If you can play the piano, it's because your parents had you take lessons and encouraged you to learn how to play. All of your experiences here give you opportunities to learn, beginning at birth and continuing until you die. After death, you move into the next life, where you will continue to learn until you reach your final perfected state—becoming like

God. All of this can and will happen because you're willing to allow it to happen. Let's now apply this same process to school.

You show you're willing to learn in school by wanting to learn in school. Next, you ask God to help you learn while you believe He will help you learn. Then you use this belief to motivate you while you go to work and learn. But it doesn't stop there. Watch what else happens.

When you go to work, you begin to learn. Because you learn, you see that the process actually works, and that gives you more confidence. This added confidence strengthens your faith, which increases the amount of help you can receive from God, and that makes it even easier to learn. Now that it's easier, you're able to learn more, and that again increases your confidence in the process. Can you see the cycle of certainty? This cycle never ends until you decide to quit using it.

Can you see why I said you could learn a lot? All of this will happen when you put some effort into your studies by listening in class instead of goofing off, by doing your assignments to the best of your ability instead of just handing in whatever you can quickly scribble on a piece of paper, and by making your homework a priority instead of leaving it until the last minute.

If you're willing to do your part, God will help you because He wants you to do well in school. Why? When you do well in school, you get scholarships, go to college for free, graduate with honors, and have lots of companies waiting to pay you lots of money when you work for them. With that money, you'll pay lots of tithing, which builds churches and temples and supports the missionary effort so God's plan can continue to spread until it fills the whole earth.

$$\pi$$

NOW LET ME remind you of what will happen if you don't do well in school. Hidden in this example is a point I don't want you to miss. See if you can find it.

In this example, those who are not willing to do well in school think they don't want to do well or think they don't care about school. I say "think" because they don't yet understand they want it or care about it. They'll eventually want what comes from a good education, but unfortunately they won't figure it out until it's too late to do anything about it.

When students don't do well in school and start goofing off and getting into trouble, other students who are trying to stay out of trouble ignore them. That leaves them feeling isolated and alone. No one likes to be alone, so they start looking for those who have the same attitudes and desires. Unfortunately, they find them. Since all of them are unhappy in school and in life, they start looking for ways to have fun so they can be happy.

This fun usually leads to immorality, drugs, and alcohol, because those things make them feel temporarily happy. Since these behaviors and products are their only source of happiness, they do it more and more often, and that prevents them from graduating from high school. When they don't graduate, they can't go to college, get a degree, or get a good job. That leaves them at the mercy of society, but society has no mercy. So those who don't get an education have to go to work wherever they can find a job, or they have to live on some type of assistance, which robs them of self-esteem. Assistance and the jobs they can get never pay enough money to support a family, so the frustration builds at home. If they got married, the unhappy couple to starts fighting. This fighting eventually leads to divorce, and that makes the kids suffer. What's really sad about this example is that their kids usually end up doing the same thing, because they didn't have a good example to follow.

Did you find what I wanted you to see? The point I didn't want you to miss was the cycle of uncertainty this lifestyle creates for future generations. When parents don't do well, the cycle usually continues for several more generations.

Some may think my school example was too simple, and others may even think I'm being cruel to those who aren't doing well. How you feel depends entirely on how you choose to look at it. I feel like I need to tell you the truth, because the truth will set you free from the miserable life I've described. I believe those who aren't doing well need to honestly look at their future so they don't end up living that lifestyle.

I hope you know that I would never purposefully try to be cruel, but I believe it's crueler to know the truth and not tell you. Now that you know what will happen, I hope you'll use the power of faith so you can do well in school.

$$\pi$$

ARE YOU READY to choose to believe that the four steps, with God's help, can help you become successful in life? Here's how you use each of the four steps.

The first step requires you to decide what you want in life. I'd suggest making a detailed list of the things you want and the things you want to accomplish. The list might include a good marriage, kids, a great career, a beautiful house in a perfect location, places you'd like to travel, or your dream car.

The items on your list can be anything, but you need to be specific. For instance, if you want a car, don't just say, *I'd like a car*. Decide what car you'd like. For me it's a Celestial Black Shelby GT 500KR with a flat metallic gray stripe, twenty-inch polished wheels, auto transmission, gray leather interior, navigation, and the best sound system money can buy. Can you see the difference between any car and my car? Which one creates more excitement? For me it's the Shelby, but you can have whatever you want. After you've made your detailed list, you've completed step number one.

The second step, asking for God's help, is also easy. Here's how you do it. When you ask for God's help, you shouldn't say, "I want this car; help me buy it." You should say, "Help me make good choices so I can become successful." Then sit down and make a plan that leads to success, and that success will give you what you need to buy the car you want.

Are you wondering how many times you'll need to ask for help? You must continually ask while you're following the plan you've developed. While you're asking, always remember to thank God for the help He's already given, the help He's currently giving, and the help He will give. Then you're ready to move to step number three.

Step number three is harder because you must believe it will happen before it happens—every single day until it happens. This is the step that stops most of us. Most of your wants or goals in life will take years to achieve, so it's easy to quit believing.

How do you keep believing? You choose to keep believing—the same way you choose to do everything else in life. You wake up and choose to believe it will happen, and then you move on to step four.

Step four requires you to go to work and stay at work until it happens. This step is also hard because it requires you to work, but all work isn't the same. For example, you must first work on your plan, and then you must inventory your resources that could help you complete your plan. Then you use your resources to acquire the additional resources you still need to complete step four. All of this is work. It all must be done, so find something you love to do, and it will get done.

That is the *Reader's Digest* version of how to use the steps to become successful. They will work if you continue to use them. Never forget that your life is an open book, full of blank pages waiting to be filled. Now that you understand how to use the four steps, I hope you'll choose to use them every day, because your successful life is waiting to be created!

$$\pi$$

BEFORE WE MOVE on, I want to make sure you recognized one more point: I hope you were able to see that what I've taught you is true. If you're not yet convinced, start watching the people all around you, and see if you recognize what I've described. I'm not asking you to judge them; I want you to become convinced that what I taught you is really true. If you're convinced, you'll never be deceived. There will always be those who don't seem to care about what they do in life. I hope you'll choose to believe so you don't become one of them.

In the next chapter, I'll share something unbelievable with you. Would you like a hint? Have you ever hoped to find a hidden treasure? Me too—and I've found one. I'm going to show you how to find one too.

REVIEW OF IMPORTANT POINTS

- The darkness of not knowing can be replaced by the light of knowing.
- You learn new things by following the four steps to success.
- You can receive what you're willing to receive. God wants you to receive everything.
- Use the four steps to do well in school.
- Doing well in school will allow you to enjoy a successful life.
- God wants you to be successful.

$$A = \begin{pmatrix} 2 & -1 \\ -3 & -2 \end{pmatrix} \qquad y = \sqrt{2x-1}$$

δ

CHAPTER 12

A TREASURE GREATER THAN GOLD

WHEN I WAS young, my family owned and operated a mining and trucking company. The mines we worked were located in the mountains of Utah, Nevada, Colorado, and Wyoming, so the mining had to be done in the summer. I remember thinking life was unfair because I'd be heading out of town to work at the next mining job while the other kids enjoyed their summer.

During the late 1960s, I spent a couple of summers in northwestern Nevada on top of Buckskin Mountain, mining mercury. It was named Buckskin because from a distance you couldn't see anything green on top of that mountain.

I didn't want to go there to work, but it quickly became one of my favorite places because there were a lot of old abandoned shacks and mines near our camp. I wasn't old enough to do much of the actual mining, so I spent my time exploring. Exploring could have been dangerous, so my parents constantly warned me about everything from rusty nails and rattlesnakes to vertical mine shafts and places in the mines called dead-air pockets. Those warnings kept me from being too brave, but I still explored each mine and shack as much as I dared, because I was sure some hidden treasure was there just waiting to be found.

I found a few old colored bottles, rusted tools, and kitchen items scattered around the area, but I didn't think they were worth anything. I thought they were junk. I did find a really neat old heavy-cast iron cooking stove that I thought would be fun to have, but I couldn't figure out how to get it out of the shack and up the hill to the road. I guess that's probably why it was still there: if it could have been easily moved, someone else would have taken it a long time ago.

I was disappointed I didn't find any hidden treasure. Or did I, but I didn't recognize it? The realization that I had found some treasure came several years later when I visited my first antique store. The minute I walked in the door, I discovered that many of the items I had passed over—the ones I thought were junk—may have actually been valuable antiques. The treasure I had spent so much time looking for was right there in front of me the whole time.

I share this story to help you understand there are things in life that have great value all around you that you may not yet recognize. For instance, take a look at my book. Believe it or not, it's like a hidden treasure, but you'll have to read it and then do what it teaches before you'll be able to find its value.

Somewhere along the way to becoming old, I discovered my hidden treasure, and like all the antiques I had passed over, it had been there right in front of me the whole time. I didn't recognize it because I didn't know what I was looking for.

The treasure I found is special thoughts and feelings that tell me what I *should* do. Sometimes these special thoughts and feelings are barely noticeable, but at other times they're loud enough to hear. I've mentioned these thoughts and feelings several times, but now it's time to teach you how to use them to create your successful life.

Before I learned to recognize them as separate thoughts and feelings, I believed they were coming to me from my conscience. I didn't think they were special because they had always been there telling me what not to do. Then one day, something pretty amazing happened.

Do you remember my hero Nephi, who wrote the first two books in the Book of Mormon? Nephi had many special abilities, but there was one I thought was extra special. He was able to have conversations with the Spirit. I was so impressed that I decided I wanted to grow up and talk to the Spirit like Nephi. Sadly, I knew it would never happen because every time I thought about it, a thought would say, "You can't be like Nephi. Nephi was special, and you're not." That thought would cause me to think about all the good things I had done in life, but another negative thought would always come and tell me I wasn't special.

These thoughts often went back and forth like the ball in a tennis match. I'd serve up a thought trying to score a point, and then a negative thought would be hit right back at me until I either gave up or got distracted by something else. After I gave up, I would always have one last negative thought to make sure I got the message loud and clear: "You're not special, and you'll never be special, so don't think you could ever have a conversation with the Spirit." I figured since I wasn't special and probably never would be special, it would never happen. And guess what? It never happened.

Don't get the wrong idea. I wasn't spending my whole day talking to myself. These events take a bit of explaining on paper, but in my head they only lasted for a few seconds. Occasionally, they did happen more than once on an average day, and that's why I was finally able to notice the pattern.

For some reason on that one special day, I finally realized what was going on. I was having the conversation I always wanted to have while the evil team was telling me that it couldn't happen.

This recognition helped me to believe that if Nephi could do it, I could do it, because God is the same today as He was in Nephi's day. For the first time in my life, I began to believe that God is no respecter of persons. This is important, so I'll explain what it means.

God is a perfected being, so His love for you is also perfect. You can't make Him love you any more or any less because He already loves you perfectly. Since you can't make Him love you more, you can't become better or more special than anyone else.

You also can't make Him love you less, so He doesn't love anyone else more than you. That's what "no respecter of persons" means.

You might have just had a flood of negative thoughts that sounded like this: "This is so much baloney. God loves others more than you, and you know it." Or you might have heard the old standby, "If God loves everybody the same, why does He let bad things happen to some and not to others?" Maybe some of your thoughts started with the word *why*.

If they did, did you notice that all of those thoughts were negative, and they all caused you to have doubts about God's love for you? If you answered yes to any of my questions, then you just had a conversation with the wrong spirit as well.

If any of this did happen, then I need to help you get beyond those feelings by sharing a scripture that explains your relationship with God. It's found in 1 Nephi 17:35: "Behold, the Lord esteemeth [looks upon] all flesh in one; [but] he that is righteous is favored of God." This verse clearly explains that God looks upon and loves everyone equally, but He favors the righteous!

I know this is a simple question, but if you had a choice, would you rather be favored by God or not favored by God? I'm sure you would rather be favored. Why? If you're favored, what do you get? You get more blessings. How can you become favored by God so you can receive more blessings? You can become righteous. You become righteous by obeying the commandments and repenting quickly when you don't. If obeying the commandments and repenting make you righteous, and being righteous is how you receive blessings, what would happen if you obeyed more of the commandments and became more righteous? You would be more favored, and you would receive even more blessings.

If you're wondering what all this has to do with having a conversation with the Spirit, or finding a hidden treasure, then you're right where I hoped you would eventually be. You're now ready to cross the bridge over to the knowing side of the canyon. So let's cross.

YOU'VE NOW CROSSED, and you're trying to be more righteous so you can receive more blessings. How are these blessings given to you? They're given as stronger feelings and thoughts that will help you make more good choices and experience more good consequences. Who gives you these stronger feelings and thoughts? It's the Spirit of God. How far can this cycle of certainty go? The answer is—I don't really know.

I can almost hear you saying, "What do you mean you don't know? How can you answer the question if you don't know?"

The reason I don't know how much spiritual help you can receive is that I'm not you. You're the only one who knows how many commandments you're willing to obey, and that's what determines the amount of spiritual help you'll be able to receive. But I do know how much is possible. Nephi gave us the answer in 2 Nephi 32:2–3, 5. In those verses, Nephi said the Spirit will tell you (verses 2 and 3) and then show you (verse 5) all things that you should do. How does the Spirit tell you and show you? Nephi's life story answers these two questions.

If you're familiar with the story of Nephi, you know that he was told what he should do during several one-on-one, in-person conversations with the Spirit. For example, he had the vision of the tree of life and the experience with Laban. The Spirit also taught him how to build a ship. The Spirit showed Nephi what he should do on many other occasions too. For example, when his family was starving in the wilderness, Nephi made a bow and some arrows, and the Spirit showed him where to find food for the family. The Spirit also showed him the more fertile areas while they were in the wilderness.

From the outside looking in, these experiences would cause you to think he really was special in the eyes of God—and I would quickly agree—but what made him special? I'll give you a hint. Change the word *special* to *favored*; he was favored because he obeyed the commandments and learned to repent quickly when he didn't.

What, you don't think Nephi ever had to repent? I thought that too, until I read Nephi's lament in 2 Nephi 4:17: "O wretched man that I am!" As hard as it was for me to believe, Nephi wasn't perfect either, but he could still talk to the Spirit.

I hope you'll choose to believe that if Nephi could do it, you and I can do it, because God is no respecter of persons. All you have to do is want it, ask for it, and believe it can happen. Then go to work and make it happen by obeying the commandments. Remember, you don't control the timetable; God does. You just have to continue doing your part until you receive the promised blessings. Whatever you do, don't give up or put a limit on the amount of spiritual help you could receive by limiting the amount you're willing to receive.

Do you believe you can receive spiritual help? Good. Now all you need to do is figure out how to get it. But wait—you're already getting it, so what are you missing? You're missing faith, or a belief, that it really is happening. How do you get faith? You choose to have it. Let's talk about what you can expect when you choose to have faith.

$$\pi$$

NEPHI SAID THAT the Spirit helps you by telling and showing you all things that you should do. When I first read those verses, I wondered if Nephi really meant *all things*, because that would mean the Spirit's influence must be available to you all day every day. Is it really possible for the Spirit to be with you all the time? Honestly, I don't understand how He could be, but I still choose to believe He is, and that belief is enough to make me want to have Him with me all the time.

Did you notice in 2 Nephi 32:2–3, 5 that Nephi said the Spirit will tell you and show you what you *should* do, not *what* to do? Think about what happens when you make a choice. Two different thoughts or feelings enter your mind, and each wants you to make the choice they are suggesting. One thought tells you to do one thing, and the other thought tells you to do something else.

How can you tell if the evil team is trying to deceive you? You can look ahead to see the true consequence of that choice. If you'll just look, you'll clearly see which thought is telling you what you *should* do. The things you should do are things that qualify you to receive God's blessings. This is what Nephi was trying to teach you when he said the Spirit will tell you what you should do—you should always do what's right.

Now let's go back and look at the process you go through every time you make a choice. When you make a choice, you'll have at least two different thoughts. For as long as I can remember, I've used thoughts to help me make choices, but I never realized how much they were actually influencing me. I thought they were created in my mind, so I never made a connection between them and the two opposing forces here on earth. However, now that I'm older, I can plainly see that most of my thoughts and feelings are coming from the good team or the evil team.

Can you see how these thoughts and feelings could create problems for you? Let's look at it again. When you're making choices, the good team and the evil team send you thoughts and feelings that influence you. Both *sound* good, but only one really *is* good.

The evil team knows if they told you the whole truth, you would never consider their thoughts, so they twist their thoughts into something that sounds good, hoping you'll choose quickly before you take time to think about the consequences. The evil team's thoughts look good because they always include some form of short-term gratification. This means they make you feel good for a short time. This is why you must train yourself to look at the consequences of each thought before you make your choice.

You might think looking at the consequences of each choice would be hard, but it really isn't. God knew the evil team would try to confuse you, so He gave you a gift that helps you discern each thought. In fact, this gift will help you know which choice you should make before you even think about the consequences. This gift is your conscience. But here's another warning: you will lose your conscience unless you listen to it and obey it often.

The Spirit also communicates with you by sending you subtle, almost unrecognizable feelings and thoughts that help you make the right choices. They will feel natural, but it's important for you to learn to recognize them. Why? If you want to increase the intensity and frequency of these thoughts, you must ask for them. If you don't recognize them, you won't think to ask for them. You also must recognize when the Spirit is helping you so you don't think it's just you having the thoughts. If you think it's just you, you won't be motivated to obey the commandments or remember to thank God for His help. Thanking God is important if you want Him to continue helping you.

The last way the Spirit communicates with you is by speaking directly to you. In my life, this hasn't happened often when you compare it to all the other thoughts I normally have. But when it does happen, it really gets my attention. These special experiences normally happen right before I realize I'm going to need help. But as rare as they are, they can happen more often than you think. If you want them, ask for them, believe they will happen, and then go to work to make them happen.

These are the three ways the Spirit of God communicates with you. Now let's look at how the evil team communicates with you.

$$\pi$$

THE EVIL TEAM will always be waiting for an opportunity to send you a thought or feeling that influences you to do something wrong. Their thoughts can be random, meaning they can come at any time, or they can be situational, meaning they come when you're in a certain place or when you see something. The situational thoughts are the easiest to control because you can choose the places you visit and what you look at. The best rule is, if you're not there, they won't happen. Random thoughts are more difficult because you can't completely stop bad thoughts from popping into your head. But you can push them out when they do.

Now that you understand how thoughts influence you, Nephi's teaching in chapter 32 should take on a whole new meaning. He said the Spirit will tell you all things you should do, so all you have to do is learn to identify the right Spirit and do what He tells you. Identifying the right Spirit is easier than you think, because you have your conscience to help you.

Let me plug these principles into a real-life example so you can see what happens when you make a choice.

A choice needs to made, and at least two thoughts enter into your head. One thought tells you to do one thing, and the other thought tells you to do something different. If you make the right choice, then life goes on, and not much happens other than you seem to enjoy better luck, or blessings.

If you make the wrong choice, then one or two things usually happen. If it's just a bad choice—meaning it's not good for you— you'll eventually suffer the consequences. If the choice is bad— meaning it's evil—then you'll eventually suffer the consequences, and you'll also feel bad until you repent. Make sure you remember that this bad feeling helps you recognize you've sinned and need to repent; it doesn't mean you're a bad person.

You also don't want to confuse this bad feeling with the really bad feelings you'll eventually get if you choose not to repent. This immediate bad feeling helps you recognize you've sinned and need to repent so you can start to feel good again. If you choose to repent and finish the repentance process, you'll start feeling better pretty quickly. If you choose not to repent, a really bad feeling called guilt or shame will begin.

The evil team wants you to feel ashamed, so they'll tell you it's no use trying to repent because you're just going to sin again, or they'll say you've committed a horrible sin so you'll become depressed and discouraged and want to give up.

Never forget that in the eyes of God, there are no good or bad sins. The evil team just said, "There are too bad sins." In a way, I guess they're right. There really are sins that are bad because they have bad consequences, and it should also go without saying that no sin is good in any way, shape, or form. But my point is this: God looks at all sin as just sin. He said, "I . . . cannot look upon sin"—notice He didn't say good or bad sin—"with the least degree of allowance" (D&C: 1:31). This means He looks at all sin as just sin.

If you'll look at all sin as just sin, you won't fall victim to an evil team trap—the trap of putting sins into categories. This means you think some sins are bad but others aren't.

Here's an example. When I was young, I used to say a few swear words, but I never said any bad ones. Did you see it? What was I doing? I rated that sin as small. But can you guess what happened later on? That's right. I started saying other words I thought I'd never hear myself say. But I never used the Lord's name in vain.

Did you see it again? I rated the sin by saying I started with little, meaningless words and then graduated to stronger words, *but I never took the Lord's name in vain.* Lucky for me, I came to my senses and eventually was able to get rid of all the words from my speech pattern. The reason? I nearly swore when I was giving a talk in church! That was the day I knew I had to straighten up my act.

If you choose to rate sin, you'll probably commit sins you think aren't bad, but God can't ignore any sin. That means you must repent for every sin you commit. If that sounds depressing, then I want to make something perfectly clear. I don't want you to sin, I hope you don't sin, and I'm not saying sin doesn't matter. Sin matters, so try hard not to sin. But don't get depressed when you sin, because agency is part of the plan. God knew you would sin, so He put a Savior in the plan. He will save you if you try hard not to sin and repent when you do.

Did you just hear what I heard? When I said you needed to repent, the evil team said, "Why bother repenting if it's impossible not to sin?" These guys never give up.

The answer is simple. You must repent *because* it's impossible not to sin. Again, I'm not telling you to sin, but what you do isn't as important as what you do about it. Could it really be this easy? It can, if you don't let the evil team discourage you or talk you out of believing.

The Book of Mormon explains how the plan works in 2 Nephi 31:13. This verse teaches you how you can sin and still be saved: "Ye shall follow the Son [Christ], with full purpose of heart, acting no hypocrisy and no deception before God, but with real intent, repenting of your sins." This verse might be hard to understand, so let me help you. It teaches you that you can sin, repent, and be forgiven—unless you try to sin on purpose. If you think you can sin and just repent later, that's deception and hypocrisy. If you really try not to sin but sin anyway, then repentance works. Your ability to be forgiven depends entirely upon your desire or intent.

Let's review the repentance process for those who are trying not to sin:

- Recognize the sin. This isn't hard, because you know you're committing sin before you even do it.
- Feel remorse. Having remorse means to feel bad. If you're trying to not commit sin, you'll immediately feel bad after you sin. Don't confuse this feeling with guilt. It's not yet guilt, it's just a feeling God gives you to help you recognize sin.
- Confess. *Confess* means apologize to God, which you probably already do when you start feeling bad. This simple apology works for 99 percent of the sins you commit. Sins that involve immorality or addictive products must be discussed with your bishop so he can help you not become addicted.
- Try hard to not sin again. This step is the hardest.
- Take the sacrament each week.
- Make restitution. This is what you do if you're really trying to repent.

This simple process is a real blessing because it allows you to carry the burden of sin for just one week. You start the week by taking the sacrament. You try really hard not to sin, and use the repentance process when you do. The next Sunday, you finish the steps by again taking the sacrament and starting over. If you'll choose to complete the steps of repentance as outlined, you can avoid most, if not all, those really bad feelings called shame or guilt that come when you choose not to repent.

For the longest time, I thought that my shame and guilt were coming from God because He was mad at me. These bad feelings kept me from wanting to get too close to Him. Would you want to get close to someone who's mad at you or someone who wants you to feel bad? I know I don't.

If you're also thinking God is mad at you, stop thinking that way. He's not. He loves you more than you will ever understand—even when you sin. Why then do you feel bad? There are two basic reasons. You feel bad either because you know you did something wrong and need to repent, or because the evil team doesn't want you to feel like you can go to God and ask for forgiveness.

God loves you even when you sin, but you still must repent of every sin. If you choose to not repent, His Spirit will leave. The evil team then moves in and tries to stop you from repenting by sending you bad feelings called guilt. When you feel bad, you aren't the only one who does. God also feels bad because He wants to bless you, but He can't until you repent. This is why you want to train yourself to always turn to God, not away from Him, when you sin. All throughout the scriptures, you've heard the Savior say, "Come unto me." You come unto the Savior by not turning away from Him when you sin. He's not mad, and He doesn't want you feeling bad. He really is on your side, and I hope you'll choose to believe it.

This ability to believe that God loves you is another bridge you must cross before you can see what's on the other side. Once you're on the other side, you'll be able to use the treasure, or spiritual help, that's available if you want it, ask for it, believe it will happen, and go to work to make it happen. You won't believe how much help is available until you see it. In the next chapter, I'll teach you how to use it so you can see it.

REVIEW OF IMPORTANT POINTS

- You have a hidden treasure right in front of you.
- The treasure is the thoughts and feelings that come from God.
- These thoughts will tell and show you all things you should do.
- Satan will deceive you by making his thoughts and feelings sound good.
- You won't be deceived if you look at the consequences of your choices.
- All sin is sin. You must repent so God can bless you.

- Guilt and shame are not part of the repentance process.
- God uses a feeling we call remorse to remind you to repent. The evil team uses shame to keep you from repenting.
- Turn to God, not away from Him, when you sin.
- Unlimited spiritual help is waiting to be used, if you want it, ask for it, believe it will happen, and then go to work and make it happen.

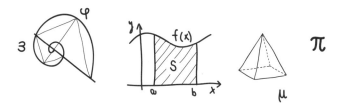

CHAPTER 13

USING YOUR TREASURE

MOST OF US struggle when we have to make choices. This struggle often stops us from making a choice or causes us to make choices that make no sense whatsoever. Wrong, or no-sense, choices always have bad consequences, which are easy to recognize because they hurt. Good ones don't hurt, so naturally you will focus on the ones that hurt. But that's not what you should focus on. This is what you should focus on.

Whenever you're about to make a bad choice, three words will fly through your mind. If you're still young, you should be able to hear them loud and clear. If you're older and have ignored them for a while, they may not be quite as noticeable as they once were. What are these words? *Don't do it.*

I did a little scientific research and found that these same three words go through everyone's mind right before they make a bad choice. Okay, maybe it wasn't exactly scientific, but it did involve quite a few test subjects. If you want to have some fun next time you're in front of a group, ask them what three words go through their minds right before they make a bad choice. It may require a little coaching to help them actually slow down long enough to remember, but when they do, it's always the same answer—*Don't do it!*

When I was young, I thought these words just came from my conscience, but that isn't exactly right. I now understand that they come from the Spirit through my conscience, and that's why I didn't recognize them as help from the Spirit. Here's how it works.

You're about to make a bad choice, and you hear the words *don't do it*. You think it's just your conscience and that the experience is anything special. The evil team continues to entice you by pointing out all of the good in their bad choice, so you decide to just go ahead and do it. After you've done it, the Spirit withdraws, and you suffer the consequences of your bad choice. Those consequences hurt, so they get your attention, and that's when you see the Spirit was trying to help you. This is another easy question: What would have happened if you'd listened to the warning and didn't do it? You wouldn't be hurting, and you might even be able to enjoy a good consequence.

Do you see the treasure? Can you see how it works? The treasure is that thought or feeling that tells you what you should do before you do it. It starts as three simple words—*don't do it*—and continues to grow in frequency and intensity when you don't do it. Can you imagine what it would be like to know what you should do before you do it? Wouldn't that be a treasure worth more than gold? I promise you it would, and all you have to do to enjoy your treasure is start obeying those three simple words that always come right before you make a bad choice.

Can the evil team also say "Don't do it"? I guess they could, but for some unexplained reason, I don't think they do. They instead try to tempt you by offering you another choice that sounds even better than their first. For instance, if you have a thought that tells you to go to church, the evil team won't say, "Don't do it." They'll instead say, "Church is no fun. You can have more fun doing . . ." You can fill in the blank. Maybe there's an unwritten law about who gets to say *Don't do it* that the evil team can't violate. We'll just have to wait until we get to the other side to see.

Can you remember hearing the words *don't do it*? If you can't, it's probably because you've gotten older and have quit paying attention to them. That's what happened to me. I would never intentionally ignore them, but that's what happened when I quit paying as much attention to them.

If you continually ignore this warning, it will weaken until you can't hear it. And if you don't hear it and use it, you'll eventually lose it, and then you're on your own in this spiritually and physically dangerous world. *On your own* means you will be left to make choices without any spiritual help. That isn't good because the evil team is really good at what they do. God knows you will need help, so He sends His Spirit to lead, guide, protect, and prosper you.

If you listen to the spiritual warnings and choose to follow them by doing what they tell you, the promptings don't become weaker. They become stronger, and that makes them more noticeable. This cycle of certainty continues until you recognize the Spirit when He's telling you all the things you should do.

If you're thinking that being able to have the Spirit speak to you isn't possible or He only speaks to other people, you're thinking wrong. As incredible as it sounds, it's actually quite common. We even have a name for it—it's called *sharpening your conscience*.

The evil team knows you have a conscience, so they are going to sprinkle little bits of truth into their messages to confuse and deceive you. They don't ever tell the whole truth, but they do sprinkle a little truth in with their lies, or you would never consider listening to them.

Here's an example. It's late at night, and you're ready to go to bed. As you approach your bed, a thought tells you to say your prayers, and then another thought tells you that you're tired and can pray tomorrow. Can you see the sprinkling of truth? Aren't you tired right before you go to bed, and couldn't you say your prayers tomorrow? Yes, you could. But is either of those suggestions a valid reason not to pray? Do they change the fact that you should pray? No. This is how the evil team operates. They sprinkle a little truth in your thoughts and feelings so you won't think the thoughts are coming from them. They know if you knew where the thoughts were coming from, you'd never listen to them. Another way to keep from being deceived is to slow down long enough to compare each feeling and thought to the commandments. If the feeling or thought is in line with the commandments, then go ahead and do it. If not, don't do it.

π

NOW THAT YOU know how you receive thoughts and feelings, the next step is to start following only the good ones. Always wanting to do good things can be hard, especially when you really don't want to. Like it or not, you're going to have some bad days when nothing seems to go right, and that can cause all kinds of negative feelings. There will also be other times when it's equally hard to keep yourself from doing something you want to do, even when you know it's wrong. Want an example? At this very moment, I have a pack of Oreo cookies staring at me, waiting for me to eat them, but I know I shouldn't. I guess that's why these feelings are called temptations. Maybe I could share them with my wife. That would make it better, right?

Resisting the evil team's temptations will require you to choose to believe God's way is better until you convince yourself that it is by experiencing the good or better consequences. Will you always be able to resist the evil team's temptations? No, because doing what's right doesn't come naturally to you. You live in an imperfect world, and that makes it hard to control *the beast*. I'll tell you all about the beast later. For now, just know you're normal if doing what's right doesn't always come easy.

If you'll consistently try to listen to and obey the thoughts and feelings that come from God, they will become stronger until, on special occasions, they sound like a voice. I know this because I've felt and heard them. I'm not exactly sure which best describes the experience, feeling or hearing, but once you've had the experience, you'll never forget it.

Most of the time, good thoughts and feelings come quietly, or what you might call naturally. If you choose to listen and obey, a bond of trust will be created between you and the Spirit. This trust allows your faith to increase, and that allows the volume of the thoughts to also increase.

When I was teaching you how to listen to and use the Spirit, did any doubts enter your mind? If they did, remember that the evil team is not just going to sit there and let me teach you this without a fight. They don't want you learning any of this, so don't allow doubt to stop you from choosing to believe you really do have a God who sends you thoughts to help you make good choices.

How many times in an average year do you really need God's help? When I asked that question, I almost felt guilty for asking it because you always need God's help. So let me ask the question a different way. How many times, on average, will you find yourself in the wrong place at the wrong time? I've found from experience that if you're careful, it will only happen a few times a year, and that's why you don't get to have this experience often. If I likened these experiences to a cake, the cake would be your life, the frosting would be the subtle feelings and thoughts you receive every day, and these stronger feelings would be just a few sprinkles on top of the icing.

The feelings and thoughts I likened to the icing aren't as strong as the ones I likened to the sprinkles, but they're every bit as important because they're the ones that lead, guide, teach, preserve, protect, and prosper you every day. Here's how you can use these gifts from the Spirit.

First, you must choose to believe that every one of your thoughts and feelings comes from one of three places. We've talked about two of those places, good and evil, and we'll get to the other one in a minute. Next you must learn to sort out your thoughts by comparing each one to the commandments so you can know which spirit sent you that thought or feeling. Then you must act on each feeling or thought—if it's good, do it; if it's evil or bad, don't do it.

If you will do these simple steps, then the Spirit can lead you through life. If you think following these steps is too simple to actually work or that sorting out your thoughts is impossible, it isn't. Let me explain.

Think back to when you learned to ride a bike. How long did it take? Didn't you get on, pedal a few feet, and crash? But you got back on and kept trying until you were riding it without even having to think about it. Learning to sort out your thoughts works the same way. All you have to do is work on it until you learn how, and then your mind will do it without you even having to think about it. But I need to give you another warning.

When you start sorting out your thoughts, you'll notice that you have quite a few bad thoughts. Don't get depressed. Remember, thoughts are just thoughts until you do something with them. So do something with the bad ones—get rid of them as quickly as possible. The evil team will tell you that you're bad because you have bad thoughts, even when they just sent them to you. Bad thoughts are part of our test in life, so when they come, get rid of them as quickly as possible and you'll be fine.

After you learn to sort out your thoughts, the next step is to work on increasing the intensity of the good ones so you can recognize them more easily. When you obey them, this will happen automatically. Obeying qualifies you for blessings, blessings help you make good choices, and good choices create better consequences. These better consequences increase your confidence, more confidence gives you more faith, and more faith increases your desire to obey even more commandments. Can you see the cycle of certainty?

Now that you're in the cycle of certainty, the increased spiritual help will allow you to avoid most of the challenges or trials you would normally experience in an imperfect world. I can make this promise because I've been there and done that. I don't have any idea about what the future will bring, but because I've been able to miss some in the past, I believe that I can miss more in the future as well. Here are a few examples of what I've been able to miss by listening to and obeying spiritual promptings.

First there was the time I lost my brakes in a loaded semi halfway down a steep canyon freeway. The Spirit told me what I should do to avoid an accident that would have cost me my life. Then there was the time I was trying to reach one hundred miles per hour on a snowmobile and was told to stop before I crashed into a ravine I couldn't see in front of me. There was also the time the Spirit reminded me to put on my safety glasses when I was trimming the lawn. And of course there was the time I *didn't* listen when it told me to wear my safety glasses, and now I'm blind in one eye. I've also been able to avoid multiple car accidents.

Then there was the time I was thinking about putting our life savings into the stock market. That experience was especially meaningful because I got to plainly hear both spiritual voices. One said, "You can make 18 percent in the stock market." The other quite forcefully said—you guessed it—"Don't do it." Remember my other stories about the exploding ball, the four-wheeler trip, and my reason for early retirement? All of these incidents helped me understand that I do have God on my side, and He is willing to help me avoid challenges if I'll listen and choose to follow His spiritual direction.

This is what the gift of agency is all about. You get to choose to believe and exercise faith that the Spirit is really there to help you. This help comes to you in the form of feelings and thoughts, and sometimes even voices. These influences help you live a happier, healthier, safer, and more prosperous life, and these blessings will make your life successful.

Everything you've just learned is in your contract with God. He promised if you're willing to obey the commandments, you will prosper in the land, because the Spirit will help you make good choices. These good choices create good consequences, which increase your faith. More faith increases the intensity, until it's like you're having conversations with the Spirit.

π

I'VE NOW IDENTIFIED and discussed the two main sources of your thoughts and feelings. Most come from God or from the evil team, but there's also one other source: you. You're the one who ultimately decides what you're going to think about. Let me show you how you can control what you think about.

When I was young, I thought the evil team could read my thoughts, which gave them an unfair advantage. Unfair because they could just keep feeding me one bad thought after another until they led me right into their trap. Lucky for us, the game wasn't designed to be played that way. I've been told the evil team can't read our thoughts. Who then controls your thoughts? It's you—sort of.

The evil team still has an uncanny ability to know what you're thinking even though they can't read your thoughts. I believe they know what you're thinking by reading your body language. Over time, they've discovered all humans act pretty much the same when they're thinking the same thoughts. All they have to do is take a look at how you're acting, and that tells them what you're thinking.

The evil team also loves to go fishing. When someone goes fishing, they take a pole, attach bait to a hook, and cast it or drop it into a place where they hope to catch a fish. They don't know if there are any fish there; they just hope one will be there willing to take the bait. This is exactly what the evil team does. They take a hook, attach a thought to it that appears to be good, and cast it into your mind to see if you're willing to take the bait. Has that ever happened to you? You're just sitting there, minding your own business, and all of a sudden, an undesirable thought came out of nowhere and dropped right into your head. It happens to me all the time.

Obviously, once the evil team has made their cast, the thought is in your mind whether you want it or not, so you have to do something with it. You could just leave it there and try not to take the bait. But the longer you think about it, the more the odds increase that you'll take it. So what do you do with this unwanted thought? You must learn to throw it back at them.

You know, that brings up an interesting thought: Could that be why fish don't have arms? Can you imagine casting your bait into the water, only to have a fish throw it back at you? Come to think of it, that wouldn't be such a bad idea. At least then you'd know if the fish are there even when you're not catching anything. Hey, two more mysteries of life solved! We now know why fish don't have arms and why they call it fishing, not catching. I'd better get back on topic.

The evil team casts a thought into your mind, and you have to go get it and throw it back at them. Can you see how that could be dangerous? You have to think about it before you can throw it back, and when you think about it, it's in your mind. If it's in your mind, you have to consider it, and what usually happens when you consider something that seems good—especially if you consider it for a long time? You end up doing it.

This sounds like another no-win situation, doesn't it? It doesn't have to be because you can close the pond to the evil team's fishing by always thinking good thoughts. This works because your mind can only think of one thing at a time.

Is it even possible to always have good thoughts? Honestly, it may not be 100 percent possible, but I believe its 99.5 percent possible. The evil team doesn't want you to think it's possible because they don't want you to close your mind to fishing. They know they can't catch you if they can't go fishing. Before I tell you how to close your mind, let me tell you how I came up with the 99.5 percent number.

If you go to bed at 11:00 p.m. and get up at 5:00 a.m., you're awake for 1,080 minutes. Now, 1,080 x 99.5 percent is about 1,074 minutes. Subtract the 1,074 from the 1,080, and that leaves just 6 minutes or 360 seconds, which is a long time. If you don't believe me, stop and watch one full minute pass on a clock. It seems like it takes forever.

Now apply this to a bad thought. It comes into your mind, you recognize it, grab it, and throw it back. How long did that take—maybe five seconds? Okay, let's say it took ten seconds because you're still learning how to throw it back at them quickly. That means you could have thirty-six bad thoughts in a single day and still be bad-thought-free for about 99.5 percent of the time.

Think about it. Even on a bad day, with all that's going on in your mind, how many times on average can a bad thought even make it through? If you're trying, couldn't you limit it to about twenty or less each day? I'm sure you could, but you don't have to have twenty, because it's possible to have just a few or no bad thoughts at all. Here's how you do it.

As I said earlier, the best way I've found to limit or even eliminate bad thoughts is to constantly think good thoughts. Your mind can only think of one thing at a time. If that one thing is good, then your thoughts will be good. How do you make your mind think only good thoughts? I've found the best way is to listen to good, spiritually uplifting music. When that's not possible, just memorize the melody and a few lines of good music, and play it over and over in your mind. If you'll give it a try, you can limit or even eliminate most, if not all, your bad thoughts.

After the bad thoughts are eliminated, the Spirit can move in and really start to help you make your choices. When that happens, you'll begin to notice a positive difference in the consequences of your choices—and you know where that leads. Noticing increases your confidence, confidence increases faith, faith increases the amount of help you can receive, and receiving lots of help turns your life into a successful life.

This spiritual help is the hidden treasure that's right there in front of you, waiting to be found. Can you even begin to imagine what you can accomplish in life with God's help? The sky really is the limit. If you want it, ask for it. Believe it's going to happen. And go to work and make it happen by choosing to obey the commandments and repenting quickly when you don't.

REVIEW OF IMPORTANT POINTS

- God, through His Spirit, always uses these same three words: *don't do it.*
- The evil team rarely uses those words. They instead try to entice you with other equally desirable thoughts.
- When you don't do it, the intensity or volume will increase.
- Every thought comes from one of three places: God, the evil team, or you.
- You must learn to sort out your thoughts. Keep the good ones; throw the others away.
- The evil team can't read your thoughts, but they can read your body language. They also love to fish.
- You can limit bad thoughts most the time by continually playing good, spiritually uplifting music in your mind.

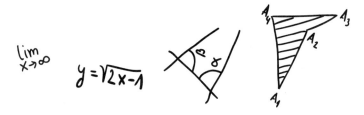

CHAPTER 14

CONTROLLING THE BEAST

OU'VE NOW LEARNED two of the three steps you'll need to create a successful life. First, you learned how things in this imperfect world actually work, and then you learned how you can control a lot of what you experience in life. Both of these steps are important, but step three—learning to control the beast, or your body—is by far the most important. Why? If you don't learn to control it, it will control you. You don't want your body controlling you, so let me show you how to control the beast while it can still be controlled.

If you're young, you may not yet know why I call your body a beast. If you're older, you know exactly why.

Have you noticed there are actually two of you? What are these two different parts? One is the spiritual part, and the other is the physical part. The spiritual part is the real you. You're a spirit son or daughter of God having a get-your-physical-body experience.

When I was young, I didn't understand that my spirit and my body were two separate parts, and that created all kinds of problems for me. I don't have the space or the time to mention every one, so I'll just share an example.

As I entered my teenage years, my body began to act like a stubborn, hard-to-control beast. Have you noticed that yet? If not, give it a little more time. I noticed it when I tried to make my body do physical things, like exercise, play sports, ride a bike, or just get off the couch. I also had a hard time keeping it from eating and drinking too much, and it never wanted to go to bed or get up early in the morning. I could go on and on, but I think you get the picture.

If you're having any of these same problems, you can breathe a sigh of relief, because you're normal. But being normal doesn't make it right. Learning to control your body is important because an out-of-control body is the root cause of most problems you'll face in life. It could be difficult if you don't get started right away. In fact, the longer you wait, the harder it will be. If you wait too long, it could become almost impossible.

Let's begin by identifying the ways your body helps your spirit learn new things. Your body has the ability to gather, process, and store information from everything you see, hear, touch, taste, and smell. These are your body's five basic senses. This information is then used to help you make choices. You also can use two of these senses, sight and hearing, to gather information from others' experiences as well. Learning from others' experiences is often better because it's easier, safer, and less painful.

While your body is gathering, processing, and storing all this information, it's also running a complex manufacturing and warehouse plant. In your plant, raw materials enter through one door and are converted into things that help your plant run efficiently. Your plant then uses what it needs, stores what it might need later, and sends what's left out another door as waste. All of this is being done without you even thinking about it, because up above the factory floor there's a small, powerful computer that continually monitors and controls everything that's going on below. This computer is your brain. What powers your brain? I believe it's your spirit, because when your spirit leaves, your brain and all other parts of your body stop working. This is why I believe there are two of you in you.

I'm sure you know you have a spirit and a body, but have you recognized what they've been doing since the day you were born? They've been locked in battle to see which one is going to control you. Your spirit, or the thinking part of you, is always trying to control the physical part of you, and the physical part of you is always trying to overpower the spirit. Which one is winning my battle? My body is winning most of my battles, but my spirit is winning the war. How can my spirit lose and still win? When I lose battles, it just means I've chosen to learn something the hard way, but that doesn't change the outcome of the war. The war will eventually be won as long as I don't get discouraged and give up. Why do I keep learning things the hard way? My body loves to ambush or surprise my spirit. See if this sounds familiar.

You're watching an old western movie. A good guy enters a town, and then a bad guy hiding in the buildings jumps out and takes him by surprise. This is exactly what my body does to my spirit. It just sits there and waits for an opportunity to ambush my spirit. I wish it wasn't true, but I haven't made it through every single ambush without committing a sin. I do understand that losing a few of these day-to-day battles is all part of the plan, but that doesn't mean God wants me to sin or that I can sin without any consequences. It just means God knew I'd lose a few battles here at the university, so He created the repentance process.

How does my body ambush my spirit? Again, see if this sounds familiar. You're just sitting there, and your body is acting like it doesn't really care about anything. So you relax and let your guard down. The second you do, your body surprises your spirit with all kinds of feelings that come in the form of wants, needs, emotions, drives, desires, and passions. You must decide whether you're going to give your body what it wants or tell it no.

You're human, so making the right choice every single time is impossible. But the good news is, you don't have to—if you will recognize your sin, feel bad, confess, try really hard to not sin anymore, and take the sacrament so you can be forgiven of your sins. If you're really trying to not sin, you can use the repentance process when you lose some battles and still win the war. Repentance is possible because every sin you could possibly commit has already been paid for by the Atonement of Jesus Christ.

This simple repentance process really will work if—and only if—you're really trying hard to not sin. Really trying hard means you're not looking for or creating opportunities to sin. You're instead just out there living life, trying to make good choices. If a choice creates a sin, you recognize it and try not to make the same mistake again, even if it was fun. Whether or not you receive forgiveness depends entirely upon your intention. If you didn't intend to sin or if you learned your lesson after you sinned, repentance works. If you try to sin or look for ways to commit sin, repentance doesn't work until after you change your intentions.

Did you notice that earlier I said your body surprises your spirit with all kinds of feelings? I said it that way because your spirit is the real you. Again, you are a spirit son or daughter of a loving Heavenly Father and Heavenly Mother. They created you and raised you until you were ready to receive your physical body here on earth. Then they gave you your body and a lifetime to learn how to control it. Knowing you started out as a spirit son or daughter of God is an important point. This life is just a continuation of your previous life. You're a boy or a girl now because you were a boy or a girl back then. I'll discuss this topic more in a later chapter.

Your body is able to surprise your spirit because it came with a long list of God-given standard equipment that creates all the wants, needs, emotions, desires, drives, and passions you experience. Some of these feelings are hardly noticeable, while others are incredibility strong, and any of them can change several times on any given day. For instance, you may have no desire to have a boyfriend or a girlfriend on Friday morning, but then you see someone later in the day that creates an incredibly strong desire to make that person part of your life. This type of experience, and hundreds more like it, are all part of the earthly learning-to-control-your-body experience.

So here you are, locked in a battle for control with a strong-willed body that acts like it has a mind of its own, with an endless list of God-given feelings as standard equipment. Can you see how this could create a big problem for a teenager? How many bodies have you had? This is your first one, and since you've never had a body before, how are you going to know how to control all these new feelings? My body didn't come with an owner's manual. Even if it did, I probably wouldn't read it because I'm a guy, and guys don't read owner's manuals.

Since you don't have an owner's manual, you have just two ways to learn about your body. You can use the trial-and-error method, which works great until you make an error. Or you can read my owner's manual, which I've written while growing old. Using my manual is better because you can learn from my experiences instead of experiencing everything yourself.

π

WHEN I BEGAN writing my owner's manual, I thought I could teach you everything you needed to know about your body in just a few chapters. But I was wrong. Your body is a complex machine, and it's constantly changing as you grow older. If I waited until all my growing older was done, my manual would never get finished because my life would be over. So I decided to help you understand just the basics. The basics should be enough to keep you out of trouble while you figure the rest out on your own. Let's begin with a personal story.

One of my goals in life was to own a new car or truck every few years. I remember looking forward to my annual visit to the local Ford dealership at the beginning of each new model year. I loved the new-car smell of the interior, the new designs, the different options, and the more powerful engines. I could continue telling you why I love new cars, but I'll sum it all up by simply saying, I just love new cars and trucks. I believe I inherited this love from my dad. I can't remember a time when my dad didn't drive a new car or truck.

This addiction to new cars lasted until I finally understood that new cars were not a good investment. I can't remember how many new cars and trucks I bought before I was forced into recovery for my addiction, but my best guess would be somewhere around twenty-five. I do remember the ones that I absolutely loved—the 1970 Ford Torino Cobra, which happened to be one of the fastest cars in the county, but don't ask me how I know that. I also owned a 1971 Boss 351 Mustang. I only got to drive it a couple of times because I had a hip-to-toe cast on my right leg from a football injury when it arrived from the factory. The cast made it impossible for me to drive it safely, so my dad gave it to my sister. There were others I'd love to mention, but I'd better explain what owning new cars and trucks has to do with controlling your body.

First, since driving a new car or truck was one of my main goals in life, I had to make my body get up and go to work so I could earn enough money to buy them. My love for new cars was greater than my love for my time in bed, so I used this greater love as motivation. It wasn't easy to make my body do something it didn't want to do, but I had to do it or I couldn't buy a car. If you're also having a hard time making your body do things, find something you love and use it to motivate you. A successful life will require you to do things you may not want to do.

The next lesson I learned from buying new cars was that nothing in life is free. Once I signed the sales contract, the price had to be paid. I also learned that every new car has a price posted on the window, but it's not the price you'll have to pay. To find the real price, you must add in the finance charges, the dealer fees, license fees, taxes, insurance, and whatever else they can think of before you can see what the car really costs.

The evil team understands this truth perfectly, so they'll never tell you how much you really have to pay, either. For instance, you might think that stealing a candy bar from a store is no big deal because it only costs a dollar, but it will cost you a lot more when you have to face your parents and the owner of the store and pay a penalty for shoplifting. All these added costs are attached to that stolen candy bar, but you won't see any of them until you get caught.

There's another, even greater cost attached to a stolen candy bar. This cost is the shame or guilt you'll feel every time you think about what you've done. These feelings won't ever go completely away until you fix the problem. But you won't want to fix the problem because you'll have to face your parents and the store's owner and pay the penalty for shoplifting. Can you see the cycle of uncertainty? This is not a road you want to travel.

The next lesson I learned from buying new cars is the one I really wanted to share with you, because this one is by far the most important. When you go to a dealership, you'll see on the window of every new car a long list of standard equipment that comes with the car from the factory. Your body also comes with a long list of standard equipment, but the list isn't posted on the outside where you can see it. You can see a few items from the list, but there's a lot more hidden inside. All of them are there for a reason, but you won't find the reason until you take your body on a long test drive. Not understanding the reason for my standard equipment created a lot of problems for me. Since I didn't know they were there, I had to use the trial-and-error method to find them. Trial and error is dangerous because the trials can be fun, but the errors can be life changing, or even life ending.

You won't have to use the trial-and-error method to find your standard equipment because you now have my owner's manual that explains what I've learned while test-driving my body for over sixty years. If you're willing to read it and use what's in it, you'll be able to avoid a lot of the problems you could face while test-driving your new body.

$$\pi$$

BEFORE WE START discussing your standard equipment, let me give you a warning. I believe some of the topics in these chapters should only be discussed with your parents, but because of my experiences with single young adults, I decided to put them in the book anyway. As I spent time counseling these beautiful young sons and daughters of God, I recognized that many of their parents made the same mistake I'd made—they didn't teach their kids about their bodies. Instead, they had taken the easy way out by letting the schools and their kids' teenage friends do it for them.

Letting the schools teach you about your body is a mistake, because schools can't talk about God. If God can't be part of the discussion, you'll never be able to really understand why you have a body. If you don't understand, you'll use it wrong, and then it will become an uncontrollable beast that will eventually destroy you.

Your teenage friends also can't teach you about your body for at least two reasons. First, they haven't test-driven their bodies long enough to know what they're talking about and it's unlikely their parents have taught them. Who then taught them about their bodies? The world—and that's a problem because the world wants nothing to do with God, or they've remade God into someone He isn't.

The second reason friends can't teach you is that they're also teens. During your teen years, your body will fully develop, but you won't yet have enough experience to gain common sense. Fully developed bodies with new and exciting feelings but no experience and no common sense is the perfect recipe for a life-changing, or life-ending, event. If you don't believe me, watch the evening news.

Recognizing these truths has forced me to step out of my comfort zone and teach you about your body. I'm going to be blunt, but I'll try to explain it in a way that doesn't offend you, your parents, or the Spirit.

Let's start by discussing two of the most powerful, most used, and most misunderstood items on your body's standard equipment list. These features are your physical and emotional feelings. Physical feelings are those your physical body feels. Emotional feelings are those you mentally feel. Both make you feel either good or bad, but they're different as night and day. Let's take a look at physical feelings first.

Your physical body only wants to feel good, so the evil team is only going to offer you things that make it feel good. Do they offer you them because they like you and want you to be happy? I promise they have their reasons, but none of them have anything to do with your happiness. Even though their offerings make you feel good for a short time, that's not why they want you to have them. They know that once your body has felt good feelings, it's going to want to feel them again and again. This constant desire to feel good is what makes your body hard to control.

Look at the world you live in. What does the evil team offer that makes your body feel good? You could make a list, but you don't have to, because they'll use anything—if it can destroy you. Take food, for instance. Food is good, but it can also destroy you if you overeat or eat too much of the wrong food. What eventually happens to a body that overeats? It becomes overweight, and that increases the probability of many different diseases. I know it sounds harsh, but you must never forget that the evil team wants to destroy you as quickly and miserably as possible—quickly, so you can't score as many points, and miserably, because they don't like you.

You must be honest with yourself. The products and actions the evil team offers really do make you feel good for a short period of time, or no one would consider them. These good feelings may last for a few seconds, minutes, or hours, but when that feel-good time is over, those good feelings are always replaced with bad feelings. How bad? That depends entirely upon what you took or what you did to feel good. If you're lucky, the misery may only last a short time. If you're not, it could change or even end your life.

Here's an example. After I purchased a brand-new car, how do you think I felt when I drove it off the dealer's lot? I felt good. But did my happy, good feelings last forever? No. I always eventually lost those good feelings when I made the car payments. What did I do so I could feel good again? I bought another car so I could experience the good feelings of driving a new car off the lot again.

So what changed in my life that stopped me from buying new cars? Two things: my level of debt and my relationship with my wife. If you buy a new car before you finish paying off the old car, the dealer adds what you still owe to the cost of the new car. So by the time you buy two or three new cars, you owe more than the new car is worth. This affected my relationship with my wife because she doesn't like being in debt—especially for unneeded new cars. Ever heard the saying, "When Mom's not happy, nobody's happy"? I learned this saying really is true.

So if no one was happy, why did I keep buying new cars? I wanted to feel good again. This desire created my addiction to new cars. An addiction is an unbelievably intense desire to feel good physically or emotionally again and again. I'm not sure if my addiction to new cars was physical or emotional, but the type I had really didn't matter. The only thing that mattered was that I had an addiction, and I needed to get rid of it.

The evil team understands that your body's desire to feel good is powerful. They also know that once your body has experienced good feelings, it will be difficult at first and next to impossible later for you to tell your body it can't feel them anymore. Once you become addicted, your body will crave those feelings all the time. To stop the craving, you give your body what it wants. But it will always want more, and it will be hard to say no.

The only real way to break an addiction is for you to go through a miserable experience called withdrawal while you try to regain control of your body. How bad do you feel during withdrawal? In my case, it wasn't too bad since I only had to deal with the feelings when I saw a new car or truck. But I've watched withdrawal almost destroy other people. How bad your withdrawal is and how long it lasts depends entirely upon your addiction. For some, it's just a bad experience for a few days. For others, it's so bad they can't do it, and that makes the addiction stronger than it was before.

You can't underestimate your body's desire to feel good. This is the only thing it cares about. If you let your body have whatever it wants whenever it wants it, it will be hard at first and next to impossible later to tell it that it can't have it. This is why your spirit must win the battle for control with your body. I'm not exaggerating when I say that your future happiness depends entirely on which you—you the spirit or you the body—wins this battle.

$$\pi$$

NOW THAT YOU understand that your body only cares about whatever makes it feel good, you should be able to answer this question: Why did Satan want Adam and Eve to eat the fruit in the Garden of Eden? What was he thinking? If they hadn't eaten it, they couldn't have a physical body. No physical body means they'd have no children, and if they had no children, God's plan would have been destroyed right at the beginning. So why did Satan want Adam and Eve to eat the fruit?

Want a hint?

What is evil really all about? Evil is about control. Satan wanted them to eat the fruit because that's the only way they could receive a hard-to-control physical body.

Do you remember the war in heaven between God and Satan? What did Satan want to do? He wanted to take away your agency so he could make you do things. From the beginning, Satan tried to gain control over God's children. He didn't win the war in heaven, so now he's trying to control you by making your physical body feel good.

That last paragraph might make you think you can avoid all life's problems by simply not allowing your body to feel good, but it's not quite that simple. For instance, right now I'm eating a good-sized jar of mixed nuts. As of today (who knows what they'll say tomorrow), many experts agree that nuts are good for you. So is the evil team trying to help me do something good for me? No, because they're telling me to eat the whole jar. I need to go put them away in the pantry.

The nuts are now in the pantry, and I'm happy to report that I ate just two more handfuls before I put them away. Yes, my body loves nuts—and chocolate, buttered popcorn, and just about everything else. When I give my body something it likes, it creates physical cravings that cause me to want more. If I give in, it will continue to want more until it eventually destroys itself and me with it.

Does this help you see why the battle between the spirit and the body must be won by the spirit? It's going to be a battle, so make sure you never underestimate the power of your body. A body's desire for things it likes is strong, and that's why you sometimes see otherwise normal people doing unbelievable things after they've become addicted. When the body is in control, it can't be controlled, and the end of that road, after years of unhappiness and misery, is almost always death and destruction.

Now you must ask yourself this important question: Is a few seconds, minutes, or even hours of feeling physically good really worth it? The answer is clearly no, especially after you suffer years of misery battling an addiction.

Can we take a short break? I think it would be a good idea because my beast needs a short rest. When it thinks it needs a rest, I better listen!

REVIEW OF IMPORTANT POINTS

- There are two of you, body and spirit. You are a spirit son or daughter of God who came to earth to get a body.
- Your body will be hard to control if you don't learn to control it while you're young. You must learn to control it; never let it control you.
- An out-of-control body creates most problems you'll experience in life.
- Your spirit and body are locked in a battle for control.
- Your body loves to ambush your spirit using a long list of standard equipment.
- Two most used but most misunderstood items on your standard-equipment list are physical feelings and emotional feelings.

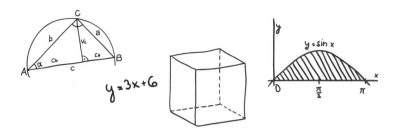

CHAPTER 15

THE BEAST HAS FEELINGS

'M BACK AND all rested up. Let's pick up right where we left off.

In addition to physical feeling, the other type of feeling on your body's list of standard equipment is emotional feeling. Physical and emotional feelings both make you feel good—or bad—but they are as different as night and day. Physical feelings come from your physical body. Emotional feelings come from your mind, but they can also affect your physical health if they aren't dealt with.

Your mind controls the way you think, the way you act, and your emotional well-being. It also controls the way you feel about yourself and your relationships with others. Physical and emotional feelings are both powerful, but I believe emotional feelings are more destructive if they're not handled correctly.

When I worked with young single adults, I got to see first-hand the destructive power of two bad emotional feelings: depression and discouragement.

The world our young singles are growing up in is much more difficult than the one I grew up in, even with all the technology we enjoy today. Having lived back then and now, I can plainly see how technology has made it much more difficult today. For instance, let's take a look at what you'll have to go through just to get a job.

When I graduated from high school, I simply went out and got a job. If I didn't like that job, I could quit and find another one fairly quickly. All I had to do was walk into an office and fill out an application. Odds were pretty good I'd get hired if they were looking for help. In today's job market, you must go to college or trade school and graduate with a degree before you'll even be considered for any decent job. It doesn't necessarily matter what degree you have, just that you have one, because it shows employers you can stay with a project until it's completed. My experience has shown you'll rarely get an interview unless you have a degree.

The next step in the hiring process requires you to prepare a resume that introduces you to your future employer. It details your work history, qualifications, and hobbies and explains why you want to work for that company. Resumes are extremely important, and they take time and effort to produce. Several years ago, when I managed my lighting company, I didn't ask for resumes. I just set aside a couple hours and invited four or five applicants in for a one-on-one fifteen- or twenty-minute interview. That rarely happens today, because it's common for many people to apply for the same job. Instead, employers request that potential employees send in a resume electronically. It can take weeks to sort through the resumes to find the applicants who look most qualified on paper. During this period of time, it's easy to become depressed or discouraged because you don't even know if you're being considered.

At some future point, after the employer has looked at all the resumes, a few applicants will be selected for a phone interview. The ones who look good will get a call, and the ones who don't may not even get notified. During the phone interview, they'll ask you a few questions to see if you sound qualified. If they like the sound of your voice, they'll schedule you for a one-on-one interview.

I could continue, but I think I've made my point. All the things you have to do to find a job today can create more discouragement and depression than simply walking into an office, filling out an application, doing an interview, and getting hired. But finding a job is just a small part of what you have to deal with. You also have to finish school, date, deal with parents' expectations, find a way to support yourself until you get a job, have some fun, do your church callings, and the list goes on. All these demands will create opportunities for you to experience discouragement and depression. And all of these bad emotional feelings must be dealt with correctly, or you're probably going to have some serious emotional problems.

There is one other big reason people experience discouragement and depression in today's world. These bad feelings are created because people are obsessed with the way they look. In this age of computer imaging and photo touch-up, the evil team has been able to create the deception that you must look beautiful or you can never be happy. This would be a great time to ask *why* the evil team wants everyone to try to look beautiful. It's because most of us can't, and because we can't, most of us become depressed and discouraged.

When I worked with young single adults, I spent most of my time helping them deal with problems created by depression and discouragement. Their bad feelings ranged from mild to extreme, and most were caused by low self-esteem or trying to do too much at once. These negative emotions often caused them to do things that made no sense whatsoever. I could list what they did, but that's not as important as the consequences they experienced afterward. Those consequences always led to more problems and more misery, and this created an endless number of opportunities for more discouragement and depression.

Have you ever felt discouraged or depressed? If so, you probably felt physical discomfort. What do most people do when they feel physical discomfort? They take medicine to relieve the pain. Today's medicines are great at relieving pain, but wouldn't it be better to eliminate the cause of the pain? Doing so would also eliminate any future pain.

Here's how you eliminate the discouragement and most of the depression you'll feel in life. Again, I have to say "most," because some forms of depression are caused by chemical imbalances in the body. If you suffer from this type of depression, you should get professional help. The type of depression I'm referring to is the type caused by trying to do too much and the desire to look beautiful. I found these two types are the most common.

To eliminate discouragement and depression, you must first identify what's causing it. Let's look at what causes low self-esteem. Why would you suffer from low self-esteem? It's because most everyone you see on TV, in the movies, in magazines, and on every street corner appears to be more talented and more beautiful, and they all have near-perfect lives. Constantly seeing these people allows the evil team to fill your head with thoughts that you must be like them or you can never be happy. Of course this isn't true, but that's hard to believe when you're the one who isn't talented or beautiful and your life is far from perfect. So why are you, *you*?

When I was a teen, I remember wondering why I looked, acted, and felt the way I did. Eventually, after some challenging experiences, I realized that I'm no different from my Shelby Mustang dream car. Why is my Shelby a Shelby? It's a Shelby because the Shelby Car Company created it. Who created you by putting all of the things into you that made you, *you*? It was your parents and your ancestors. When they created you, they gave you your eye and hair color, your character traits, and your physical size and shape.

For example, I have a son who weighed ten pounds, ten ounces when he was born, and he was taller than most of the other babies in the hospital. My wife and I couldn't decide whether to be happy or sad, because all the people who visited the hospital kept pointing at him and saying, "Wow, look how big that one is." Why was he so big? He's big because I'm big, and he's taller because I'm also taller. His hair and eye color are also like mine because he received more from me than he did from my wife. When my second son was born, he was built more like my wife's side of the family. He wasn't quite as big or tall as his brother, and his hair and eye color were different from mine.

These two examples should help you understand that everything that makes you came from your parents and your ancestors, going back in some cases many generations.

Did your parents and your ancestors influence only the way you look? No, they also influenced the way you think, the way you feel, and even the way you act. Could your strengths and even your weaknesses have come from them? Of course they could, but don't try to use that as an excuse if you decide to mess up your life. In today's world, few people are willing to take responsibility for their own actions, saying it's always someone else's fault. It's true that your ancestors made you, but what you decide to do is completely up to you.

The way you were raised also had a big effect on you. While you were growing up, your parents and those around you either knowingly or unknowingly helped you become you. For instance, when I was young, I had a temper and thought nothing of it because my dad, my brothers, and a couple of my sisters had one as well. We were all quite often passionate about things we cared about. In fact, we were so passionate that we often spoke quite forcefully about the things we cared about. How's that for rationalization? It was pretty good, wasn't it?

Because I had grown up with my temper, using it seemed like a normal and natural way for me to express my feelings—until one day when I was watching my son play high school basketball. My wife and I had traveled to a distant high school to watch the game. After it began, I noticed the referees weren't calling the game fairly—again—so I began to yell, like I did at all my son's games. I guess my son had finally had enough, because he stopped right in the middle of the game, looked at me, and said, "Dad, sit down and shut up." I'm now grateful for my son's courage, but at the time I wanted to die. Every single person in the gym turned around and looked at me. I was so embarrassed.

That was the day I was finally willing to admit that not being in control of my passionate feelings was a problem. Something inside me had always told me it wasn't right, but since I'd been that way my whole life, I didn't think much about it. Besides, I wasn't the only one yelling at the referees, the coaches, the time-keeper, or the other team's fans. That was also a great rationalization. I think I'll send it to the Rationalization Hall of Fame.

Where did my temper come from? Was I born with it, or did I learn it? I believe it could have been either or both, but how I got it really doesn't matter. All that mattered was that I needed to change. It took a while, and at times I have to control the passion building inside me, but I'm happy to report I am now better able to control it. That keeps me from making a fool of myself—most of the time.

Understanding why you are you is the first step toward learning to love who you are, while you work on changing what needs to be changed. Can you love who you are when you know you need to change? Yes, you can. While it's normal to feel embarrassed or discouraged when you see character traits that need to be changed, you must remember you can't do anything about your ancestors or the way you were raised. Changing can be hard, but you can do it if you're willing to try. I know this because I've had to do a lot of changing.

Recognizing why you are you is also important because it stops the evil team from filling your head with negative thoughts about yourself. If I didn't recognize that my temper might have come from my ancestors, it would be easy for me to think I'm a bad person because I have a temper. I'm not a bad person. I'm a good person with a bad character trait that needs to be changed because bad traits lead to bad actions, and continued bad actions will eventually turn me into a bad person.

Because none of us are perfect, we all have bad character traits that need to be changed. While you're working on the needed changes, don't let the evil team discourage or depress you. Feeling good about yourself will help create positive self-esteem, and that will help you deal with negative thoughts from the evil team and thoughtless friends. Having the right amount of self-esteem may not be easy, but it can be done if you'll take the time to understand why you are you, while you work on who you'd like to become.

God never intended for you to just accept who you are. The Book of Mormon teaches this principle clearly in 2 Nephi 28:24: "Therefore, wo be unto him that is at ease in Zion!" *At ease* means you're content or complacent. It's okay to be at peace, but not content or complacent. Those who become content won't want to improve, and one of the main purposes of life is to give you time to improve. Positive self-esteem will allow you to be at peace while you work on self-improvement.

The way you were raised can also have an effect on your physical health. Here's an example. My wife and I absolutely love chocolate. So we can't have chocolate in the house or we'll probably eat it. A little chocolate now and then isn't a bad thing, but too much of it definitely is, so we keep it out of the house.

Where did our love of chocolate come from? It came from the way we were raised. Our parents loved chocolate, so we had lots of opportunities to enjoy chocolate. It really doesn't matter how we got our love for chocolate; we just needed to recognize we should limit the amount we keep in the house. I realize this makes us look weak, but it is what it is. Would the evil team use chocolate against you? Of course. They'll use whatever makes you feel good because they know when you experience good feelings your body is going to want more of them.

You're probably saying, "Okay, you and your wife love chocolate, but what's the point?" My point is, does our love for chocolate make us bad people? I'm sure you think that's a silly question, and I hope you answered no, but don't stop there. Think about how that same answer applies to every character trait, desire, and weakness you may have received from your ancestors. Every single feeling that makes you *you* came from them, and none of it makes you a bad person. What you do with your character traits through your actions will determine whether you're a good or bad person.

In this day and age, I often hear people say they are who they are because God made them that way, but that's not true. It is true that God placed their spirit into their body, but their parents and ancestors created their body. All bodies have the same standard equipment, but each person's emotions are different because they came from different parents and ancestors. Does that mean you can't do anything about it? No. If you choose to separate who you are from God's will, you'll see that anything is possible. You simply go to God with perfect faith and confidence and ask Him to help you become what you want to become. Will it be easy? In some cases, yes; in others, no. But in all cases, God will be there to help you if you want it, ask for it, believe it will happen, and go to work and make it happen.

I hope you will choose to believe that changing really is possible. You can become whatever you want to become. Just accept who you are while you work on changing what needs to be changed. But you need to be careful. Your body is a strong-willed, complex machine that runs on physical and emotional feelings. Once it decides it likes something, it will make your life pretty miserable until it either gets it or becomes convinced you're not going to give in. You can win the war between the spirit and the body, but it won't be easy. If it were, everybody would be doing it.

Winning the war between the spirit and the body is in God's plan for you. He called His plan the plan of salvation; *salvation* means success, not failure, and that's why I know you can win this war.

REVIEW OF IMPORTANT POINTS

- You are you because of your ancestors and the way you were raised.
- You aren't bad just because you have character traits that need to be changed.
- You can change if you want it, ask for it, believe it, and go to work and make it happen.
- You can be at peace with who you are while trying to improve.
- You can lose battles and still win the war. God's plan is called the plan of salvation, not the plan of failure.

$$A = \begin{pmatrix} 2 & -1 \\ -3 & -2 \end{pmatrix} \qquad y = \sqrt{2x-1}$$

δ

CHAPTER 16

TAKING CARE OF THE BEAST

HAVE YOU NOTICED how the evil team encourages you to try to look like the near-perfect people you see in the movies, on TV, or in magazines? Why do they do it? It's because most of us can't.

The evil team uses these perfect-looking people to create a standard of personal perfection that's almost impossible for you to reach. This standard requires you to be a certain height and weight, and it requires your eyes to be the right color and your hair to be styled a certain way. You also must wear a certain brand of clothes, drive the right car, live in the right house, have the right hobbies, get the right job, and live single for the rest of your life, because your career is the most important thing in life. This is the world's standard of personal perfection you must meet or you can never be happy.

The evil team just said, "We never said you can't be happy." I hate to admit it, but this time they may be right. They may not say it, but let me show you how they make you think it.

They make you think you can't be happy by making sure you notice all the perfect people when they're having fun in some exotic place. Then they send a thought that says you'll never be able to live that lifestyle because you're not as beautiful or talented.

These thoughts make you feel envious and jealous. Are you happy when you feel envious or jealous? No.

If you think my example is too simple, listen to what goes on in your head the next time you see someone more beautiful or more talented. If you'll listen to your thoughts, you'll see how the evil team makes you unhappy without you even realizing it.

If you're not convinced, look at this real-life example. When I worked with young single adults, a colleague and I taught some classes on dating. In one of the classes, we asked those attending to write down their thoughts and feelings about dating. We gave them a few minutes and then gathered up their papers. When we read their answers to the class, it was obvious many of the students were not happy because every comment was negative, and some were even mean.

For instance, a young lady said, "I'm going to dye my hair blonde, change my eyes to blue, lose thirty pounds, become six inches shorter, lower my standards, and flirt more, and then I'll be able to date more." Another came from a young man who wrote, "Why do all the girls want to date just the bad boys?"

I asked, "What does 'bad' mean?"

The kids described a bad boy as one with no standards, sloppily but fashionably dressed, with long, shaggy hair and a full week or more of facial hair. They had taken in the world's standard of perfection and that made them feel unhappy. As I looked at the class, I thought, "If all of you could see yourselves through my old eyes, you'd be able to see how beautiful you really are."

Beauty may allow you to have fun, but fun always ends. Physical beauty won't last forever. You'll eventually get old, and age will rob you of the beauty of youth. If beauty is all you're living for, the happy feelings that come from being beautiful will turn into feelings of envy and jealousy, and these feelings can't lead to happiness. I know this is true because I'm old.

Will seeing yourself as a beautiful son or daughter of God be easy? If it were, everybody would be doing it. Not fitting within the world's standard of perfection will naturally cause you to feel some frustration, but that's normal. I'm confident you can deal with it, because most older people already have. Just remember, your teen years won't last forever. Be patient and accept who you are while you work on improving. Have fun and obey the commandments, and you'll enjoy your once-in-a-lifetime teen experience. After you've made it through your teen years successfully, you'll be able to see that most of what the world values really doesn't matter.

Are you wondering what getting through your teen years "successfully" means? It means you'll be able to make it through without experiencing any big problems, or you'll be able to deal with the problems you experience in a way that doesn't destroy you. The sad truth is, only a small percentage of today's youth make it through this critical time of life successfully.

If you want to successfully make it through your teen years, you must recognize what's going to eventually happen to your body. This is important, because the habits you form now will determine what's going to happen later. I'll use what happened to me as an example of what could happen if you're not careful.

When I was born, I was taller and weighed more than most other babies. During my school years, my height and weight stayed pretty much in proportion, but it changed when I got married because my lifestyle changed. I didn't get any taller, but I did get bigger. I went from 6'3" and 190 pounds to 6'3" and 260 pounds in just thirty short years. I didn't pay much attention to this change until I visited the doctor. He got my attention when he told me my added weight and my family health history (ancestors) were steering me toward a possible heart attack at a young age. He said if I'd start exercising and lose some weight, I could decrease the risk or even avoid a heart attack altogether.

Being in shape doesn't guarantee you won't have a heart attack or catch a life-threatening disease, but it does improve your chances, because the law of probability and outcome also applies to health. If you'll try to stay in shape, you'll increase the probability of better health now and enjoy better health later.

If I had taken better care of myself when I was young, I wouldn't be heading toward a heart attack now. So why didn't I do it? I was blessed with good health when I was young, so I didn't think much about it. I ate what I wanted and rarely exercised, and now I have to live with the consequences of that lifestyle.

When you grow older, your overall health normally declines, but that doesn't mean you just have to accept it. You can slow your body's decline if you're willing to stay in shape, and that will help you be able to better enjoy your later years. One of the consequences of my earlier lifestyle is that now I can't do everything I want to do. But I'm not complaining, because it could always be worse.

One of the best ways to take care of your body is to limit the amount of junk food you eat. When I was young, my body loved junk food, so I fed it what it loved nearly every day. I was probably one of the burger joints' and convenience stores' best customers. Now that I'm older, I can see what that lifestyle has done to me every time I look in the mirror. But that's not all junk food did to me. Recently I had a body scan and discovered some of that junk food was still inside me. So here I am, about sixty-two years old and overweight, my arteries are filling up with plaque, and I have several kidney stones in each of my kidneys. How could this have happened? Let's take a look and see.

In addition to the junk food, I've gained a few extra pounds because I have a bad habit of eating too much at every meal. When I was young, my mom told me there were kids in the world who would starve if I didn't eat everything on my plate, so I thought I would help them out by eating two full plates every chance I got. My body also loves big chocolate donuts, chocolate muffins, and soda, so I made sure it got what it loved way too often.

After I married, my daily exercise routine was trying to stay awake while I drove a semi-truck. I did this by filling up on donuts, muffins, soda, and anything else I could stuff in my mouth. This lifestyle has made me what I've become, but that wasn't the only thing it did to me.

Remember the kidney stones? A kidney stone is a tiny piece of hard, stone-like material with jagged edges that hangs out in your kidneys until it decides to leave your body. When it starts moving, those jagged edges scratch and tear at everything they come in contact with. Some say the pain is worse than having a baby. Being a guy, I wouldn't know anything about that. When the first one passed—*passed* means that it came out of my body—the doctors analyzed it to see what it was made of. Imagine my surprise when they told me it was made up of soda.

Life is not fair. Others drink soda by the gallon and nothing happens. I drink it and get kidney stones.

I could continue, but I'll just give you the bottom line. Don't kid yourself like I did. How you take care of yourself when you're young will eventually determine the number of physical problems you'll enjoy later. If you're eating too much and not exercising, your body is going to become difficult to live with later. In some cases, difficult things build character, but in this case, it merely ruins lives. Start preparing for a better future by taking care of your body right now.

π

JUST FOR FUN, answer this question: Which would you rather have—lots of money or good health? The answer should be obvious, but while you're young and enjoying good health, what do you spend all your time trying to get? Money. If you spend all your time making money, you won't have time to take care of yourself, and that increases the odds that you won't enjoy good health later in life. If your health isn't good later in life, you'll spend the time you have left and all the money you made at the doctor's office, trying to regain the health you lost while you were making money. Sounds like another no-win situation, doesn't it? It doesn't have to be.

You can increase the odds of good health later by doing a few simple things when you're young. If you'll choose to eat right, exercise at least three times a week, avoid stress, and be careful, your later life will be better. The type of exercise you choose really doesn't matter. It just needs to make your heart beat faster than normal for about thirty minutes. You should also do some weight lifting three times a week, because it will help keep your muscles strong. Strong muscles keep your bones in line, and that relieves stress on your joints. Exercising is good for your body, but make sure you don't overdo it. The reason you're exercising is to keep your body in shape, not wear it out. Some exercise is good, but too much can be bad if it wears out your joints.

Did you notice I also said you need to be careful? Trying to be careful will help you avoid a lot of potential bad experiences in life. You won't be able to avoid all of them, because cuts, scrapes, scratches, and broken bones are part of the mortal experience. Being careful helps you avoid bad experiences because of the law of probability and outcome. If you're careful, you won't do as many things that could get you hurt. Doing fewer things that could hurt you decreases the odds that you'll get hurt.

Thinking this law doesn't exist or apply to you is why a lot of young people get hurt or even killed. People of all ages will do things that are dangerous or just plain stupid for the adrenaline rush. When nothing happens, they keep doing them until they experience a life-changing or life-ending event. After the event happens, if they're lucky enough to still be alive, they might wish they weren't, because they'll spend the rest of their lives physically impaired. The excitement you get from the rush of adrenaline really is fun, and there is nothing wrong with feeling it, but please be careful. Stop and think before you act. Always weigh the probability of a bad outcome against the potential good feeling before you make your choice.

In this imperfect world, life-changing and life-ending accidents do happen, but you can decrease the odds of them happening to you if you'll just be careful. My best advice is don't do stupid or dangerous things. Once an accident happens, what's done is done, and you'll have to live with the consequences whether you like them or not. Being careful really decreases the odds of having a bad experience, and it's easier than you might think.

Here's an example that shows you how you can increase the odds of a good experience. Let's say you want to cross a busy street. What are the odds of crossing safely if you try to cross without first looking both ways? I'll bet you'd be lucky to even make it across one time. What would happen to the odds if you looked just one way before you crossed? What would happen if you looked both ways? Looking one way or both ways would increase the odds of crossing safely, but because you're relying on your own judgment, you could still have a problem. What if you went to an intersection with crosswalks and traffic lights, waited for the light to turn, and then looked both ways before you crossed? What would that do to the odds? The odds would greatly increase, but there would still be a small amount of risk. What would happen to the odds if you used a pedestrian overpass?

Speaking of crossing roads, I'd like to share an experience that recently happened. I was driving in the middle lane of a three-lane road. Just as I came to a red light, it turned green. As I started to go, I noticed a kid on a bike who rode up to the crosswalk and kept going. The car on my right was stopped, and I was able to stop. But the car on my left couldn't see the kid, so they started to accelerate. I was sick because I knew the car was going to hit him unless I did something.

I would have stuck my arm out the window, but it was rolled up, so I did the only thing I could do: I honked the horn. My horn startled the kid. He swerved out of the crosswalk and into the intersection, and that gave the driver time to stop.

Guys, please be careful. You live in a tough, unforgiving world. That kid was lucky. I hope he'll be more careful next time.

Being careful while you use the law of probability and outcome is how you avoid experiencing almost all the possible bad events in life. I said "almost" because in this imperfect world, *almost all* is about the best you can hope for. But it's also all you really need. When you're playing the odds, *almost all* is pretty much a sure thing. Here's why.

The average person may fly in an airplane a few times a year, but airplanes are flying tens of thousands of times each day all around the world. Once or maybe twice a year, one goes down, and it makes the evening news. Seeing the crash might make you to think flying isn't safe, until you actually consider the odds of it happening to you. You fly a few times a year, but planes fly hundreds of thousands times a year. What are the odds that you'll be on one plane that happens to go down once or twice a year? The odds are low. Conversely, the odds are really good—in fact, you could say it's almost a sure thing—that you'll be able to fly to your destination safely on any given day. *Almost all* is all you really need when you're playing the odds.

Once in a while, things will happen that are totally out of your control, but many of those can be avoided if you stay away from dangerous activities, keep the commandments, and learn to repent quickly when you don't. Avoiding dangerous things lessens or eliminates the probability of experiencing a life-changing or life-ending event. Obeying the commandments and repenting allows God's Spirit to be there to warn you before you experience an event that would normally be out of your control.

But here's another warning. You can't start thinking that because you're trying to obey the commandments you don't need to be careful. Obeying will give you spiritual guidance and warnings that help you make good choices. These good choices do increase the odds of good consequences, but you still need to be careful.

Everything in life requires you to make choices, and all of these choices either increase or decrease the odds of good or bad things happening. If you want to increase the odds that you'll be healthy later in life, eat good foods and do some exercise. If you want to increase the odds that you'll be able to avoid life-changing or life-ending experiences, then carefully consider all the possible consequences before making your choice.

I hope you now better understand why being healthy is important. Your body is an amazing machine, but it needs to be taken care of. If you don't take care of it, it will eventually break down. Unlike other machines here on earth, you can't throw your body away and get a new one. Problems create unhappiness or even misery, and experiencing these feelings will not allow you to enjoy life. If you want to enjoy life—especially your later life—take good care of your body now while you're young.

REVIEW OF IMPORTANT POINTS

- The world created a standard of perfection that is impossible to meet.

- Beauty can create temporary fun, but not happiness.
- Habits developed now will determine your future later.
- By eating right, exercising, and being careful, you can increase the odds of a better life later because of the law of probability and outcome.

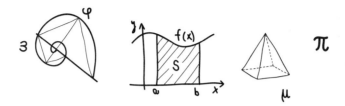

CHAPTER 17

TAKING CARE OF YOUR MIND

I F YOU'RE GOING to make it through you teen years success-fully, you must also learn to take care of your mind. I briefly touched on this subject when we discussed emotional feelings, but I need to dig a little deeper so I can help you keep your mind from messing up your life.

See if you can answer this question: What do most of us absolutely hate but spend much of our time trying to get?

The answer is stress.

What? Don't believe me? Think about it. What causes you to experience stress? My stress comes from living life with everyone else, because they rarely act how I think they should act. Did you notice that I said "I think"? Regardless of what anyone else does, *I'm* the one who decides how I'm going to feel about it. No one can make me feel anything unless I let them, because I control how I feel about everything. So who really creates my stress? I do.

You can experience stress for many different reasons, but I believe most, or even all, of those reasons could be avoided or eliminated. How? Just living in today's world gives you plenty of opportunities to experience stress, but I believe it's the choices you make that create most of the stress you feel. If choices create stress, you should be able to avoid some or eliminate most of it by making better choices. Better choices bring better consequences, and those better consequences can help you avoid or completely eliminate your stress. Still not convinced? Let's identify the different types of stress you could experience, and then you can see if better choices could help you avoid it or eliminate it.

What is stress? Stress is pressure you feel physically, mentally, or emotionally. For example, if your body is feeling weak or burdened, that's called physical stress. If you're feeling mentally burdened or tired, that's mental stress. If you feel depressed or discouraged, that's emotional stress. Any of the different types of stress make it almost impossible to enjoy life, and they can also affect your health.

Since all types of mental, physical, and emotional stress make you feel bad, where are these feelings coming from? They're coming directly or indirectly from the evil team. While you're living life and making choices, the evil team sends you thoughts and feelings that influence you to make bad choices, and it's those bad choices that create the stress you feel.

Let's look at each of the different types of stress so I can show you how to beat the evil team at their own game.

Physical stress is caused by what you do or don't do physically. That may sound like another no-win situation, unless you understand that doing things like exercise and work creates muscle, which is a good type of physical stress, and not doing anything creates a bad type of physical stress. I've already discussed the benefits of regular exercise, but talking about it is easy; making your body actually do it is hard. In fact, just trying to make your body exercise could cause you to experience some physical and mental stress.

When the doctor told me to start exercising, I decided to start riding a bike, even though I didn't enjoy it until after my ride was over. During my ride, my body constantly complained, especially when it saw a hill in front of me. But after the ride was over, even though my muscles ached and I was tired and sweaty, I found that I felt better the rest of the day.

Feeling better for the entire day certainly had an effect on the amount of stress I felt. I can honestly say that if I go on a good bike ride, I rarely feel any stress for the rest of the day. But knowing I won't feel stress is not enough motivation to make me want to ride my bike.

Here's what I have to do every day to make sure I don't miss my ride. First, I have to make my body get out of bed early in the morning, around 5:00 a.m. If I don't get up early, the odds of going on a ride decrease dramatically. I usually spend an hour or two working on my book. I love writing, so it's never easy to make myself quit and go on my ride, but I still have to do it. My ride usually lasts about an hour, and it's always an hour that I could, or maybe even should, be doing other things. I have to choose to ride instead of doing those other things that might need to be done. I also have to make my body complete the ride even when the ride is hard. My body is lazy, and it doesn't like to do anything hard. I have to fight and win the spirit-versus-body battle every day or I'd never ride my bike.

Having to do all this just to go on a bike ride could make you wonder if it's worth it. It is, because riding really does make me feel better, and feeling better helps me avoid or even completely eliminate the stress I normally feel during the day.

But feeling better isn't the only benefit I get from riding my bike. It's been about three years since I started exercising, and I just received some pretty good news at my last physical exam. About a week ago, I reluctantly took another test that would give me an update on my heart condition, and much to my surprise, the results were impressive. I was told my heart was now acting like the heart of a forty-year-old man.

Even though I don't put a lot of stock in tests, those results made me feel a lot better than the test I had three years ago. If the results of my test showed I was still on death's doorstep, I would have felt bad, and that would have caused more stress. But it didn't, so I was able to avoid or eliminate that stress because I started exercising.

Where did the time go? It's now 7:00 a.m. I need to stop writing, even though I don't want to, and go for my bike ride. I'll be back in about an hour. See you then.

π

I'M BACK. THE ride was great, but it's now early the next morning. I would have liked to spend more time writing after my ride, but when I came back, I got busy doing other things, and before I knew it, the day was over. Even though I'm retired, my days are still busy. My bike ride is important, so I have to set some time aside and make myself do it before I get busy or it won't get done. Let me use my bike ride story to show you another important point you may have missed.

Obviously, I had to make myself quit writing or I wouldn't have gone on my bike ride. But consider this: Why didn't I want to quit writing? I enjoy writing, and I believe if you read what I've written, it will help you, which makes me feel good. Feeling good lessens stress, which lessens the odds of me having a heart attack. Can you see how I have two good things competing for my time? I love to write, and I need to exercise.

The evil team often uses two good things against us. Which activity would best decrease the odds of a heart attack—writing or bike riding? Both are good because they lessen stress, but in my case the bike ride is probably better. Since the evil team knows I need to ride, would they try to keep me from riding by encouraging me to keep writing? The answer is yes. Consider this: When I finish and publish this book, what are the odds everyone will read it? I'd be happy if everyone did, but I know that probably won't happen. Only a small percentage of possible readers will read my book, and an even smaller percentage will use what's in it to make their lives better. Think about this as we look at the odds of me having a heart attack.

The doctor told if I wanted to avoid a heart attack I needed to start exercising and eating better. If I keep writing, I won't have time to exercise. Could the evil team be playing the odds by trying to keep me from exercising, hoping I'll have a heart attack before the book gets finished? I'll never know, but it does make sense. If I don't finish the book, no one will be helped. If my life is cut short, I won't have time to do good things, like finish the book. I'd call that a win-win for the evil team. This is an example of how the evil team uses two good things against you.

π

THE NEXT TYPE of stress is mental stress. Living in this imperfect world gives you plenty of opportunities to experience it, but the good news is you can avoid, manage, or even eliminate a lot of it by following a few simple steps. Again, the first step is for you to figure out what or who is causing your stress.

Who causes most of your mental stress? You do.

Here's an example. You're in school and you didn't pay attention, so you're now behind. Being behind in your classes increases the odds of bad grades, and that makes school no fun. No fun causes you to lose interest. When you have no interest, you'll find friends who also have no interest, and then you'll start missing classes. Missing class means you won't graduate and go to college. No college means a bad job, a bad job increases stress, and stress creates all kinds of mental and physical problems.

In this example, where did the mental stress start? It started way back in school when you weren't paying attention, got behind, and refused to do something about it. Can you see how all of that added stress could have been avoided if you had just kept up in school?

Here's one more example. You're out in your car with a group of friends. Somebody says, "Let's see how fast this car will go." You feel the rush of excitement as you consider how fun it would be to push the pedal to the metal, but you decide to say no, as in, "No, I'm not going to do that." That decreases the probability of a bad outcome and increases the probability of a good outcome. Bad creates more stress; good creates less stress. Who is controlling your amount of stress? You are.

Can you think of another everyday experience that could cause mental stress? How about looking in the mirror? Just for fun, think about the last time you looked in the mirror. What did you focus on? You probably focused on things you don't like about yourself. But how did you know you didn't like those things? You compared yourself to someone else. In an imperfect world, you can't meet every requirement of the world's standard of perfection. It might be hard for you to hear, but there really are people who are more talented and more beautiful than you. Life is not, and never will be, completely fair. How do I know there will always be better-looking people? I also look in the mirror.

There will always be people more talented and beautiful than you, so you have to make a choice. Do you just accept who you are and live unhappily ever after, or do you accept who you are while trying to improve what needs to be improved? If you want to be happy, you'll accept who you are while trying to improve. Personal improvement is one of the purposes of earth life, but there are a few things that can't be improved. For instance, if you're a tall girl, you can't make yourself shorter. All you can do is accept it, stand up straight, put a smile on your face, and be happy that you're tall—and it doesn't hurt to remember that most supermodels are also tall.

I could give you hundreds of reasons why life isn't fair, but the evil team has probably already pointed them out to you. I hope you'll choose to ignore them, but that's easier said than done, unless you've developed the right amount of self-esteem. Will developing it be easy? If it were, everybody would be doing it. But it can be done. One of the biggest challenges you'll face in life is developing the right amount of self-esteem. The right amount is just enough for you to be able to make right choices regardless of what others might think.

Here's an example. You're out with a group of friends, and someone suggests you do something you know is wrong. You think about it and decide to do it so your friends will like you. How much stress did your choice create? Stress is created when you do something you know is wrong, and when you do it for the wrong reason. Doing things so your friends will like you is not a good reason. The stress you create will be determined by the outcome your action created and how hard it will be to fix it—if it can be fixed. Some consequences can never be fixed, because once they're done, they're done; there's no way to undo them. I hope you never experience any of those, but you do need to recognize they exist.

In this example, let's assume the consequence can be fixed. Now that you have a problem to fix, the evil team will try to talk you out of fixing it. Their suggestions will sound good, but you'll know deep down that it's not right. They'll also fill your head with fears by saying the punishment will be so bad that it would be easier to just live with it. The evil team always exaggerates the punishment when they're trying to keep you from fixing the problem.

Is this all the stress your choice created? No, not even close. More stress will be created by your family's disappointment and by countless other unforeseen consequences. The evil team may say, "It's your life. You can do what you want," but don't be fooled. It may be your life, but your actions will always affect those who love you.

Have you ever thrown a rock into a pond? Did it just plop in the pond and that was it? No, the plop was only the beginning. When the rock landed in the water, it created a circle of ripples that moved away from where it landed. The bigger the rock, the bigger the ripples. The ripples are like feelings. Some are yours, while others belong to those who love you, but they all create stress.

Can you see how my example created all three types of stress? If the evil team just said, "There's no physical stress in your example," think about it. Could my example create physical stress? Yes, because your brain controls your entire body. When it suffers emotional stress, you'll feel tired, sick, and depressed. As usual, the evil team was just trying to cause doubt, so don't listen to them.

How could you avoid most, if not all, the potential stress created in my example? You know the answer, because I've already given it to you. All you have to do is say no to doing something you know is wrong, and most, or even all of it, goes away. It may sound too easy, but it isn't. It works every time.

Saying no is a good choice. Good choices increase the probability of a better outcome, a better outcome creates confidence, and confidence creates self-esteem. Self-esteem gives you the confidence to make choices based on what's right instead of what others think. Those right choices then produce even more better consequences. These better consequences create more confidence, and more confidence strengthens your self-esteem. This cycle of certainty will continue as long as you're willing to make good choices.

Will you be criticized and made fun of when you make good choices? Sometimes, but you'll be okay because you have self-esteem. Remember, the evil team will never give up, because there's a lot at stake. When they see an opportunity to make you feel bad, you can bet they'll use it. Constant opposition is just part of the ongoing battle between good and evil.

In the next chapter, I'll share a personal experience that shows how things can turn out surprisingly well—eventually—when you have the courage to make the right choice. I've learned from this experience and many others that having the right amount of self-esteem will give you the courage to make the right choice quickly, which will keep you from suffering most, or possibly even all, of the physical, mental, and emotional stress that comes from making a bad choice.

REVIEW OF IMPORTANT POINTS

- Since you create most of the stress you experience, you can also control or eliminate it.
- Life is not fair, but that shouldn't be your focus.
- Having the right amount of self-esteem allows you to base your choices on right and wrong, not on what others think.

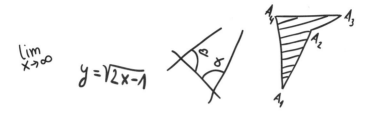

CHAPTER 18

WHY DIDN'T I JUST SAY NO?

A FEW YEARS AFTER I was married, I went to work for a truck and auto parts company as an outside salesman. My territory included parts of Utah, Nevada, Arizona, New Mexico, and Colorado.

After I had worked there for only a few months, the owner of the company invited me to go on a business trip back East in the company plane. To this day, I have no idea why he asked me to go, but I did enjoy the flight, because the weather was perfect and the pilot seemed to know what he was doing. I even got to sit in the copilot seat and fly the plane several times. Being up front, watching the pilot, and flying the plane helped increase my confidence that we would actually get there.

Worrying we might not make it was silly, but that's what I was thinking. I inherited an intense fear of flying from my mom. We tried several times to get her into a plane, but she always said, "If man was supposed to fly, he'd have wings."

After we arrived, we went out and had the best shrimp dinner ever. It's been over thirty years, but I still remember the shrimp. The safe flight and the shrimp dinner made the trip fun, but all of that was about to change.

When we left the restaurant, I looked down the street and saw what looked like a bad part of town, so I started walking the other way. As I did, one of the guys shouted, "Hey, Ted, we're going this way," and pointed toward the bad part of town. I should have just said, "No, thanks. I'll see you later back at the motel." But I was afraid they'd make fun of me, so I followed them.

As soon as we entered the bad part of town, I knew I shouldn't be there, so I frantically began looking for a way out. Off in the distance, I saw the tallest building in the city and said, "Let's go there." I started walking toward it. The scene must have been almost comical—a twenty-four-year-old kid leading four older guys down the street. I was in front, and they were several feet behind.

We arrived at the building and rode the elevator to the top floor. When I looked out the window, I remembered I was afraid of heights, so I took one quick look and headed back to the elevator. When we got back down to the street, I headed off in the direction opposite from where we had just come. But that same guy said, "Hey, Ted, we're not going that way. We're going this way," and pointed back toward the bad part of town.

What should I have said? I didn't say anything. Now it was four older guys walking ahead with a twenty-four-year-old kid trailing several feet behind. I didn't want to make a scene, so I just followed them back.

By the time we made it back into the bad part of town, I was quite a ways behind them, so they stopped in front of a business and waited for me to catch up. When I arrived, they grabbed me and pulled me into the business, laughing. I tried to tell them I wasn't interested, but that made them laugh even more. I was so embarrassed. It was then I realized the scene I had tried to avoid was now happening, and there was nothing I could do about it.

After they pulled me inside, they stepped back and laughed, which caused everyone nearby to turn around and look at me. They were having fun, but when I saw what was on the stage, I completely lost it. I wanted no part of it, so I pushed and shoved everyone out of my way and left.

Outside, I ran to the curb where a taxi was waiting. When I opened the front passenger door, the driver said, "If you get in, I'll have to shoot you!"

The look of confusion on my face must have told him I wasn't a threat, because he laughed and asked, "Where you from, boy?"

Without thinking, I said, "I'm from Utah." He continued to laugh as he told me to get in the backseat. I managed to tell him the name of the motel, and he took me there even though I didn't know the address.

During the ride, I experienced severe stress because I was sure I'd be fired and be told to find another room and another way home. At the motel, I went to the room and waited. Later that evening, the owner of the company walked into the room, and I braced myself for the worst.

To my surprise, he didn't say a single word to me. He just got undressed, got into bed, and turned on his side. He was snoring within a minute or two. Even though nothing even close to what I thought would happen actually happened, I lay there for quite a while, thinking about what I had done. Those thoughts caused even more stress until I eventually fell asleep.

The next day, I again braced myself for the worst, but nothing happened. Not a single word was said about the night before. We completed our business, boarded the plane, and headed home. The owner told me to sit in the copilot seat, which was fine with me. I really didn't want to talk to the others, and I was sure they didn't want to talk to me. I don't remember all of my thoughts then, but I do remember one: "How could I be so lucky? Here I am stuck inside a small twin-engine airplane with guys who didn't obey the commandments."

For a while, the flight home was uneventful, but that was about to change. After two hours, I noticed we were headed right into a big, black wall of storm clouds. You can't imagine the fear I felt when I saw those clouds, and I knew I wasn't alone because of the look on everyone's face. Even the pilot, a retired Air Force combat veteran, showed signs of concern as the plane started to bounce and jerk. He said, "It's going to get a little rough, so buckle up tight and hang on."

"A *little* rough"—I thought the wind was going to rip the plane apart!

I could tell you all about the wind, the lightning, the rain, the hail, and losing two of our three radios before we landed in Omaha, but I'll leave that to your imagination. I hoped we'd stay on the ground in Omaha, but after we fueled up, the owner said the same words every small-plane pilot probably says right before crashing: "Let's go. I think we can make it!"

We took off, and I was just getting comfortable when the plane hit a bad wind shear that caused it to drop a couple of hundred feet. I thought we were dead, but we made it and flew a few more hours through the storm until we reached Denver. The owner wanted to continue to Salt Lake, but the pilot refused to fly over the mountains at night. We spent another uncomfortable night in Denver and took off the next morning.

After takeoff, we climbed until we finally broke through the clouds into the sunshine. As we did, I heard a slapping noise outside the airplane. I asked the pilot what it was, and he calmly said, "Oh, that's just ice coming off the wings. It's nothing to worry about." Ice on the wings; now I understood why the pilot refused to fly over the mountains at night!

The flight over the mountains was uneventful, and my life returned to normal. Two weeks passed, and no one said anything about the trip, but there seemed to be an uneasy tension in the air when I went into the office. After a while, I began to wonder if the feeling was real or if it was just the evil team messing with my mind.

Then one day, I walked into the building and saw a group of guys in a circle, looking at a book. They were having a good time, but when they saw me, one of them grabbed the book, held it up to the window, and yelled, "What do you think of this, angel pants?"

I remember thinking, "Angel pants? You've got to be kidding. Is that the best you can come up with?" His remark was really stupid, but it still hurt to hear it.

As I stood there wondering if I really liked my job anymore, I felt an arm grab me from behind and pull me backward. I turned and was shocked to see the truck shop foreman, who had been with us on the trip back East. This guy was big, bearded, and looked like a poster boy for Harley-Davidson motorcycles. He was the nicest guy you'd ever meet and had always treated me well, but I had never felt comfortable around him. When he grabbed me, I thought my time here on earth was over.

Then something unexpected happened. He pulled me around behind him like he was protecting me, and he let those guys in the office have it. I don't remember exactly what he said, but they got the point in a hurry, because they all just kind of melted into their office cubicles. He then turned around, looked right at me, and said something I'll never forget: "Ted, don't let those guys bother you. I want you to know you're the only Mormon I've ever met who actually tries to live his religion."

If that was true, he must not have met many Mormons, but I'll never forget how I felt. I felt happy and sad at the same time—happy because he got to see a Mormon try to live his religion, and sad that he had to wait so long to see it.

I soon quit that job and moved on, but I've often thought about him. Did that experience make a difference in his life? I'll never know, but it made a difference in mine, and for that I'll be forever grateful.

Do you see how all my choices had consequences? For instance, there were several opportunities to leave the group and return to the motel, but I choose to stay even though I knew it was wrong. If I had chosen to return to the motel, I could have avoided all the stress.

Did you also see the choice I made that could have cost me my life? I chose to get back on the plane in Omaha. The storm had shorted out two of the three radios we used to speak to air traffic control on the ground, so we couldn't know how bad the storm was ahead of us. It was like we were flying blindfolded, but I got back on the plane anyway. I could have increased the odds of making it home safely by taking a commercial flight, but I didn't dare do it. I reluctantly got back on the plane. I was worried I might get fired if I didn't. But would that have changed anything in the end? No, because I left the company later anyway. If I had gotten fired, I could have lessened the amount of stress I felt during those final few weeks with the company.

Because everything eventually worked out, you might think I must have made a few good choices. I did. I made one: I left the group and went back to the motel, but I handled it poorly. All of my choices during that trip increased the probability of a bad outcome. As I now look back, I can see I was just lucky—or blessed—to make it home safely, but let's jump ahead and see if people on that plane were always that lucky.

After I left that company, a friend told me the plane I had flown in had crashed while trying to land. It had run out of fuel a few miles short of the airport and had to make an emergency landing in a field. Those onboard were lucky—or also blessed— because everyone walked away from the crash. I don't know why they ran out of fuel, but I can think of one possible reason. In my mind, I could again see the owner saying to the pilot, "Let's just go. I think we can make it."

Can you see how I could have increased the probability of better outcomes if I'd had the courage to make the right choices on my trip? Looking back, I can, but I didn't have enough self-confidence or self-esteem. That caused me to make the bad choices that created stress.

$$\pi$$

LET ME SHOW you how to develop the right amount of self-esteem so you can have the courage to make right choices.

The right amount of self-esteem must come from inside you. You can't take it from another, nor can anyone give it to you. Some people may be willing to help you find it, but it must still come from you.

When you look in the mirror, it's normal for you to notice things you don't like about yourself. If you want to see this actually happen, look in the mirror and listen to what goes on in your head. Which team made sure you noticed those things? It's the evil team. Since you'll never be perfect in your own eyes, how will you ever be able to be happy? You know the answer, because

I briefly mentioned it in the last chapter. You must learn to accept who you are—while you work on improving what needs to be improved.

How do you learn to accept you? It's a choice like every other choice you make every day. Think of it this way. When you look in the mirror and see things you don't like, you've made a choice not to like them. Your choice to accept yourself is no different from your choice to not accept yourself.

Choosing to accept you is important for at least two reasons. First, you must accept yourself before you can develop self-esteem, and it keeps you from wasting a lot of valuable time worrying about who you aren't. When you worry, you have negative thoughts that invite the evil team into your thought process. Once you let them in, they'll continue to send more negative thoughts that cause you to feel discouraged and depressed so you won't try to improve. If you don't try, you won't improve, and no improvement means more negative thoughts, more discouragement, and more depression. Do you see the cycle of uncertainty the evil team uses to destroy you?

Must you always try to improve? The answer is yes—if you want to find real happiness. When you try to improve, you move toward your goal of becoming like God. For you to become like God, you must obey the commandments. Obeying brings blessings, and blessings bring real happiness.

Here's another reason you can't be happy unless you try to improve. See if this makes sense.

Why do you do things in life? For instance, why do you mow a lawn, clean the house, or wash the car? Why do you take a bath, comb your hair, and wear nice clothes? Why do you get an education or a job and do community or Church service? Aren't you always trying to improve whatever you're working on? I know I am. I never try to do anything to make it worse. I only do things to make them better. After you've made something better, how do you feel? You feel better or happier. But let's not stop here.

Where did you get this desire to improve everything you touch? Were you born with it, or did you learn it while being raised? I believe you were born with it.

Take a look at young children. They're happiest when they're building, drawing, coloring, or learning a new way to make something better. While it's true that they may not be able do any of these things well at first, they'll keep trying until they succeed or until someone convinces them that they can't do it, because this desire to create or improve is built into them. They are sons and daughters of God, and God is always trying to create or improve everything He touches—including you.

Personal improvement is one of the main purposes of life. You must try to improve in order to be happy. But I'd better give you another warning. The evil team knows you need to improve, so they're not going to let you do it without a fight. I want to help you avoid the evil team's traps, so here's how you travel the road to improvement safely.

Make a list of things you like and things you don't like about yourself. As you create your list, don't be surprised if the evil team tells you that you don't like anything about yourself. You and I both know that's not true. All they're trying to do is depress and discourage you. If you find a few things you'd like to change, don't look at them as bad things. Just look at them as things you need to work on.

Next, break your list down into different categories, such as education, character, spiritual, and physical. Pick one or two to work on. These will become your long-term goals. I taught you how to make goals earlier, but it would be good to review the steps.

First, make sure the goal is realistic. Nothing will destroy your motivation more quickly than trying to reach an unrealistic goal. Next, define in writing what reaching your goal actually means. This is important because you won't know when you get there unless you know where you're going. After you've defined your long-term goals, break each one into several smaller short-term goals that are easier to reach. Reaching a smaller goal allows you to feel successful, and that's what keeps you going until you reach your long-term goal. Success is important because it builds confidence, and confidence creates self-esteem. But here's another warning.

Make sure you're trying to improve for the right reason. The evil team will influence you to want to change so others will love and accept you. But there will always be someone who doesn't like something about you. Don't try to change for others; change so you can accept and love yourself. And never forget that there are things that can't be changed. You can always improve, but you can't change into someone you're not. You will always be you, and you must learn to accept that or you'll never find real happiness.

Where should you look to find character traits to define your goals? Look at the character traits of Jesus Christ. Grab a piece of paper and put two columns on it, side by side. In one column, list the Savior's character traits. In the other column, list yours. Then compare both columns. The traits that don't match are the ones you need to work on.

In 2 Nephi 31:12, we are counseled to "follow [Christ], and do the things which ye have seen [Him] do." I've heard those words more times than I can count, but I never made the connection between what they were saying and what I was doing. I guess I didn't think He was talking to me. Then one day, the light of understanding clicked on, and that led me to create the two lists. When I compared them, I saw things I needed to change, so I started working on them. As I did, a good change began to happen, which made me feel better about life.

Here's why you'll feel better when you do the things the Savior did while He was here on earth. You're living life in this imperfect world, and you notice life isn't fair because others are prettier, smarter, taller, shorter—the list goes on and on. This recognition naturally creates feelings of envy and jealousy. I say *naturally* because they feel natural, but they really aren't natural. The evil team is just influencing you to feel that way.

Feelings of envy and jealously eventually cause you to covet. *Covet* means you really want what someone else has. Those feelings will eventually turn into hate if they're not corrected, because the evil team is never content. They'll always continue leading you down the road to destruction for as long as you're willing to follow.

Since there are people who have things you don't and there's nothing you can do about it, you're faced with two choices. You can continue to allow these feelings of envy, jealousy, and hate to make you miserable, or you can work on improving. If you're willing to try to improve, here's what you can expect.

A while back, I was called as bishop in our home ward. To make a long story short, serving my ward members taught me how to love them even though they were just ordinary, everyday people. It didn't matter if they were attractive, tall, short, gifted, or not gifted. None of that changed the way I felt, and that really surprised me. The change was so noticeable that my wife once asked, "Who are you, and what have you done with my husband?"

What caused the change in the way I felt? I already mentioned it. Did you catch it? I'll give you a clue. What do bishops and the Savior have in common? In my case, there wasn't much, but there was one thing. We both served others and expected nothing in return. Can you think of a time in the scriptures when the Savior refused to help someone? I can't, because it's not there.

Did you just say, "Okay, you helped others, and your feelings changed. What does that have to do with me loving who I am?" That's a great question. When you start doing what the Savior did, you will experience a change of heart. This change of heart can be summed up in one simple statement: you want to do unto others as you would have them do unto you. How do you want others to treat you? You want them to treat you well, so that means you need to treat them well. One of the blessings that comes from being good to others is a positive change in how you feel about yourself. But I'd better give you another warning. Just because you do good to others doesn't mean they'll always treat you well, and that may cause you to feel like it's not fair. Feeling like things aren't fair causes discouragement and may cause you to want to quit trying. What can you do in these situations? You should look at it as you would any other goal. Just choose to believe they will treat you well until it happens, and in most cases it will happen—eventually.

This change of heart doesn't happen overnight. Keep reminding yourself that it doesn't happen because of what others do; it happens because of what you do. How does it happen? I don't exactly know. Like all gifts from God, you'll wake up one day and realize the change has taken place.

After that, you won't feel envious, jealous, or hateful, because all those negative feelings will be replaced by positive feelings of caring. Is it caring or love? I'm not even sure what I should call it. I just know I felt different. These positive feelings create confidence, which creates positive self-esteem, which allows you to accept and learn to love who you are. It really is hard to explain how it works, but it does work, so get out there and start serving others, and watch what happens.

It will still hurt when others don't treat you well, but it won't matter. When you're trying to be like the Savior, another interesting change will happen—and for the record, I didn't see this one coming, either. When others didn't treat me the way I treated them, I noticed that instead of feeling angry, rejected, or hurt, I just felt sad for them, because I didn't have a problem—they did. At some future point, we'll all have to answer for our actions. When that happens, it's not going to be a good day for them unless they experience a change of heart. Doctrine and Covenants 88:32 states that you receive what you receive because you're not willing to receive what you might have received. What they'll receive on Judgment Day will be less than what they might have received, and that's why I feel sad for them.

As you're trying to become like Jesus Christ, a bond of trust will develop that allows you to live your life with more confidence. More confidence creates more trust, and that creates more positive self-esteem. Self-esteem frees you from the concerns you may have about yourself and what others think. Once you're free, you can enjoy life while you work on becoming who you want to become. But that's not the only blessing. You'll also be able to make choices based on right and wrong, not on what others think. When you do that, you'll make fewer bad choices and experience a lot less stress.

I've also learned that you see things differently when you're older. For example, everyone who is happy, confident, and trying to be like Jesus Christ radiates a beauty that comes from within. You may not always notice it in passing, but you will when you get to know them. Which type of beauty is the best? While you're young, you may not understand it. But now that I'm old, I can see it's the beauty that radiates from within.

If you don't understand how that could be possible, slow down for a minute and look around you. If you'll honestly look, you'll see beautiful people who are nice, and beautiful people who are not nice. Which person would you rather be around? I'd rather be around those who are nice. So which is more important, their beauty or them being nice? See how it works? I use the word *nice* because it best exemplifies the character traits of the Savior.

Regardless of where you start out in life, try to accept it while you work on improving. If you can do this, you'll be happy, confident, and beautiful in the eyes of those around you. If you can't or won't, all I can promise you is a lot of unnecessary heartache and disappointment.

Is it easy to follow the Savior's example until you receive a change of heart? If it were, everybody would be doing it, but you can do it because you have God on your side. He is there, and He is more than willing to change your heart if you want it, ask for it, believe it's going to happen, and are willing to go to work so it can happen. You get to choose. I hope you choose wisely!

REVIEW OF IMPORTANT POINTS

- Control or avoid stress by making good choices.
- Others will notice when you make good choices.
- Learn to love yourself while you work on changing. Change to improve, not to impress.
- Create your list of needed changes. Work on one or two at a time.
- Use the Savior's character traits to guide you in changing.
- Serving others and expecting nothing in return will help you learn to love yourself and others.
- Beauty from within creates noticeable beauty from without.

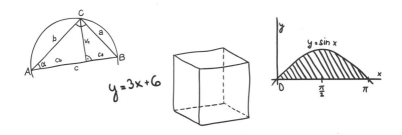

CHAPTER 19

FEELINGS ARE JUST FEELINGS

DO YOU NOW understand the importance of developing the right amount of self-esteem? Have you started working on it? I hope so. Self-esteem will help you manage or even eliminate a lot of stress in your life.

Speaking of unneeded stress, have you noticed your body has started to physically change? Since the day you were born, your body has been growing up. As it grows, it changes not only on the outside but also on the inside. Both will create stress unless you understand why the changes are happening.

When will these changes start? I can't say exactly because it's different for just about everyone. For some, the changes could start as early as ten or eleven, but for others it could be fourteen, fifteen, or later. For reasons I can't explain, they usually start earlier for girls than they do for boys.

God has given you a strict set of rules called commandments to help you make it through your time of change safely. Unfortunately, you won't get a warning when your changes start. You'll just be living life as a kid without a care in the world, and then you'll start feeling all kinds of new and exciting feelings you won't understand. This is the time when you must learn to control your body or it will become an uncontrollable beast.

This reminds me of a picture my wife once showed me of a big bear. Above the image, it said, "In the Next Life, I Wanna Be a Bear." Below it were listed several reasons you would want to be a bear: bears sleep through the winter, give birth to their young while they're asleep, eat all they want, and never have to shave their legs. My wife and I thought it was really funny.

Now that you have a big bear pictured in your mind, would you want to get into a cage with it if you could only *almost* control it? I know I wouldn't. I would never get into a cage with a bear unless I could *completely* control it.

Your body will become no different than that big bear unless you can learn to control it. Controlling it means your spirit must be able to tell your body what it can have and when it can have it. Your body can't control itself, and the best time to learn to control it is while you're young. If you wait until you're older, your body will have developed bad habits that are hard to break. Because I'm old, I know that it's much easier to make a new habit than it is to break an old one.

$$\pi$$

I'VE SPENT A lot of time teaching you about your body so you can learn to control it, but there's one more important part of this complex machine we haven't yet discussed. Your body can create little copies of itself called babies.

If you're a teenager, you probably know how babies are created, but that's only a small part of what you need to know. Anyone old enough can make a baby, but just being old enough to make one doesn't mean you're prepared to take care of one. Babies are completely helpless, incredibly selfish little bundles of joy—or misery, if you're not prepared. I hope you're looking forward to that time of life, but just like every other time of life, you must follow God's plan or your body will become your worst enemy.

The feelings, emotions, drives, and desires you'll experience while growing up are strong and dangerous. I want to help you understand why you have these feelings. Experience has shown that if I leave it up to you to figure them out, you'll spend your time fixing problems instead of preventing them. When you're dealing with the consequences of these feelings, preventing is a lot better than fixing, because once it's done, it's done, and there's no right way to make it undone.

The feelings I'm referring to are the emotions, drives, and desires that make you want to procreate.

Let's start with a question I've asked before. What makes a Shelby Mustang a Shelby Mustang? It's a Shelby because the Shelby Car Company created it. Your body, just like a Shelby Mustang, had a Creator, and that Creator was God. When He created it, He intended for it to be used a certain way. If you'll choose to use it His way, it will be your best friend. If you decide to use it some other way, it will become your worst enemy.

So how does God want you to use your body?

Your body has a feeling that's even more powerful than the need to be loved and accepted. It's the feeling that makes you want to be intimate with another human being. *Intimate* means sexually involved. If you're a teen and haven't yet felt these feelings, you soon will. These powerful feelings are sacred to the Creator of your body. Because they're sacred, He placed strict limits and restrictions on how, when, and where you can use them. God calls these restrictions, or this commandment, the *law of chastity*. I believe all the commandments have a reason they were given, but I can think of at least four reasons why God gave you the law of chastity. Let's go back and review how this commandment was given.

God gave Moses ten basic commandments, and He added to each of them as time went on. The law of chastity, or the commandment He gave Moses, said, "Thou shalt not commit adultery" (Exodus 20:14). Later He added, "Nor do anything like unto it" (D&C 59:6). He stated, "Whosoever looketh on a woman [or man] to lust after her [or him] hath committed adultery with her [or him] already in his [or her] heart" (Matthew 5:28). Can you see how each additional commandment builds upon the previous one?

In this commandment, there are two words—*adultery* and *lust*—you need to understand. The sin of adultery happens when a married person has sexual relations with someone they're not married to. *Lust* means a person wants to have sexual relations with someone they're not married to, so these commandments could apply to everyone.

Can you see how God is teaching you step by step, and how each step requires you to gain greater control over your body? First, you can't do it. Then, you can't do anything like it. And finally, you can't even really think about it. You did notice that I said "really think about it," right? *Really* means you're often seriously thinking about it. The evil team will send you bad thoughts to try to make you feel ashamed or guilty, but if you'll just push each one out, then you won't really be thinking about it.

If you don't yet know exactly what having sexual relations means, that's okay. Just understand that in God's eyes, sexual relations between men and women are sacred. If they're sacred to Him, they must be sacred to you or you're not following His plan.

Here are the four reasons why you need to obey the law of chastity. First, if you break these commandments, it could affect more than just you and your partner. Breaking this commandment could cause a pregnancy before you're ready or able to handle the responsibilities that come with it. If you're not ready, you, your partner, and the baby will suffer. Babies are completely innocent when this commandment is broken, but they're usually the ones who suffer the most.

The evil team just complained that babies don't always suffer, so let me explain what I mean. Babies must be taken care of. They must be fed, clothed, protected, and taught. All of this requires time, money, patience, and commitment. Young parents haven't had time to prepare for any of these necessities, and that can cause unnecessary suffering for the baby. In addition, babies will eventually grow up, and that will require even more time, money, patience, and commitment. If young parents spend all of their time taking care of the baby, where will they find time to finish their education? No education means the child could be raised by a low-income family. It may not seem fair, but more money creates more opportunities for a child's future success.

If you'll look at this issue honestly, you won't have any problem recognizing the truth. Babies born to young, unprepared parents have fewer opportunities than babies born to older parents who are prepared.

The second reason for this commandment is that once you break it, it can never be unbroken. Once a sexual act is committed, all those involved can never be the same again. You can repent, but repentance doesn't change what's been done. You just have to live with it, and sometimes living with it can be hard.

The third reason for this commandment is to protect your spirit from your body. The feelings and desires that come from intimacy are the strongest feelings you'll experience in life. Once you feel them, you can become addicted to them. Overcoming any addiction is hard, but breaking a sexual addiction is extra hard. I'm not trying to scare you. I'm just trying to help you understand what you could be dealing with if you choose to break this commandment.

The last reason is that a good, strong marriage relationship must be built step by step. When you break this commandment, you skip over several important steps in the relationship-building process, and that lessens your chances for a happy marriage. Can you complete the missing steps after you're married? Yes, but it's a lot harder.

These are four good reasons you must control the desire for physical intimacy. God gave you the law of chastity to protect you. If you choose to obey this law, you'll be able to enjoy true physical intimacy in a secure, committed marriage relationship.

$$\pi$$

GOD CREATED YOUR body, and He put the desire for sexual relations in it so you could enjoy physical intimacy with your future spouse. Real intimacy is necessary and good because it helps you build a strong, secure marriage relationship. The world you're growing up in is a lot different from the one I grew up in. In this day and age, the evil team is doing everything they can to confuse and mislead you about the proper use of intimacy. If I remember correctly, I was introduced to sex at about age fourteen. I had heard about it, but it wasn't until I made a bad decision one night that I really started learning about it. I'd better tell you about the decision I made so you don't get the wrong idea about me.

One night, two friends and I were on our way to see a movie. We were walking toward the theater when one of my friends stopped and said, "Let's not go to the movie. Let's go have some fun."

My other friend said, "No, we need to go to the movie because that's where we told our moms we were going."

They argued back and forth for a minute. Then they turned and asked me, "What are we going to do?"

Regretfully, I didn't make a good choice that night. I chose to go have some fun. I soon learned after I made that choice that my less-than-obedient friend's life was almost entirely focused on sex, and he was only fifteen at the time.

I know now I was way too young to be thinking about sex, but today you don't have to wait until you're fourteen. All you have to do is open your eyes and turn on your ears, because the evil team is using the radio, TV, movies, the Internet, newspapers, magazines, and billboards to encourage immoral behavior. This is why I often call this imperfect world a sewer. Just living life will require you to wade through this sewer. Let me show you how you can do it without getting anything on you.

$$\pi$$

IN THE BEGINNING, God presented His plan to you. That plan allowed you to have many different experiences on this earth so they could prepare you to eventually become like Him. God has a body just like yours, but His is a perfected body. It looks and functions basically the same as yours, but there are some differences. For instance, His body doesn't deteriorate with age, has no physical impairments, has no aches, has no pains, and the list goes on. I'm not sure how all that works, but I choose to believe it, and I hope you'll also choose to believe it.

God is a male god, and His wife is a female god. We don't know much about Her, but we do know She exists. He told us in the scriptures that we are all patterned after Him. I am a male like

Him, and my wife is a female like Her. The reason there are males and females is that it takes two—one male and one female—to create a baby through the act of procreation.

God's plan for His children is simple. His children are to follow the law of chastity. This law states there can be no intimacy or anything like it until after marriage. Why? It's so a man and a woman can really learn to love each other before they marry. They then marry and join together in intimacy to create bodies for God's spirit children here on earth. God also encourages the married couple to use intimacy to express their love for each other.

If you choose to follow God's plan, His work will continue moving forward until it is completed. When will it be completed? Only God knows, but I suspect it will be completed after all His children assigned to this earth receive their bodies.

I realize there will be some, maybe even many, who will disagree with His plan, and that's okay. God gave them the right to follow or not follow it. But they can't receive His blessings unless they follow the plan. I choose to follow His plan, and they choose to follow their feelings. This is why I spent so much time teaching you about feelings. I wanted to make sure you understand why you have feelings. The feelings that encourage you to follow God's plan comes from God. Feelings that encourage you to not follow God's plan come from the evil team.

Let's take another short break.

REVIEW OF IMPORTANT POINTS

- Your body will go through several different stages of change as it prepares you for adult responsibilities.
- God put the desire to join with another human being into your body so children could be created.
- Your body will be able to create a baby before you're ready to take care of it.
- The ability to create children is sacred to God.
- Most people base their choices on feelings.

$$A = \begin{pmatrix} 2 & -1 \\ -3 & -2 \end{pmatrix} \qquad y = \sqrt{2x-1}$$

δ

CHAPTER 20

ATTRACTIONS DON'T MEAN ANYTHING

I HOPE AFTER READING the last few chapters you better understand why you are you and why you feel the way you do. Everyone has challenges, but we still have to learn to deal with them the way God commands if we want His blessing. How do you deal with them? You have to learn to control them. This means your spirit must win the spirit-versus-body battle.

Let me share with you a couple examples I hope will show you why feelings and attractions must be controlled. In these examples, I'll use some of the feelings and attractions I've had to learn to control while growing old.

You know that I am attracted to Shelby GT 500KR Mustangs. Every time I think of one, I feel like I really need to have one. Even though I want one really bad—or to put it another way, even though I'm strongly attracted to them—I know buying one now would be wrong because I can't afford the car.

Does knowing it's wrong to buy a Shelby Mustang stop me from wanting one? No, I still feel like I really want one. In this case, *wrong* means if I bought one I wouldn't have enough money to feed my family or have a house, a regular car, and everything else I need to sustain life. That's why buying a Shelby is wrong and it makes absolutely no logical sense whatsoever—yet!

The feelings and attractions I have for Shelby Mustangs really don't mean anything. I have them, and they're intense, but they're just feelings, attractions, and desires that I need to learn to control. Here's another example.

A guy who doesn't understand feelings all of a sudden finds he is attracted to girls. It could be the way they look, act, or walk, or the clothes they wear—or in this day and age, the lack of clothes. It could be the way they hold their heads or talk, or even the perfume they wear. In fact, he may not even know why he's attracted to girls; he just knows he's attracted to girls.

Since he has these strong feelings of attraction to girls, is it okay for him to be intimately involved with every willing girl? No, it's not okay according to God's plan. Here's another example. Let's say the guy doesn't want to be intimate with a girl. He's just feeling strong attractions, so is it okay for him to look at pornography? Again, no, it's not okay, because looking at pornography is wrong according to God's plan.

Here's one more example. Let's say a girl is married with a couple kids. One day, she feels really attracted to someone at work, at the mall, or on the street. Since she feels this intense attraction, is it okay for her to act on that and leave her spouse and kids? She's only attracted to one person, and the attraction she feels is strong, so is it all right for her to pursue this new attraction? Some may think it is, but I can guarantee you that God doesn't. This same principle would also apply to a guy who develops an attraction outside of his marriage.

These examples should help you clearly see that the feelings, attractions, and desires you feel are just feelings, attractions, and desires—nothing more, nothing less. They really don't mean anything, and they cannot be used as an excuse for not following God's plan. They may be real and powerful, and they're certainly not fair, but they must be dealt with the way God commanded us.

His commandments are clear. He said in the scriptures and through His prophets that physical intimacy is only for a man and a woman who are legally and lawfully married.

You may have noticed that some states have recently started allowing gay and lesbian couples to marry, but that still doesn't make it right. Being legally married fills one part of the commandment, but it doesn't fill the part that restricts physical intimacy to a man and a woman.

God, through His prophets and scriptures, clearly tells us that marriage is between a man and a woman. The evil team is going to tell you God created you and gave you feelings, so it must be okay to act on them. But don't believe them. Saying God created you is just an example of how the evil team uses partial truths to deceive you.

It's true that in the beginning God created your spirit. He then sent you to earth to receive a physical body. But who created your earthly body? It was all of your ancestors. They are the reason you are you.

Could it really be this easy? No, it's not always easy. Denying yourself something you really want is hard but not impossible. I know this because I've often had to deny myself things I've wanted.

If you're having unwanted or unnatural feelings and attractions, don't feel guilty, picked on, or cursed. Just recognize that you have them and try to follow God's plan. No feelings make you a good or a bad person until you act on them. What you become will depend entirely upon what feelings you act on.

Did you just hear the evil team? They said, "If unwanted or unnatural feelings and attractions are part of God's plan, then it must be okay to act on them." If you heard that or anything like it, don't believe it. Attractions and God-given feelings (or desires) are not the same thing.

π

GOD GAVE YOU the desire to join with another human being in physical intimacy. This desire was given so bodies could be created for His spirit children. Out of necessity, this desire had to be strong or the human race couldn't continue to accomplish His purposes. This *desire* to join with another human being comes as standard equipment in your body, but *attraction* is something different. Attraction helps you decide whom you'll join with. Being able to understand the difference between these two feelings will keep you from falling into another evil team trap: the idea that you can't change your attractions.

When God created the plan, He created rules that teach you when, how, and with whom you can be physically intimate. He then gave you agency, which allows you to choose whether or not you'll follow His rules. If you want God's blessings, follow His rules. It really is that simple.

If people can't change their attractions, how do they choose which people they want to date and then marry? Don't they base their choices on attractions, and don't those attractions often change? In almost all cases, people date different people until they decide whom they're going to marry.

I said "in almost all cases" because that's not what happened to me. When I saw my wife for the first time, I was attracted to her and only her. My strong attraction eventually created a relationship, and the rest is history. But I guess I was just different from everyone else.

Now why did I say that? When I wrote how other people date several people before they choose whom they'll marry, the evil team slipped a thought into my head that told me I must be different from everyone else because I only wanted to date one person. Thinking I'm different could have made me feel self-conscious and less confident, and that would have prevented me from building a lasting relationship. No relationship meant I wouldn't marry, and not marrying meant I wouldn't be following God's plan. Lucky for me, that didn't happen because I followed the plan and eventually married my wife.

π

CAN YOU SEE how living your life according to God's plan just makes sense? I hope so, because it will make your life a lot easier.

Now that you understand your role in His plan, you can live your life with confidence. You shouldn't feel embarrassed or self-conscious when you feel desires, attractions, and passions. These feelings aren't dirty, wrong, or sinful. They only become dirty, wrong, and sinful when they're used in a way contrary to how God wants you to use them.

The evil team wants to destroy you, so they're going to tell you that you shouldn't even have desires, passions, or attractions. They'll want you to feel embarrassed and self-conscious about these feelings so you won't feel comfortable asking for help or advice. If you won't ask, you won't be able to understand why you have the feelings, and that leaves you with just four choices. The first three rarely work, because they increase the probability of bad outcomes:

- Figure out your feelings on your own
- Ask your friends about them
- Follow the examples you see in media

The evil team wants your body to become your worst enemy. If these God-given feelings aren't understood and used correctly, they'll most certainly lead you to regrets, addiction, and eventual destruction.

What is the fourth choice? You can read this book, and it will help you understand why you have those feelings and why they really don't mean anything. They're just feelings your body creates, and you must decide how you'll use them.

$$\pi$$

YOUR BODY IS an amazing machine. It comes with everything you'll need when you're young and everything you'll need when you get older. The things you'll need when you're older are now dormant inside you. *Dormant* means they're just sitting there doing nothing while you grow up.

As you grow up, your body will change as it prepares itself for the responsibilities of adulthood. These changes affect the way you feel, think, and act. During this critical time of life, you need an open relationship with your parents so you can use their experiences to help you make good choices. Parents have an unlimited amount of helpful information you can use to make your teen years a lot easier.

God doesn't want you experiencing intimate relations until after you're in a secure, committed marriage relationship. In the next chapter, I'll explain why He has commanded you to wait. When you understand why, you'll be much more motivated to follow God's plan.

I hope you understand now how God intended for you to use your body. If you choose to use it the way He intended, it can be your best friend. If you don't, it could be your worst enemy. As always, the choice is yours. I hope you'll choose wisely.

REVIEW OF IMPORTANT POINTS

- Strong feelings and attractions don't excuse you from God's rules.
- No feelings or attractions are sin until after you act on them.
- The desire to join with another human being comes as standard equipment. This desire and your attractions aren't the same.
- You can change your attractions.
- Many body parts should remain dormant until they are needed.
- God's plan is simple. Sexual intimacy is only acceptable in a marriage between a man and a woman.
- Your body will be your best friend if you use it correctly.

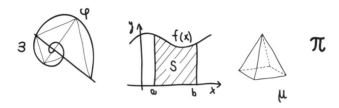

CHAPTER 21

IT TAKES TWO

HAVE YOU HEARD of Sonny and Cher? They were famous singers back in the sixties and seventies. I still enjoy some of their old songs. I used their cover song as a chapter title because it takes two to create a secure, committed marriage relationship.

Let's begin with a question. Why would you want to marry? In my day, that would have been a silly question. It seemed like everyone looked forward to getting married. Today, fewer people are choosing to do so. I can think of several reasons to marry, but I'll mention just two. First, marriage is the fourth step of the five basic steps you must take to be eligible to continue your eternal progression toward godhood. The second reason is that it's a lot easier to find real, lasting happiness in life when you're in a secure, committed marriage relationship.

Creating this kind of relationship will be a lot easier if you know how. But even if you don't, you can still create a marriage relationship; it just won't be secure or committed. Anyone can create a relationship because God put in every body a strong desire to join together with another human being.

$$\pi$$

GOD WANTS YOU to be intimate with your future husband or wife, so what does the evil team want you to do? Usually, they want you to do the opposite. In this case, the opposite doesn't work because of the desire that's built into our bodies. This built-in desire forces them to use the same plan they've been using since the beginning of time. God calls their plan "immorality," and unfortunately it has been successful.

For God's plan to succeed, new human life must be created. For new life to be created, a husband and wife must have sexual relations. God wants His plan to succeed, so He made intimacy the most enjoyable physical feeling you'll ever experience. That's why sexual relations before marriage are so dangerous. Your body wants to feel good. Sexual relations makes your body feel good, so the evil team will try to get you to experience it before you're ready to handle the responsibilities that come with it. Most people are physically ready in their early teens, but they're not emotionally ready until they're in a secure, committed marriage relationship. I know this sounds old-fashioned, but you must be in a secure, committed marriage relationship before you can emotionally handle all the responsibility that comes with intimacy.

Both types of feelings—physical and emotional—can destroy your relationship if your needs aren't being met. Everyone is constantly thinking about physical feelings but rarely consider emotional feelings until those needs aren't being met. You can create a relationship with just about anyone, but if you focus only on physical feelings, it won't last. Why? Because physical feelings can't satisfy your emotional needs.

If you didn't understand that last paragraph, don't feel bad; it's difficult to understand until you're in a relationship. That leaves you with two choices: obey the law of chastity before you're married, or don't. I really hope you choose wisely!

$$\pi$$

NOW THAT YOU understand physical intimacy is only for married people, this would be a great time to ask why. Why would the evil team want you to experience the feelings of physical intimacy before you can emotionally handle them? The answer is always the same. They want to destroy your opportunity to become like God, and nothing will destroy that opportunity faster than sexual relations before marriage. Let me help you understand why they're so physically and spiritually dangerous.

If you let the evil team talk you into having sexual relations before marriage, at least two really bad things are going to happen. First, you'll turn on some parts of your body's standard equipment that can't be shut off. This means your spirit will have to fight to control this desire until the day you die. Once your body has experienced these intense feelings, it's going to want to experience them again and again.

That might have caused you to think you should never allow your body to enjoy sexual relations, but that's not what I'm saying. God gave you the desire for physical intimacy for a good reason. First and foremost, it was given so you would want to bring children into the world. (Did you notice I said *children*, not just *a child*?) But that's not the only reason for physical intimacy. Physical intimacy also helps a married couple eventually become one.

The second reason you can't let your body experience sexual feelings early is that there's no end to the list of good feelings your body is going to want to experience. If you don't control your body's desire to feel good, it will become a selfish beast that can't be controlled.

Look at it this way. Will you make choices that encourage you to break the law of chastity, or will you choose to strictly follow the law? If you choose to follow the law, life will continue on normally. If you choose to break it, then everything that's normal in your life immediately changes. Here's why.

First, because you have broken an important commandment, the Spirit of God can't be with you to bless, guide, and protect you until you repent. Repentance is certainly possible, but in this case, it's extremely difficult because complete repentance requires you to forsake the sin. *Forsake* means you won't commit that sin again. Think about it. You've just allowed your body to experience the most intense physical feeling it can possibly feel, and now you can't let it feel it again. What are the odds of you winning that battle? Surprisingly, they're really good if you can never allow yourself to be in a place where it could happen, but that requires you to be extremely disciplined. I'm sure there are teenagers who are that disciplined, but I wasn't. Never being in a place where it could happen means you can never be alone with a member of the opposite sex. But what do teenagers like to do? They like to be alone with members of the opposite sex. Can you see how the odds of completing the repentance process are stacked against you?

That's just one of consequences of breaking the law of chastity. You could also experience real emotional problems—loss of self-esteem, feelings of isolation, loss of respect for yourself and your partner, and never-ending feelings of guilt and shame.

Why would those who break this law feel guilt and shame? It's because they know deep down inside that what they're doing is wrong. Everyone is born with a conscience that helps them know the difference between right and wrong. This God-given moral compass is a real blessing. When you break the law of chastity before marriage, a process begins that weakens your conscience until it's no longer there.

$$\pi$$

REMEMBER HOW I mentioned most of us put a rating on sins? Sexual sin is always considered one of the most serious sins. Knowing you've committed a serious sin creates bad feelings. While you're experiencing these bad feelings, the evil team will tell you God is mad at you so you won't try to repent. If you choose not to repent, the evil team can continue to send you additional guilt and shame, causing you to become depressed.

These bad feelings always make you feel even worse about your relationship with God, so you'll naturally turn farther away from God and His spiritual influences. These feelings continue until you've completely separated yourself from God, His Spirit, and all the help His Spirit can give you.

Here's one more point you need to consider. When a person involved in sexual sin feels depressed, where do they go to find someone to help them feel better again? Do they go to church or some other place that promotes moral behavior? Some do, but most don't. They feel like God is mad at them, so they go back to the place that promotes immoral behavior, because that's where they feel comfortable.

So there you are in a place that promotes sexual sin. You feel bad, but you know sexual relations made you feel good. What are you going to do? See why it's almost impossible to give up that lifestyle once you've started living it?

Just to be sure, let me share another personal experience with you. This experience was funny until you slow down long enough to think about what my friend actually said.

Several years ago I worked with a guy whose lifestyle wasn't good. One day, he was telling everyone about his latest adventure, and I told him he'd better change his ways or he was probably going to hell. He quickly replied, "That's okay. That's where all my friends will be." This helped me see the power of friendship. All his friends were stuck in the same lifestyle, and that made it almost impossible for him to leave it all behind.

π

SO FAR WE'VE only discussed a few of the problems that come from breaking the law of chastity. If I tried to explain every single problem, this chapter would never end, but I would like to give you one more really good reason to obey the law.

Odds are good that you will catch a disease if you break the law of chastity. A few years ago, I watched a DVD that showed all the different sexually transmitted diseases just waiting to destroy your quality of life or perhaps even kill you if you're unlucky enough to catch one.

Did you just hear what I heard? I almost laughed out loud when the evil team said, "That's not right. Married people have sexual relations, and few of them ever get any diseases." Again, they may be right. People who obey the law of chastity can enjoy intimacy in marriage without having to worry about catching a disease. Why? The answer is the law of probability and outcome.

The probability of catching a disease increases every time you have sexual relations with a different partner—especially if those people have also had relations with other people. All these different people having relations with all of their different partners dramatically increase the odds that you'll eventually catch a disease.

Also, consider this: you might only have to break the law of chastity one time before marriage to catch a disease. How could that happen? It may be your first time, but you won't know if it's your partner's first time. Also, don't listen to those who promote so-called safe sex. The only safe sex is intimacy after marriage with a partner who also obeyed the law of chastity.

If you and your future spouse obey the law of chastity, you'll both end up having sexual relations with just one person. That greatly lessens the odds of catching a disease.

Most of us live in a sheltered world when it comes to sexual diseases. That DVD made a real impression on me. If every teen could watch it, I'm confident it would cause them to have second thoughts about breaking the law of chastity. Remember, after you've broken the law and caught a disease, there may be nothing you can do about it, except live with it or die from it.

$$\pi$$

THIS WOULD BE a great time to ask another question. Think about the world you live in. How does the evil team encourage immorality? Not sure? Let me help you. What are the two main things the world seems to be focused on today? They are money and immorality. Actually, there is only one, because money is really just the means, or the way, to immoral behavior. Let me show you how money is used to encourage immorality.

If you'll honestly look at the world you live in, you'll see that many of the things you see and hear—including movies, songs, TV shows, magazines, and clothing advertisements—are designed with just one purpose in mind: to encourage immorality. How well are all these things working? Think about the people you see on the streets, in the malls, at sporting events, in church, or just about anywhere. What are a lot of these people trying to be? Some people call it *hot*. In my day they called it *cool*, but regardless of what it's called, it means the same thing.

We live in a world where people spend millions of dollars and thousands of hours every day on clothes, exercise equipment, diets, makeovers, plastic surgery, cars, and anything else they can think of to make themselves look hot. Why do they do it, and why is looking hot so important? *Hot* is the new code word for *sexy*. Is looking hot or sexy a bad thing? Let's look at where the road leads, and then you can decide for yourself.

I'll start with a simple question. Why do people want to look hot? It gets them noticed. What happens when you notice someone hot? I don't know about you, but I feel attracted to them. You can be honest. Remember, attractions don't mean anything; they're just feelings you must learn to control. If you control them, you'll be fine, but if you don't control them, you won't.

$$\pi$$

SINCE ALL OF us are going to feel attractions, let me show you how to control them. When you cross paths with someone blessed with stunning beauty, dressed to impress, or not dressed enough, you're probably going to notice them—especially if you're a guy. I'm not making excuses for guys, but guys are visual. They notice cars, boats, snowmobiles, and women. My honesty with you may get me in trouble with my wife, but somebody needs to be honest with you. I don't want all you guys thinking you're bad just because you notice girls. Guys notice girls. I'm not sure why. Maybe it's part of the standard equipment they are born with.

When something or someone gets your attention, don't be surprised if you feel some level of attraction. The reason I say "some level" is that every day may be different. On any given day, the attraction could be strong or weak, or you could feel no attraction at all. I'm not sure why it works this way. I just know it does. Regardless of the reason, all attractions must be dealt with in a way God would approve. In the cases concerning worldly things—like Shelby Mustangs, snowmobiles, boats, paintings, houses, yards— these attractions can be dealt with by simply saying, "Someday when I can afford it, I'd really like one of those." Then you can use your desire to have one as motivation to go to work and get it.

If the attractions you're feeling are for another human being, then the way you deal with it needs to change, because human beings aren't worldly possessions. They're sons and daughters of God, so you need to treat them respectfully. How do you do it? You simply train yourself. After you notice their beauty, immediately push any thoughts of attraction out of your mind.

Here's another warning. When I was young, the evil team had great success in making me feel ashamed every time I noticed a beautiful girl. This shame caused me to feel like I was a bad person for even noticing her. Then one day, something interesting happened. I realized I felt the same type of feeling when I saw a good-looking car, a fast snowmobile, and anything else on my worldly wish list. This realization helped me understand I wasn't bad. I'm just a guy, and guys notice things because we're visual.

Now, when I notice a beautiful woman, a nice car, a new model-year snowmobile, or anything else, I simply recognize it instead of pretending I didn't see it, and I focus all my efforts on controlling my thoughts. Remember, you can't stop a bird from landing on your head, but you can stop it from building a nest there. My recognition of beauty in all its forms is just a bird landing on my head, but I will not allow it to stay there long enough to build a nest. That is how you control your thoughts so that they don't turn into improper attractions.

Why can't I continue to think about pretty girls when I see them all around me? Recognition creates thoughts, thoughts create feelings of attraction, feelings of attraction create desires, and desires create actions that lead you right into physical relationships that are not approved by God.

Now that you understand how to control your thoughts, let me make another point. When I said money leads to immorality, the evil team said, "What's wrong with trying to look good? Do you want everyone to look ugly so nobody ever feels any attraction?" No, I don't want everyone to look ugly. I just want to help you understand how you should deal with attractions. Learning to deal with them correctly is important, because every single relationship starts with an attraction and grows from that point. Are all relationships bad? Of course not, but depending on your age, your physical development, and whether or not you're married, they could become bad if you think attractions mean something.

$$\pi$$

LET'S TAKE A look at how relationships develop. I'll use myself in this example. At what age do people start feeling attractions? For me it was early. I felt attracted to my future wife in first grade. For reasons I can't explain, I was attracted to her from the first moment I saw her. Those early attractions were totally innocent. But when I became a teenager, they began to change. At the time, I didn't understand why. Now I know it was because my body was preparing to assume the God-given responsibilities of adults. I began to feel physically drawn to her, and that attraction created all kinds of wild and crazy thoughts. Some were good and some were bad, but they all increased the level of attraction I felt for my future wife.

Because I felt these attractions, I repeatedly tried to get her to like me. To make a long story shorter (ten years shorter), she finally decided to like me. We made plans to marry right after high school graduation, and now, forty-four years later, the relationship is still growing.

Are you wondering why I was so attracted to my future wife? During my early years, I honestly don't know. But during my teenage years, I was attracted to her because she was hot. My friends and I would often rate the girls in our school, and without exception, my wife was always numbered in the top five.

Since I was a teenager and my future wife was hot, what do you think the evil team was always influencing me and probably every other young man my age to do? Was I just rationalizing my bad thoughts? I probably was when I said "every other young man." Every young man may not have felt those same feelings, but I know a lot of them did. What feelings? The evil team used my feelings to try to get me into situations where I could have experienced sexual relations before I was ready for them. None of this was my wife's fault, but they made sure I noticed her clothes, her makeup, her hair, the perfume she wore, and, of course, her physical features. All of these things got noticed and increased the attraction I felt for her. This same attraction made it possible for us to develop the relationship we now share.

You live in a world filled with people who look hot. Are they all trying to be sexy? I'm sure they're not, but it doesn't matter because of the unintended consequences. Unintended consequences means the actions you take often create consequences you never intended.

Here's an example of the law of unintended consequences from a guy's perspective. You're a gal. You eat right and exercise to keep fit. You dress nice, wear makeup, style your hair, and wear perfume—even though you're happily married. When you go to the mall, will guys notice you? Yes, they will. It's just an unintended consequence of your actions, but the guys still must deal with the feelings that seeing you created. That's the law of unintended consequences in action. By the way, who made sure the guys notice you? No surprise there. Of course it's the evil team.

A gal's desire to look hot has another really bad unintended consequence for guys, which could literally cost them their eternal kingdom. Many young men are not getting married because they can't make up their mind. Everywhere they look, they see beautiful girls. I feel bad for guys. They're out there trying to follow the plan, and eventually they find a beautiful girl to marry. They think they're happy until they turn around and see another equally or even more beautiful girl standing on the next corner. When they see the new girl, they feel the same physical attractions they felt for the first girl, and that confuses them because they thought those feelings were love. So they take a step back and check out girl number two, just to make sure the first girl is really the one. While they're checking out number two, they see girl number three. That confuses them even more because they feel physically attracted to her. All these beautiful girls create nothing but confusion, and that makes it hard for them to make up their minds.

This also creates problems for girls, but not for the same reason. Girls generally don't make choices based on what they see; they make choices based on what they feel. They may notice a hot guy, but the guy will get nowhere with the girl unless he pays attention to her. Girls like attention because it makes them feel good, and these good feelings create feelings of attraction for that guy. Feeling attraction makes girls think they're in love. But when another guy comes along that makes them feel even better, they feel attraction for him, and that confuses them.

Today's boys and girls are having a harder time marrying because they're basing their choices entirely upon feelings of attraction. A boy sees a pretty girl, and that attracts him to her. A girl feels good when someone pays attention to her, and that attracts her to him. Each believes their feelings of attraction are real love, until they feel the same or even stronger attraction for someone else.

Confusing attractions with real love also creates another problem. Have you ever heard someone say that their relationship was meant to be or they were meant for each other? But "meant to be" conflicts with a really important principle: agency.

Why would someone think they were meant to be with someone else? I can think of two reasons. First, they have strong attractions. Second, they asked God if they should marry them, and He said yes.

The evil team is complaining again, so I'd better explain what I mean.

You can ask God to confirm your choice, and He will, but don't expect Him to tell you whom to marry. A couple recently ended their marriage. Along the road toward their divorce, the wife said, "I never loved you. The only reason I even married you is because God told me to." Was it God who told her to marry him, or was it the evil team? I don't think she knew whom she was talking to.

The evil team does not want you to marry, or they want you to marry the wrong person so your marriage will eventually fail. They understand God's plan, so they'll do anything they can to stop you from following it. What is God's relationship plan?

Maybe you've heard this rhyme: "First comes love, then comes marriage, then comes the baby in the baby carriage." This little rhyme describes God's plan for you perfectly, and you can follow it by doing four simple things:

- Obey the commandments while you build a relationship.
- Marry for time and eternity.
- Join together to bring children into the world.
- Love, honor, cherish, and serve each other for the rest of your life.

That's all you need to do to follow God's relationship plan.

Now let's look at the evil team's relationship-building plan. Almost everyone will try to marry at some point in their lives so they can fulfill the two basic human needs we discussed earlier. The problem is they're looking in places that don't encourage them to follow the commandments, like clubs and bars. If they find someone in these places, what did they base their choice on? Attractions. And how is that working for them? From the outside, it looks like they're having fun, but let's see if this fun will ever lead to real happiness. Here's what usually happens when people base their relationships on attractions.

An average visual Joe sees an average hot Jane. He feels a strong attraction to her, so he starts paying attention to her. Jane likes the attention. So Joe and Jane start a relationship that's based on Joe's feelings of attraction and Jane's natural desire to have someone pay attention to her. This relationship is new and exciting, so they think they're in love. Because they're in love, they start acting like married people after just a few short hours, or maybe a day or two at best. They think they're happy for a while because they love the newness of their relationship and the freedom it gives them to enjoy everything a close physical relationship has to offer. All of these wonderful feelings make them think their relationship will last until the day they die. But will it? Sadly, for Joe and Jane, it won't.

What is their relationship really built on? It's Joe's attractions, Jane's need for attention, and lots of passionate physical relations. Can these three things keep a relationship from eventually falling apart? No. Those three feelings aren't the only things needed for a successful relationship. Joe is going to have strong or even stronger attractions to other women, and Jane's need for attention is not going to be satisfied when Joe quits paying attention to only her. What about the passion? Wouldn't that keep them together? It won't, because either one or both could have the same passion with just about anyone else.

Let me explain why these three realities doomed their relationship from the beginning.

Joe and Jane are now together, but the day-to-day demands make both of them tired and sometimes even depressed. These negative feelings make it almost impossible for Joe to pay attention to Jane, and Jane is too tired to give Joe the passion he thinks he needs. This causes them to start drifting apart, and that weakens Joe and Jane's relationship. Watch what happens next, and tell me that there really isn't an evil team.

As Joe is struggling with his feelings, he happens to notice hot Jane #2, who just happens to be ready, willing, and able to understand Joe's feelings. Joe pours out his heart to this new sympathetic Jane. That gives her the attention she needs, so she feels drawn to Joe. Joe starts spending more time with Jane #2, and that of course causes him to feel attracted to her. He pays even less attention to Jane #1, which causes her to feel betrayed. Joe and Jane then start fighting, and that puts even more stress on their relationship, until they eventually have no relationship. Joe then moves out and moves in with Jane #2 so they can start acting like married people.

Jane #1 feels devastated by Joe's betrayal—until someone else starts paying attention to her. This new attention causes Jane to think she's found someone who understands. A brand-new relationship develops when Joe #2 moves in with her and they start acting like married people. The same destructive cycle then starts over for both of them, only to end again in the same miserable way.

Can you see how confusing and disappointing this would be for the average Joe and Jane after this happens several times? I believe this is the reason the world you live in is in such a mess.

The world thinks following attractions or the evil team's plan will lead them to real happiness. It can't because it wasn't designed for happiness; it was designed for fun. Joe and Jane may have a few short moments of fun that they think is happiness, but it never lasts because happiness isn't in the evil team's plan. Their plan is designed to make you miserable, but they hide it by giving you a little fun along the way.

That brings us to a valid question: How has the evil team been able to hide the real purpose of their plan? They've learned how to use the God-given feelings that come as standard equipment with your body against you. God gave you all these wonderful feelings, but He also gave you a strict set of instructions on how and when you can use them. If you'll use your feelings as God intended, you'll experience true happiness. If you don't, you'll just enjoy a few moments of fun on your way to misery.

Can you see the difference between God's plan and the evil team's plan? Good.

$$\pi$$

THE EVIL TEAM'S plan is centered on you breaking the law of chastity. If you follow their plan, you take a dangerous shortcut in the relationship-building process. Relationships must be built step by step just like everything else in life.

Here's an example that may help you understand why shortcuts won't work. You're in sixth grade and doing quite well in school, so you decide to skip the rest of junior and senior high and enroll directly into college. That would save you time, effort, and money, but could it actually work? The answer is no. Even though you can walk through the doors into college, you're not ready for college.

My college example also applies to sexual relations. Your body will be capable of having relations before you're emotionally ready. If you're not ready, odds are good that you'll pay for it one way or another later on. The consequences of breaking the law of chastity are never good. I've already mentioned a few of these consequences, but there is one more that I need to explain.

The evil team wants you to believe that sexual relations cause people to fall in love. But it's exactly the opposite. According to God's plan, you fall in love first, and then you enjoy intimacy. But that's not what you see on TV and in the movies. In those make-believe worlds, two people meet in the morning, act like married people later that night, and tell each other they've fallen in love the next morning.

A classic example of this is in the movie *National Treasure* (directed by Jon Turteltaub [2004; Buena Vista Pictures], DVD) and its sequel. In the first movie, the two main characters meet and have an adventure for a few days, or maybe a week. Then the movie ends with them holding hands as they run up a hill toward a mansion. This causes us to think that this good-looking guy and gal will live happily ever after, doing what married people do. Is that what happened? We know it wasn't because of *National Treasure 2* (*National Treasure: Book of Secrets*, directed by Jon Turteltaub [2007; Walt Disney Studios Motion Pictures], DVD).

At the beginning of *National Treasure 2*, the good-looking guy isn't living with the good-looking girl in the mansion. She's living in the mansion, and he's living somewhere else. Why? They skipped most of the steps in the relationship-building process. They met, which is step one, and after a short time they started acting like married people, which is step five. They took a short-cut by skipping steps two, three, and four. And because they did, they weren't together in the next movie. What happened? They didn't really love each other. They weren't ready to be in a lasting relationship because they hadn't yet completed all the required relationship-building steps. Skipping steps caused them to love the feelings, not the person they were having the feelings with. Why? You can't truly love a person until you've completed all the relationship-building steps.

God wants you to have a successful marriage, and successful marriages are built step by step. Every step you complete increases the odds of success, while skipping steps decreases the odds of success. One way or another, you must learn to love your future husband or wife, and it's a lot easier to learn to love them before you experience sexual relations. Could it really be this easy? Yes, it can—if you're willing to follow God's plan. It's your choice. Please, please, please choose wisely.

REVIEW OF IMPORTANT POINTS

- God has a plan, and you must follow it if you want a successful life.
- God's plan requires you to marry and come together through physical intimacy to create bodies for His spirit children.
- Physical and emotional needs must be met before you can be happy.
- Sex before marriage satisfies your physical needs but won't satisfy your emotional needs.
- You can repent, but you can't change what's been done.
- You can avoid sexually transmitted diseases by living the law of chastity.
- Many of the things you see and hear in this world will encourage you to break the law of chastity.
- Guys are visual. Seeing creates thoughts, feelings, attractions, desires, and sometimes actions. Be careful what you look at.
- Strong attractions can bring people together, but those attractions are not love.
- God wants your marriage to be successful.

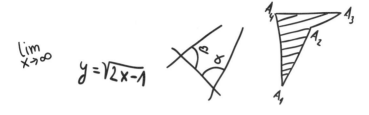

CHAPTER 22

NO NEED TO REINVENT THE WHEEL

ET'S PICK UP right where we left off. In the last chapter, I tried to convince you to follow God's relationship-building plan so you can enjoy real happiness. What is God's plan? He wants you to fall in love, marry, and join with your future husband or wife to bring new little spirits into the world. Then He wants you to work together to create a stable home environment where His spirit sons and daughters can grow up, meet someone, marry, and start the whole process over again. It sounds easy enough, so why would anyone want to reinvent the wheel?

Trying to reinvent the wheel means you try to find a new method when the old method works just fine. The wheel was invented a long time ago, and it has worked really well ever since when used the way it's intended. You could choose to ignore that it has worked and try to invent something to take its place. But why spend all that time and effort trying to replace something that works so well? Wouldn't that be a big waste?

The same principle applies when you try to replace God's relationship-building plan. His plan works every time it's used, so why look for a new plan? After all, God created the plan, so what could you, a mere mortal, do to improve it? I believe the answer is nothing.

If you're going to follow God's relationship-building plan, you must learn how to date. Dating can be fun and exciting, but learning how to date the right way is important. Dating determines whom you'll marry and whether you'll be able to stay married. I'm sure you plan on staying married, so let me show you how to increase the odds of success by learning how to date.

Let's start with a question. When should you start preparing for marriage? If you said, "Right before I get married," that's a good answer. But can you see a problem with it? How long do you think it will take you to prepare for marriage—one or two years? I can't say for sure, because everybody is different. Some may be able to prepare more quickly than others, but if you wait to start preparing until right before you want to get married, what will you have already been doing? A lot of dating. If you date without understanding how to date, will all of your dating experiences be good? No, they won't, but you'll still want to continue dating—at least for a little while. If your dating experiences continue to be bad, you'll eventually decide to give up. I've met with quite a few young people who had given up on dating because they had one bad experience after another, and that made them think living alone for the rest of their lives was better than dating. I don't want that to happen to you, so let me teach you how to date so you won't ever want to give up.

God's plan would fail if His sons and daughters were content to be alone, so He put an intense desire in each of us to be with someone else. You find your someone else by dating, and then you get married. Does your dating stop after marriage? No, it just changes.

When should you start preparing to date? According to God's plan, you should start preparing right after you enter into those wonderful, magical, exciting, but very dangerous teen years. When do you actually start dating? You've been counseled by a prophet of God to wait until after you're sixteen. Why sixteen? In God's plan, all physical relationships start with dating and end with marriage. If you start dating too early, you'll probably marry too early.

π

HAVE YOU HEARD of the steps of dating? If not, don't feel bad. You're not alone. I've asked a lot of other young people if they'd been taught the steps, and they all said no. This made me wonder if the steps of dating is one of the best-kept secrets in the world.

I discovered the steps a few years back when I taught a class on marriage and family relationships. I would like to say that I made them up, but I didn't. They came from a lesson manual I used when I taught that class. One day I was preparing my lesson, and there they were. When I read them, I thought, "This makes sense. Now I finally understand why things happen in relationships."

For instance, during the past few years, I've had opportunities to counsel individuals and couples who were having problems in their marriages. As I worked with them, I began to notice many of them had the same problem. They felt like they had lost most, if not all, the feelings of love they once had for each other. The fact that every couple seemed to have the same problem made me wonder if the consequences they were all suffering could have been caused by the same action. If that was possible, then I needed to find out what that action was so I could help them.

I decided to ask those I was working with questions about their past, and it didn't take long to find a common answer. The answer came almost by accident when one of the couples mentioned in passing that they'd had a few problems with immorality before they were married. Admitting it must have caused them to feel embarrassed, because they quickly added, "But we took care of it before we got married."

That one statement caused me to wonder if there could be a connection between immorality before marriage and problems after marriage. I decided to ask everyone if they'd had any problems before they were married. To my surprise, all of them admitted they had. I know my research was limited to a few couples struggling with the same problem, but I believe that's the reason they thought they had lost their love for each other, and here's why.

I believe these couples loved what they were doing, but they didn't love whom they were doing it with. Why? They thought passion and love feel the same, so those passionate feelings made them think they were in love. Then, after they thought they were in love, they skipped the rest of the dating steps and got married before real love could be created.

$$\pi$$

REAL LOVE CAN'T be created or sustained by passion alone. It has to be created by serving each other over an extended period of time, and it's easier to create before intense passion becomes part of your relationship.

The steps of dating are simple. In fact, they're so simple the evil team will tell you they can't work because they're too simple. Don't believe them. These simple steps work because they keep you from situations where you'll be tempted to skip steps. If you'll follow one simple rule, you can avoid all of these situations. The rule is this: if you're not there, it can't happen. It doesn't get any easier than that.

I can't count the number of times I've shared these simple steps with someone who chose not to follow them. After they had a problem, I'd ask, "Why didn't you follow the steps?"

They'd answer, "Because I didn't think they would work."

Just to make a point, I'd ask, "Why didn't you think they'd work?"

And they'd usually answer, "They were so simple, I thought they were no big deal."

"The reason they do work is because they're so simple," I'd say. "Now are you ready to listen?"

Are you ready to listen? I hope so. Sit back and relax while I teach you how easy it is to build your strong, secure marriage relationship using the steps of dating. By the way, you shouldn't try to complete the steps until after age twenty-something, because the steps are designed to help you get married. Until you reach that age, you're walking a fine line because you're physically ready for marriage and intimacy, but you're not emotionally ready for the responsibilities that come with it. Don't rush into marriage. If you want your marriage to be successful, you'll need time to develop the social skills required for a successful relationship.

"Don't rush into marriage?" I had to laugh because the evil team just reminded me I got married at eighteen. I did get married at eighteen, but that's not what I meant. It's true that eighteen is early, so you could say I rushed into marriage. But you can rush into marriage at any age. Take second marriages, for instance. A husband loses his wife and remarries in a month or two. Will that relationship last? It could, but the odds aren't good because the couple hasn't had time to go through the steps of dating.

Here's one more example. A guy and gal meet, and the fires of attraction pull them together, so they think they're in love. Since they're in love, they decide to marry in a few short weeks, or at best, a couple of months. Will their relationship last? Maybe, but again, odds say it won't because they didn't follow the steps of dating.

Why did I marry at eighteen? Times were different back then. We were more responsible than most of the eighteen-year-olds today, and we were in love. How's that for rationalization? Another one for the Rationalization Hall of Fame, don't you think?

Marrying too early is on one side of the fine line, but most of the young adults I worked with are on the other side of the line. They say, "I'm not getting married until I'm at least twenty-five. I need to finish my education, get a job, buy a car and a house, and have some time for me." The list of reasons can go on.

Is there anything wrong with thinking you'll wait until twenty-five? No, but you may want to consider these points. If you don't start seriously following the steps of dating until you're twenty-three or twenty-four, you're dangerously close to the twenty-six-year-old deadline. Finding someone to marry is easier if you do it before you turn twenty-six because the pool of available candidates is larger. Why? It's because you're usually still in school. After you graduate, you'll go to work at the same job every day, and that shrinks the pool of possible candidates to how many people you meet at work.

Here's the next point to consider. Let's say you marry at twenty-five and have a baby two years later. How old will you be when your child graduates from high school? You'll be approximately forty-five. How old will you be when your third child graduates? You'll be approximately fifty. What about your fifth child? You'll be approximately fifty-six. I bet when I mentioned your fifth child, you said, "Fifth child? I'm not having five children." Can you see how the evil team is influencing you?

You can marry anytime you want, and you can decide how many children you'll have, but this is my point. We married at eighteen, and we were blessed with three children. We wanted more, but that didn't matter because that's all we were given. Did they all come according to our timetable? No, they came when they were sent. Our kids also married early according to today's standards and have given us thirteen beautiful grandchildren. Because all this happened earlier than normal, we've been able to enjoy our grandkids because we were still young when they were born. Now we're both over sixty, and we can no longer physically do everything we'd like to do with them. We're glad we married early and had our kids early so we could do things with our grandchildren before we got too old. Our activities together have given us memories we'll cherish forever.

What side of that fine line should you walk? That's entirely up to you, but now you have some real-life experiences to use when you're making your choices. I can't say which side of the line is right for you, but I do know God's plan is the line. If you'll choose to follow the plan, it will put you right where God wants you to be, and that's the best you can hope for.

Once you've decided to walk the line, what should you do during your teenage years while you're waiting for your twenty-something birthday to arrive? I'd recommend you concentrate on doing well in school, have fun with different groups of friends, do some group dating so you can start making your list of qualifications you'd like your future spouse to have, be careful, and make sure you obey the commandments. If you'll do these things, the time to start the steps of dating will be here before you know it.

Did you hear the evil team tell you everything I just recommended, other than the activities with your friends, is going to be really boring? If you did, I want you to know that this time of life doesn't have to boring. In fact, it can and should be fun, exciting, and productive. Let me show you one way to really enjoy your teen years.

$$\pi$$

WHAT IS THE purpose of group dating? It should be fun, but there is another purpose: it gives you a chance to create your wish list of qualifications for your future eternal companion. For you to be able to create your list, group activities can't just be random activities. Each activity must be planned and executed for a specific reason. Here's how you do it.

You might think that doing an activity for a specific reason will be hard, but stop and think about what usually happens when you and your friends plan activities. You get together, and someone asks, "What do you want to do?"

Another says, "I don't know. What do you want to do?"

And doesn't that continue until the group decides to do something?

What if you sat down and made a list of things you'd like to do before you got together with the group? For instance, if you love to bowl, hike, bike ride, dance, or go to movies, wouldn't you want your future husband or wife to like those same activities? I'm sure you would, or should, because you're going to marry your best friend. Friendships are created by spending time together, and you'll spend more time together if you both like to do the same things. Planning your activities will help you find those who like the same things as you.

To make your group activity have purpose, simply select what you'd like to do and plan that activity. Then when you get together, you can suggest it to the group. Watch for those of the opposite sex who like to do the same thing. Chances are there will be more than one, so after the activity, go home and write some thoughts about the activity in your journal. Make a list of the people who liked the activity and your own feelings about the activity so you can remember it later. Making this list can be fun, and you can use it later to guide you to those who like the same activities when you start dating.

But here's a warning: never leave your journal out where it can be found and read by someone other than you. It must be for your eyes only so you can write your true feelings about each activity. What you write is strictly your business. Give it a try and see what happens.

How come everyone isn't planning activities this way? It's because the evil team isn't going to just stand idly by while you plan for your successful future. They know they only have a small amount of time to destroy you, so they'll always be there, looking for every possible opportunity to do it.

Be careful, be smart, and get excited about life. Plan to live each day with purpose, try hard to obey the commandments and repent quickly when you don't, and your teen years will be one of your best times of life.

π

THE TIME HAS finally arrived. You're now in your early twenties and ready to get serious about the next step in God's plan. The evil team will tell you finding someone to marry will be hard, but don't believe them. It will be challenging, but you can do it. It will be easier than you think if you'll learn and follow the steps of dating.

I'll explain each step before giving you the next one. This method may take longer, but it's the best way. If I give you the steps without explaining them, you may be tempted to think they're no big deal, and you won't follow them. I'm not going to make that mistake, so I'll explain each one in detail so you can understand why they must be followed.

Step 1: Select Ten Candidates for Marriage

When you enter your twenties, look at your group of friends and acquaintances, compare each one to your list of qualifications, and select approximately ten good candidates of the opposite sex. These shouldn't be only those you're physically attracted to, because you may overlook some good candidates.

This is the group you start with, but they're not all you get to choose from. You can replace any or all while you're dating. Getting to know each candidate well will take time, so ten is about all you'll have time for.

You do need to be careful as you make your list. People who are complete opposites are often attracted to each other, and that's fine as long as you can live with the differences after you're married. I've seen couples who enjoyed or just ignored their differences while they were dating, but they spent the rest of their lives trying to change each other after they were married. People rarely change unless they want to, so make sure you can live with the differences before you give your heart to that person.

You must also make sure your list of qualifications isn't too long or too specific, because you may never find anyone who fits your list. If your candidates have to be perfect, you won't find any candidates. Your candidates should be those you get along with, who have a similar level of education, who enjoy some of your hobbies, are fun to be with, and are attractive.

Did you notice the order of the requirements I listed for the members of your group? First, it's somebody you can get along with; then someone with a similar level of education, interests, and backgrounds; then fun to be with; and the last requirement is someone attractive. I listed the requirements in that order on purpose. Step one is all about making friends. If your friend is someone you get along with and someone with similar interests, background, and education, then you'll want to spend time together. Love can't grow unless you spend a lot of time together, so it only makes sense to put people in your group whom you want to spend time with.

Why did I put finding someone attractive last in the order of requirements? If you only put beautiful people in your group, what are you using to make your selections? You're using attractions. If you use only attractions, what's going to happen? You'll never get married, because there will always be someone better looking around the next corner, and that will keep you from making a final choice. Once you've gotten to know each member of your group, it's time to move to step number two.

$$\pi$$

Step 2: Cut Your Group Down to Five

After you've gotten to really know each candidate, select five and continue spending time with them. If somewhere along the way you find a new really good candidate, replace one in the existing group, but don't add more to your group.

Keeping some and letting others go will make you feel like you're abandoning your friends, but that's not what's happening. You're just focusing more on the other friends so you can deepen your friendship with them. How do you deepen your friendship? You spend more time with them, doing things you both like to do.

While you're together, ask each candidate how he or she feels about debt, family traditions, the future, schooling, children, vacations, and the list goes on. Asking questions helps you see clearly what you're getting into before you move beyond step two. If you need questions to ask, look at the list I've included in the back of this book.

Deepening friendships takes a lot of time, so don't let the evil team get you involved in other, less eternally important things like school, study abroad, travel, or career opportunities. All of these are good, but make sure you leave enough time in your schedule for dating. Additional opportunities in life are not always blessings if they stop you from building a successful relationship. The evil team doesn't want you to date, so they'll try to keep you really busy. They understand the law of unintended consequences better than you do, and they'll use it every chance they get.

Here's another important point. Today a lot of emphasis is placed on being compatible with your spouse. Fortunes have been made on the Internet matching couples with the same interests.

I believe these sites are helpful, but they're not really necessary if you're socially active. You can usually find someone to marry if you'll get involved in school, church, or sports activities. But remember this: if the person you're marrying really loves to do something, make sure you also like it or that you're okay with them doing it without you. Don't be fooled into believing they'll just leave it behind for you. They may do so for a while during the early part of the relationship, but those interests will become important to them again later on. Make sure you're okay with what they like before you move on to step number three.

Getting to know the members of your group is the main purpose for step number two. It's also the step many couples skip over because it takes up a lot of precious time. This step is where you gather information you can use to make a logical, intelligent, well-informed choice. I know love is all about feelings, and it's those feelings I'm trying to help you protect. You need to really know a person before—I'll repeat that—*before* you give your heart to them. In other words, before you decide to swallow the entire hook, line, and sinker. You need to protect your heart until you're sure it's safe to give it away, because once you've given it away, you're going to be miserable if your relationship doesn't work out and you have to take it back.

After you get to know each member of your group well by asking them all the questions, it's time to move on to step number three.

$$\pi$$

Step 3: Cut Your Group Down to Three

Cutting your group down to three will be difficult because you're now good friends with all of your candidates. But you still have to do it.

After you've chosen three good candidates, it's time to put on the blinders. Blinders are what they put on horses to keep them from getting distracted by everything around them. In today's world, there is beauty all around you, and that beauty will cause attractions. Attractions create feelings, and feelings can create confusion. The evil team understands this perfectly, so they are going make sure you notice every single beautiful person you come in contact with.

Since you live in a world where beauty is all around you and there's nothing you can do about it, let me teach you how to deal with it. First, recognize that beauty is real. No matter how hard you try, you're going to notice beauty. Trying to deny or ignore it would be like trying to tell yourself you don't need air. It exists, so just recognize it and focus all your effort toward controlling how it makes you feel.

Remember my desire to own a Shelby Mustang? No matter how bad I want it or how much I'm attracted to it, I must be willing to recognize I can't have it because it's not right for me. How do I keep myself from thinking about the Shelby Mustang? I don't spend time in the Ford showroom, and I don't let myself think about it when I see one on the street.

These are the same steps you'll use to control the feelings that come because you live in a world filled with beauty. Still not quite sure what I'm talking about? Let me spell it out for you. If you're a guy (remember, guys are visual) or even a girl with strong feelings, you need to try to stay out of the showrooms as much as you possibly can. The showrooms are the Internet, magazines, movies, the gym, or any one of the hundreds of places that display the beauty these people are blessed with. Can you stay completely out of the showrooms? No, but you still must try to do the best you can.

Now that you've made the hard choice and narrowed the field of candidates down to three, those candidates get all of your dating attention. You can still be friends with the others, but that's it. Put on the blinders and focus all your attention on the remaining three. Can you still take a person out and put a person in? You can, but if you do it often, you'll never get the job done. If you've followed the steps to this point, what could you possibly gain by changing? The grass always looks greener on the other side of the fence—until you get there. You now have three good candidates, so why take a chance on losing them for an unknown?

This is where the steps get even more difficult. By now you have deep feelings of friendship for each of your candidates, but you still can't give your heart away to any of them. You must first complete this step before you decide which lucky candidate gets your heart. To complete this step, pretend you're dating each one of your candidates exclusively. But don't tell them. In my day, we called this "going steady," but I don't know what you call it now. You might think this is dishonest, but it's not, because you're still just dating. You haven't committed to anyone yet. You're simply trying to decide which of the candidates is best for you by spending more time with each of them.

As you spend time together, look for clues that will help you know what living with them would actually be like. This would also be a great time to meet their families and watch how your candidate treats them, because that's how they'll treat you later on. After you've gathered enough information, make your choice and move onto step number four.

$$\pi$$

Step 4: Select Your Future Spouse

Now you can finally give your heart away. I can't explain how that happens, but don't worry, it'll just happen—if you follow the steps. After you've given your heart to your special someone, get engaged. But make the engagement short. I'd suggest maybe two or three months.

There are at least two good reasons for a short engagement. First, since you've followed the steps of dating, you already know everything there is to know about your future husband or wife, and you've made your choice. Don't give the evil team time to confuse or distract you.

The second reason is that all serious romantic relationships eventually end up in the bedroom. God's plan and the evil team's plan both end there—God's plan with intimacy and the evil team's with immorality. After you get engaged, the evil team is going to encourage you to follow God's plan—early. Which part? It's the intimacy part. They'll tell you that since you're getting married anyway, it's okay to start following His plan a little early. Don't give in to your intense physical desires, because that increases the odds of a future marriage failure and lessens your chances for a covenant temple marriage. What's the best rule? Never be in a place alone together where sexual relations could happen, because they'll probably happen. This why you want to decrease the odds by moving quickly to step number five.

$$\pi$$

Step 5: Set Your Date and Get Married—Quickly

You must get married quickly because the evil team will work overtime against you. Don't underestimate their desire to destroy everything you have worked so hard to get. They'll be right there for the rest of your life, trying to take it all away from you by tempting you to break your sacred marriage covenants. What's the best rule? It's the same one. Never be in a place where you could break your sacred vows and it will never happen—because you won't be there.

Breaking your covenants isn't the only way the evil team will try to destroy you. Here are a couple of their other favorites. First, the evil team will always be there to make sure you notice every single fault your new husband or wife may have. While you're dating, all their faults are kept safely hidden because you're not living with them. After you're married, you're going to be with them all the time, and that makes it impossible to keep anything hidden. Just know that all these different stages of a relationship are normal.

Here's another one of the evil team's relationship-destroying tricks. After some time—it's different for every relationship—your once-exciting, sometimes-heated passionate relationship will change. For instance, the physical passion that was once so exciting will become almost routine. You'll also begin to forget to do the little things you once did for each other. Holidays will no longer be special, you'll no longer do things you once liked to do together, and the list of possible problems goes on.

Although countless problems are possible, none of them need to happen. The best way to avoid them is to continue doing all of the wonderful, positive things that brought you together. Yes, it will require a lot of effort, but that effort is worth it because that's what feeds your love so it can keep growing.

Love is a funny thing. It's either constantly growing or constantly dying. The evil team will tell you that once you're married, all those wonderful things you did together are no longer important. Whatever you do, don't fall for that one. If you want your love to continue growing, you'll have to feed it every single day with the same food that brought you together in the first place.

A successful marriage will be the best time of your life, but the years you spend together will be sprinkled with times when it's not. As the days, months, and years pass, it will be normal for you to experience a few headaches, a few heartaches, and quite a bit of frustration—and that's why I added step number six.

π

Step 6: Never Take Your Eye off the Prize

What's the prize? Becoming like God. That's the end result of His plan, and that's why you're putting yourself through all this. If you never forget why you're doing it, you'll always be able to find enough strength to handle whatever life throws at you. It won't always be easy, but you can do it because you have a God on your side who loves you more than you'll ever be able to understand. He wants you to win the prize, and He's willing to help you, but He can't do it for you. Whether you succeed or fail is entirely up to you and your willingness to follow the plan. Are you willing? I hope so, but the choice is yours. Please choose wisely!

π

CAN YOU BELIEVE it? We finally made it through the steps of dating. I could end the chapter here, but I feel like I need to cover a couple more thoughts.

Did you notice I never mentioned *kissing*? I didn't mention it because it's not in the first three steps of dating, but what do you see people doing everywhere you look? Kissing—and sometimes kissing people they hardly know.

I'm not trying to depress you, but if you're really following the steps of dating, you only get one kiss while you're dating. Are you surprised? You read it right: you get just one kiss, and that kiss happens on the day you get engaged. Don't believe me? Well, you should, because you need to kiss your future spouse at least once before you get married.

Don't get offended. I was just trying to have some fun with you. Telling you that you only get one kiss while you're dating isn't true and I'm being silly, but I'm trying to emphasize an important point. Physical intimacy starts with one kiss and ends in the bedroom if you can't or won't stop kissing. Kisses mean something. If you start passing kisses out like candy, odds increase that you'll eventually find yourself wishing you hadn't done what you just did. I can't tell you how many times I've heard someone say, "We started kissing and . . ." I won't bother finishing the sentence. I've heard it finished in more ways than you can imagine, and few, if any, were good. I hope you'll trust me enough not to start kissing too early in a relationship. "Too early" may be different for everyone, but the longer you can keep kissing out of your relationship, the better your chances will be of completing all of the steps of dating.

Kissing or any type of physical passion may cause you to skip steps two, three, and four, and jump right to step five. Every step is important, so you can't skip any of them. Relationships must be built step by step, and for that to happen, you must keep passion—even moderate passion—out of your relationships until after step three. That means there should be no kissing until just before you take step four and little after that. Your feelings or your heart will always follow passion. If you're kissing passionately and often, you'll think you're in love, and that will take you to step five before you're ready.

This next thought is for the girls. Girls are different from boys because girls have feelings. Why don't I think boys have feelings? Blame it on my wife. She often tells me I have no feelings. I have feelings; I just don't use them the way she does. Girls think feelings mean something, and boys just want to feel good. Do you see the difference? Let's plug this difference into building a relationship.

Passion in a relationship creates intense feelings that make girls think they're in love. Girls in love, real or imagined, give their heart, soul, and body to the boy they love. What do boys do? Until a boy learns to really love a girl, passion to him is nothing more than recreation. He'll say he loves you, even if he doesn't, so you'll give him more passion. Passion makes boys feel good, but it doesn't make them love girls. Love comes from service, not passion. They can't love you until they serve you by going through the steps of dating. Until they finish, all they love is what they're doing with you.

This difference doesn't mean guys are bad; it just makes them sometimes act badly. Girls think boys love them, while boys use girls to feel good—until the next girl comes along. Then he'll dump the first girl and do the same thing with the next girl. Girls, if you don't want to experience heartache after heartache, make boys follow steps one through three of dating before you give them too much passion.

If you're thinking boys won't date you unless you give them passion, you might be right. Here's how you can beat them at their own game. Boys love passion, so when you find one that's a good prospect for marriage, go ahead and give him a little drive-by passion. What's that? When the boy wants to kiss you, quickly kiss him first, but just barely touch his lips and back away. Say to him, "I really like you, but that's all you get until after you take me out, spend money on me, and show me you love me. After you do that, I'll give you all the kisses you want." Then give him a quick hug and say, "Call me. I really enjoyed being with you. Let's go out again." Drive-by passion will work if he really likes you, but it won't if he's just looking for passion. If passion is all he wants, you don't want him anyway.

A young man must complete the first three steps of dating before passion becomes part of your relationship because the steps force him to court you. *Court* has nothing to do with volleyball, tennis, or basketball. When a boy courts you, he does nice things for you, hoping you'll eventually want to go out with him.

Courting is a necessary part of the relationship-building process, but it's been badly corrupted by the evil team. Their idea of courting is to meet someone in the morning, kiss them by afternoon, and then act like married people later that night. Their plan works great if all you're looking for is passion, heartache, loneliness, and disease. But if you're trying to marry and stay married, it's not the way to go.

Boys rarely court girls anymore because they don't have to. The time-tested roles that boys and girls have played in building relationships have changed. Back in the day, boys had to court girls before they would even consider going out with them. Today, boys have girls calling or coming on to them, and that's created a big unintended consequence. Girls, you won't understand, but a boy won't appreciate or value you unless he has to work for you.

Does this mean girls just have to sit there and look pretty? No. Girls must also work, but their work is different. They have to find ways to keep a boy interested without giving him passion. If you want a great relationship, limit passion in your relationship until after you've completed the first three steps of dating—even though you're both going to want it.

Another reason relationships have changed is that our current culture has forced a change in the way girls are raised. Again, back in the day, girls were raised to depend on boys to support them so they could stay at home and raise a family. That's not the case today. Girls are being raised so they don't have to depend on a boy. Why? In today's world, boys aren't growing up to become men. A man makes sacred commitments, and he keeps those commitments regardless of what life brings. In today's world, a large percent of men just walk away from their commitments the second they encounter a problem, leaving their wives and children behind.

Who created the problems we're now dealing with? Was it the boys or the girls? It doesn't matter. We are where we are, and that's exactly where the evil team wants us to be. Boys and girls are having problems getting married and staying married because they aren't taught the steps of dating. Failed marriages and fewer marriages mean fewer kids born and more kids being raised in single-parent homes.

If the evil team told you I just said single parents are bad, don't listen to them. They're not bad; they're just in a lifestyle God doesn't want them to be in. He wants His children to grow up, get married, enjoy intimacy, and have a family so His other spirit sons and daughters can come to earth and get bodies. He also wants them to have a good, stable home environment so they can grow up to be productive citizens, marry, and start the whole process over again. Single parents have to do this all by themselves, and that's hard. God's plan is easier if you're willing to follow it. Why you're a single parent really doesn't matter. It may be your life, but it doesn't need to be your kids' life if they'll follow the steps of dating.

My dear young women, you must never forget you are the prize. Make the young men in your life court you before you agree to go out with them. After they do, don't get passionate with them too quickly. Boys need to work for you before they can appreciate you. If they're willing to follow the steps of dating, odds are good that they'll love and cherish you forever. How do you keep them interested while they complete the first three steps? Give them a little drive-by passion and then give them a little physical contact.

Boys need physical contact, and a girl fills this need by holding his hand, sitting close to him, or just putting a hand on his arm. These actions tell him, without you saying a word, that you love him. Your touch has incredible power, so never underestimate the power of your touch.

If you aren't in a relationship, you may just have to take my word for it. But if you're in a relationship, think about what brought you together. Didn't it all start with touching? Didn't you love to sit close on the couch or in the car? Didn't you hold hands when you were walking, or put your arm around him when you were together? Didn't you want to run you hand through his hair or scratch his neck or his back while he was sitting next to you? The reason you did these things is that you love to touch each other. If you'll continue doing those things that brought you together, your relationship will continue to strengthen and grow.

π

HOW LONG DOES it take to complete each of the dating steps? There isn't a set time. Some steps may require more time than others, so don't worry about the time. Just complete each step before you move on to the next one. Some people spend years on the steps, while others spend little time. I flew through steps one and two in just a few minutes because I decided I wanted to marry my wife the minute I saw her in first grade. But she wasn't as excited about the prospect of marriage as I was. I must not have been good at courting, because she wouldn't have anything to do with me for ten years. In fact, to say I wasn't good at courting would be an understatement. Today they might call my idea of courting "stalking."

Getting her to marry me must have been quite an accomplishment because my high school classmates always ask, "Are you and Glenda still together?" The first few times this happened, I was stunned. I had never seriously considered living life any other way. I'd be lying to you if I told you I *never* had thoughts about giving up, but those thoughts are normal. The evil team isn't going to let you walk into the next life without a few headaches, heartaches, and negative thoughts. But even with those thoughts, I can say without a doubt that my marriage has been by far the best thing I've ever experienced.

If the evil team has been telling you, "The steps can't really be that important," don't listen to them. They are.

Do yourself a favor. Decide now to follow the steps. Then be smart, be careful, and stay away from passion for as long as you can, and odds are good that you'll have a successful, happy marriage. That's a big piece of the successful-life puzzle.

REVIEW OF IMPORTANT POINTS

- Start preparing for marriage when you start feeling attractions.
- Strictly follow God's dating plan. Don't start dating too early or too late.
- The law of chastity helps you learn to love the person you're with, not just what you're doing.

- Intense passion is not real love. Be careful with passion because it will blind you.
- Start group dating with a purpose at age sixteen. Begin the steps of dating as you enter your twenties.
- Follow the steps.
- Step one—Find a group of ten possible candidates for marriage.
- Step two—Cut the group to five. You can still replace members of the group.
- Step three—Cut the group to three and put on the blinders.
- Step four—Select your future spouse.
- Step five—Get married quickly!
- Step six—Never take your eye off the prize.
- Boys must work for things or they won't appreciate them after they get them.
- Eternal marriage is the prize!

$$A = \begin{pmatrix} 2 & -1 \\ -3 & -2 \end{pmatrix} \qquad y = \sqrt{2x-1}$$

δ

CHAPTER 23

PUTTING ALL THE PIECES TOGETHER

*D*O YOU REMEMBER when I likened life to a big puzzle with lots of different pieces? When you're putting a puzzle together, you take each piece and find where it fits in the puzzle. Then you do the same thing with all the other pieces until the puzzle is finished.

This is what I'll be doing in this chapter. I'll pick up each of the main pieces, identify it, and then put it into the puzzle. After the puzzle is complete, you'll know what you need to do to create your successful life.

The first piece of the puzzle of life is called *purpose*. If you understand the purpose of life, you'll know why you're here. What is the purpose of this life? There are two main purposes. First, you are here to gain knowledge. This life is nothing more than a giant classroom filled with opportunities to gain knowledge by under-going all types of different experiences. You need to be careful because some experiences are good, some are bad, and unfortu-nately, some are even terrible. All of these experiences are possible and even probable because you live in an imperfect world where everyone is making choices. All of these choices come together to create consequences you must experience—unless you change your choices.

You can control only your choices, so you can never let your guard down. You must be constantly watching for others' poor choices. If you're willing to watch and be careful, you'll find you can dodge a lot of potential problems because God is on your side. "On your side" means He will always be there to lead, guide, warn, protect, and prosper you while you're here on earth.

If you're not careful, or refuse to listen to God's warnings, you could (and probably will) experience a life-changing or possibly even a life-ending event.

π

GOD LOVES YOU. He didn't just drop you off on earth and say, "Good luck. See you sooner or later." He knew you would need a lot of help, so He sent His Son, Jesus Christ, to earth. He gave you a perfect example to follow, and through His Atonement, He paid for all of your mistakes (sins) before you even make them.

God also gave you a complete set of instructions called commandments. Obeying them is important. Doctrine and Covenants 82:10 states: "I, the Lord, am bound when ye do what I say; but when ye do not what I say, ye have no promise." What does He promise? He promised if you obey His commandments, you will prosper. He made you this promise, and He'll keep it.

If you choose to follow the commandments and listen to His Spirit, you'll miss most of life's bad experiences. Why? If you're not there, it can't happen. Commandments protect you by keeping you away from experiences that could create bad consequences.

π

IT'S ALSO IMPORTANT to recognize that there are other common-sense truths not based on the commandments. For instance, if you touch something hot, you'll get burned, or if you goof off in school, you won't get good grades.

There are more common-sense truths than you can count. You can learn them by experiencing everything yourself or by

256

watching others experience them. Watching others is better because it's a lot less painful.

π

GOD ALSO GAVE you coaches to teach you how to play the game. There are good and bad coaches. Coaches are parents, grandparents, Church leaders, teachers, coworkers, and friends. The good coaches love you and want to help you make it through life safely. The bad coaches don't care about your eternal salvation, so be careful.

All this information and spiritual help was given to you so you could have a good experience on earth while you prepare for the next life. All experiences have value because they give you knowledge that can be used in the next life. Listen to your good coaches, and they will help you gain knowledge without experiencing as many bad consequences.

π

LOOKING AT THIS life as a time to prepare for the next life is important because it helps you put experiences in their proper perspective. Proper perspective gives experiences correct meaning, purpose, and value, even when they make no sense whatsoever.

Without this proper perspective, you'll be tempted to ask *why* when bad experiences happen. Asking *why* is dangerous because the evil team will tell you bad things happen because God wants them to happen. God *allows* bad things to happen, but He doesn't *want* them to happen. If you think He wants bad things to happen, answer these two questions: Why did He give you commandments that keep you safe? And why does He send His Spirit to warn you before bad experiences happen? I promise you that He doesn't want bad things to happen to you—but He'll allow it if you refuse to obey and listen. Believing He wants you to experience bad things will damage your relationship with Him, and it will make it almost impossible for you to trust Him.

When good and bad things happen, simply ask, "What can I learn from this experience?" When you focus on learning, you'll find a purpose for the experience. Finding a purpose other than God wanting it to happen allows you to go to Him in perfect faith and ask Him to help you when it's bad, and it reminds you to thank Him when it's good. This is how learning to ask *what* instead of *why* protects your relationship with God.

π

AFTER YOU LEARN how to keep your relationship with God strong, you must try to focus on things that have eternal value. Life is full of all kinds of opportunities to gain knowledge, but many of them won't bring you closer to God. When you do things that have eternal value, you'll grow closer to God, and that allows Him to come closer to you. This relationship will continue to grow until you're able to trust Him enough to let Him lead you through life.

How do you find things that have eternal value? In Doctrine and Covenants 46:7, the Lord said that you should be "considering the end of your salvation." This means you must always look honestly at what you're doing to see if it will matter in the next life. In life you'll have opportunities to travel countless different roads, and they all will eventually end someplace. When you're sitting in an intersection of choice, make sure you look at where each possible choice or road will end before you choose. Then choose the roads that give you experiences that have eternal value.

Choosing the right roads will be easier when you have a destination or goal in mind. Why? You can't know when you get there unless you know where you're going. If you make choices without a goal in mind, all your roads are going to lead to the same place, and that place is *somewhere. Somewhere* must not be great because I can't count the times I've heard someone wish they could do it all over again.

π

HOW DO YOU set a goal so you won't end up wishing you could do it all over again? First you must decide what you want, and then make sure it has eternal value so it fits within the purpose of life. Next, you need to make a list of smaller goals that will help you reach your main goal.

Reaching your goals won't always be easy. It will require you to put forth a lot of effort and determination. The evil team is also going to try to stop you by discouraging you. They'll tell you that you can't do it or that it's going to be too hard or too boring.

They'll also try to mislead you by making all their thoughts and feelings sound or feel good—if not better—than the feelings and thoughts coming from the Spirit. Don't listen to them. They are not your friends, and they never tell you the whole truth. Their one and only purpose is to stop you from reaching your goal of becoming successful.

While working on a goal, you can keep from becoming discouraged by choosing to have faith and hope as you work on it one day at a time.

$$\pi$$

WHILE YOU'RE WORKING on your goals, never forget that this life is a lot like football. Be careful. Never allow yourself to forget for even for a moment the law of probability and outcome. This law is chiseled in stone. It simply states that once an action is taken, one or more consequences will follow. They may or may not come immediately, but they will come.

The evil team will tell you that you can do whatever whenever and there will be no consequences. Don't believe them. Once actions are taken, the consequences are set into motion. If they're bad, God won't change them, but He will try to get you to change your choices so the consequences can also change. This is how He helps you avoid problems in life.

$$\pi$$

GOD LOVES YOU more than you could ever imagine, and He wants you to prosper in life. *Prosper* has many meanings, but all of them include the word *better.* Better means your life will be better than it otherwise would have been, but it doesn't mean your life will be trouble free.

God helps you prosper by sending you thoughts and feelings through His Spirit to help you make good choices. The evil team also sends you thoughts and feelings, so make sure you're not just looking for those that sound or feel good. The word *good,* like the word *prosper,* has many different meanings.

What makes one choice feel better than another? The one you want always feels better than the one you don't want, and that's what creates the problem. The evil team will always try to make their choice feel better by including some temporary form of physical or mental gratification. If you don't want to be deceived, you must look past this temporary good feeling.

Remember, fun always ends. Having fun is an essential part of life, but you can't live just to have fun. You must quickly learn the difference between fun and happiness before you have too much fun, or you may never find real happiness. Finding real happiness is easy, if you'll just slow down long enough to see where each road leads. If the good feeling ends, it's just fun. If the good feeling continues, it's happiness. Make sure each road leads to happiness before you choose it. You do this by learning to *sort out your thoughts.*

$$\pi$$

SORTING YOUR THOUGHTS allows you to see the end from the beginning. Seeing the end will help you make better choices and experience better consequences; better consequences increase your faith and confidence. More faith allows the thoughts and feelings that come from God to become more noticeable, and that helps you make even more good choices, which create more good consequences. Can you see the cycle of certainty?

$$\pi$$

NOW THAT YOU understand how feelings help you make choices and how choices determine consequences, you must decide what type of consequences you want to experience. If you want more good ones, make more good choices each day. More good choices create more good consequences, and that leaves you with less time to experience bad consequences.

You also must recognize that little actions can make a big difference in the consequences you experience. If you'll consistently do little, seemingly inconsequential things like making good choices, obeying the law, fastening your seat belt, or wearing a helmet, you'll be able to control the severity of many of the events you experience in life. Never forget that you live in a tough, unforgiving world, so be smart and don't do dumb things.

In life there are just two ways for you to learn truths and gain knowledge. You can use other people's experiences, or you can choose to experience everything yourself. I hope you will choose to learn as much as possible from others' experiences, because it's safer and a lot less painful.

$$\pi$$

I'VE NOW COMPLETED the review of the spiritual or thinking part of the successful-life puzzle. I'll finish the puzzle by reviewing how you can control the beast or the physical part of you.

$$\pi$$

YOU ARE A spirit son or daughter of God having a get-my-body experience. I liken your body to a beast because it often acts like a stubborn, hard-to-control animal. All it cares about is whatever makes it feel good, and that is why your spirit must win the spirit-versus-body battle. You must learn to control your body because it can't and won't control itself. Bodies out of control are the main cause of misery in today's world.

$$\pi$$

YOUR BODY CAME with a long list of standard equipment. Some items on the list can be seen, but most are hidden inside. Two important items on the list you can't see are physical and emotional feelings. Both types can make you feel good or bad, but they're as different as night and day. Physical feelings are created by your physical body, while emotional feelings are created by your brain.

Most of your physical and emotional feelings are created by the choices you make. The others are created by other people's choices. You can control your choices, but you can't control theirs. You can only control how they make you feel. If you'll develop positive self-esteem, you'll have control over all your feelings.

$$\pi$$

YOU ARE A spirit son or daughter of God. You lived with Him before you came to earth. Your Heavenly Father and Mother created you. As your spirit grew, you developed many abilities and character traits. These abilities and traits came with you when you were born. You also received other traits from your earthly parents, from ancestors, and from the way you were raised. The way you look, act, and feel came from your earthly ancestors. This is why you are you. What you decide to do with you now is entirely up to you.

Regardless of who you are, try to be at peace with who you are while you work on what needs to be changed. Some changes are easy and some are hard, but you can improve because God is on your side. Being willing to improve is a big piece of the successful-life puzzle.

$$\pi$$

YOUR BODY IS an amazing machine. If you feed it the right fuel, exercise it, and fix it when it can't fix itself, it will give you years of trouble-free operation—most of the time. There are times when you do everything right and still get a life-threatening or life-ending disease. This is one of the tests of mortality, and you'll pass or fail by how you handle it. Will you remain positive and learn from the experience, or will you become bitter, resentful, and discouraged? I really hope you'll never have to find out.

$$\pi$$

YOUR AMAZING MACHINE came with five basic senses. It can see, hear, smell, touch, and feel. You use these senses to create experiences that teach your spirit truths. These truths then create knowledge, and knowledge prepares you for the next life.

Your parents' experiences are a great resource of knowledge. The evil team will tell you that you don't need your parents. That's half true. Teens no longer need their parent to survive, but they do need their parents' experience to help them make good choices. You can get a lot of knowledge from your parents' experiences. Listen to them, appreciate them, and thank them every chance you get. They really do go through a lot for you.

$$\pi$$

IN ADDITION TO the five basic senses, your body can also create new life. This ability is sacred. The evil team understands this, so they've taken this sacred act of intimacy between husbands and wives, counterfeited it, and cheapened it. Heavenly Father calls their plan immorality. He has given us a strict set of rules on how, where, and when intimacy can be used to protect us. Following these rules is another big piece of the successful-life puzzle.

As you grow, your body will be physically ready for intimacy years before you're emotionally ready. Your teen years are precious because they give you time to prepare for all the responsibilities that come with physical intimacy.

$$\pi$$

YOUR LIFE WILL be divided into five time periods. Period one begins at birth and ends when you're able to survive without your mom. Then period two begins, and it ends when you enter your teens. Period three begins in your teens and ends right after you marry. Period four is when you raise your family. Period five begins after your family is raised, and it ends when your life ends.

During period one and two, you spend your life doing what kids do. Period three, or your teens, is when life gets interesting. This is a critical period of time because it usually sets the course you'll travel for the rest of your life. During this time, the evil team will be working overtime, so please listen to your parents. Follow dating step one, work hard in school, make sure you obey all the commandments, and trust the repentance process enough to use it when you don't obey. If you will do these simple things, your teen years will be fun and exciting. If you won't, then all I can say is good luck.

$$\pi$$

AS YOU APPROACH your early twenty-something birthday, start following dating step two. Each step is important, so don't skip any of them. Make sure you keep passion out of your relationships for as long as possible. Your heart will follow passion, meaning you'll think you're in love, but you aren't. Real love must be created through acts of service over time. How much time? There is no set time. Just follow each of the steps, and everything will work out just fine. Why? God created the plan, and He doesn't make mistakes.

$$\pi$$

THIS COMPLETES OUR review. Again, I'm sure I've missed a few of the pieces up to this point, but I think I've given you enough to keep yourself out of trouble until you find them.

In the next chapter, I'll add the final three pieces and finish the successful-life puzzle.

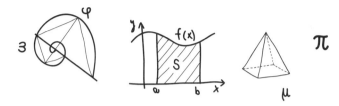

CHAPTER 24

USE YOUR FAITH—
CHOOSE TO BELIEVE

THE END IS near. You may not recognize the humor in that phrase unless you're older. If you're older, you've probably heard the end—meaning the end of the world as we know it—is near more times than you can count. But I'm going to let you in on a secret. The end really is near—or nearer than it was yesterday, and the day before that. So in that sense, the end is nearer!

Actually, it doesn't matter when the end is coming. All that matters is you believe the end is coming. All games have a beginning and an end, so try to use the time you've been given now to prepare. If you're prepared, odds will increase that you'll enjoy success in this life, and in the life to come.

Did you hear what I just heard? The evil team said, "How can you really prepare? You don't know what's going to happen in this life or the next life!" These guys never give up, but can you see what they're doing? They're planting seeds of doubt. Why? Doubt destroys faith. What, or who, don't they want you having faith in? They don't want you having faith in God or His Son, Jesus Christ.

I hate to admit it, but the evil team is right. You can't know for certain what your future holds, but you can control *almost* all of it using three simple steps:

- Choose to have and use faith.
- Choose to believe God loves you.
- Choose to believe Jesus Christ is going to save you.

Don't let *almost* make you feel uncomfortable. When you're playing the odds, *almost* is really close to a sure thing. Why? This world uses probability and outcome to teach you truths. If you'll increase the probability of good experiences by making more good choices, you'll have less time for bad experiences. Could it really be this easy?

π

THE FIRST SIMPLE step is to learn to have and use faith. Faith is the glue that holds all the other pieces of the successful-life puzzle together. Since you're already using faith every day to get things done, can you even begin to imagine what you could do if you started using faith on purpose? Decide what you want by creating your goals, ask God for help, believe the help will come, and then go to work, and it will happen. Can you see now why the evil team doesn't want you to use faith?

A successful life isn't created in a day, but it can be enjoyed every day if you'll choose to have and use faith.

The next step requires you to believe God loves you. How? Use your faith and choose to believe. This is important because it allows you to separate the everyday experiences of life from God's will. If you can keep life's experiences and God's will separate, you'll always be able to go to Him in faith when you need help.

How can you know He loves you? Everything in life begins with a choice. If you'll use faith to choose to believe, He will help you. When He helps you, you'll see that your experiences are better. Your better experiences help you recognize that He loves you.

Never forget this rule: The amount of faith you have and use determines the amount of help you can receive. How much help is possible? The only limit is what you're willing to receive.

The last step requires you to use your faith to believe in Jesus Christ and believe that He'll do what He said He will do. Believing in Him means you believe that He lived, died, and was resurrected for you.

Believing Him means you know He is going to save you, regardless of the challenges you face and the mistakes (sins) you make. How can He save you? He is full of grace.

When I was young, I wasn't comfortable with Him being full of grace, because I thought grace was a feminine character trait. Now that I understand that grace means forgiveness, I couldn't be happier. Since He's full of grace, or forgiveness, He will fully forgive my sins—if I'm willing to accept His forgiveness.

How can I show I'm willing to accept His forgiveness? I can be humble, which isn't hard when I remember I can't save myself, even after all I can do. I can also show I'm humble by using the repentance process daily, which also isn't hard if I'm willing to recognize that God—even though He's my loving, caring Father—must honor the law of justice. Lucky for me, He also honors the law of mercy.

The law of justice demands that I pay for all of my sins, unless I'm willing to repent. In Doctrine and Covenants 19:16–18 we learn that Jesus Christ paid for my sins so I wouldn't have to suffer, if I'm willing to repent. Verse 18 describes His suffering: "Which suffering caused myself, even God, the greatest of all, to tremble because of pain." This verse and others like it have motivated me to put the repentance process at the top of my priority list.

At some point between the Garden of Gethsemane and the end of His life on the cross, Jesus Christ paid for every single sin I've committed and will commit. I don't understand how His act of love satisfied the demands of the law of justice, but it did. I feel bad that I've caused Him pain, so I decided to make my relationship with Him personal. Here's what I mean.

The Savior paid for all my sins, but He didn't have to suffer for the sins I didn't commit. When the evil team is tempting me today, I can lessen the suffering my Savior experienced back then by choosing not to sin now.

Thinking you now control what He experienced back then could make your head spin, but it doesn't need to. You don't have to understand it. You just have to choose to believe it. Now let's jump ahead to Judgment Day.

I believe that someday soon, I'll be standing at the judgment bar of God. Because I'm trying hard not to sin and repent quickly when I do, the Savior is going to say, "Ted, I've got your sins covered. You made it. Go to the celestial kingdom." When I hear those words, I'm sure that I'll fall to His feet and wash them with tears of gratitude.

The Savior will allow it for a few seconds, but then He'll reach down, pull me to my feet, and say as He hugs me, "Okay, you'll have plenty of time to thank me later. You better get going, because there's a really long line behind you." I will then reluctantly leave, but as I'm walking to the door, He'll say, "By the way, thank you."

I'll say, "Why are you thanking me? You just saved me."

"Do you remember those few times you told the evil team no when they tempted you?"

"Yes, I do remember a few times."

He'll say, "Thank you. I didn't have to suffer for those sins."

Please don't think I'm being disrespectful in any way. All I'm trying to do is make my future experience real. I really do appreciate what my Savior went through for me when He paid for my sins. I also fully understand that I'll be doing all the thanking on that day, but thinking of it this way reminds me that I can lessen His suffering then by choosing to not sin today. That's how I've made my relationship with my Savior personal.

I would encourage you to also make your relationship with the Savior personal by trying hard to not sin. I hope you'll choose to look at your relationship with the Savior this new way. If you will, you'll receive great blessings in the form of better consequences in this life—and in the next life.

As you live life, please try hard to not sin. When you do, learn from your mistake, show you believe the Savior by using the repentance process, and keep moving forward. Don't look back and don't get discouraged. He said He will save you, and He will if you'll let Him.

Finding a road that leads to a successful life is easy, but making yourself actually follow it isn't. The evil team doesn't want you to be successful, so they'll try every day to discourage, distract, and depress you. Don't listen to them.

If you'll put your trust in God, and focus on things that have eternal value each and every day, you will be able to create your successful life one day at a time. Remember, there are no days off. Every single choice, great or small, really does matter, so please choose wisely!

π

THIS BOOK WAS written to help you make it through your teen years. Why do I want to help you when I don't know you? I have a Christlike love for you. And because I do, I fear for you. Please don't underestimate the evil team's desire or ability to destroy you. They're not your friends, and they're not nice. Their purpose is to stop you from scoring points, and they'll try to knock you completely out of the game of life, so please be careful.

Never forget that regardless of what life in this imperfect world brings, you can win the game of life because you have God on your side. He loves you and wants you to win. He will lead, guide, protect, and prosper you. But He can't, and won't, play for you. You're the player in the game of life, so get out there, play hard, play smart, play to win, and have fun. You only live once—so make every day count!

Well, you made it to the end of the book. You now know what to do, so what are you waiting for? Good luck and best blessings for you and those you love while you're creating your successful life!

QUESTIONS TO ASK WHILE DATING

THE REASON YOU date is to gather information so you can make a good, well-informed choice later on. Dates in our fast-paced, media-driven world often include movies, concerts, and other activities that limit the amount of time you have to talk. These questions will give you a reason to talk and to listen. The first step in building relationships requires you to find a group of friends who think and act like you, and that can't happen until you get to know each other. Some of these questions can be asked on the first date, but others shouldn't be asked until your relationship deepens. I hope they help you find your eternal companion.

- Where were you born, and where did you grow up?
  Their family, background, and culture should be similar to yours. Differences may be exciting at first but hard to live with after you're married.

- How many brothers and sisters do you have? Are you the oldest, youngest, or in between?
  Family size often explains behavior. An older sibling will be more dominant, a younger sibling more passive. It also could determine the size of your future family.

- What do your parents do for a living? What do you want to do?

  Lifestyles are created by income and spending habits, and habits are hard to break. Work ethic and the type of profession are important because different professions have different responsibilities. Doctors work long hours, and salesmen are paid on commission. Hourly workers get paid every two weeks, but they get paid less. Make sure you can live in your future lifestyle before you jump into that lifestyle.

- What are your hobbies?

  Friends marry, and to become friends you must spend time together. Hobbies allow you to spend more time together. If you don't share hobbies, make sure you're comfortable with theirs before you give your heart to them.

- What kind of movies, music, and books do you like?

  What they watch, listen to, and read are their interests. Make sure yours are similar, or you won't feel comfortable around them.

- What are your favorite foods?

  If you love meat, don't marry a vegetarian. Different cultures also have different eating habits, so make sure your lifestyles are similar.

- What are your political views? How do you feel about our country?

  Politics often make strange bedfellows, but they also create bitter enemies. Political beliefs can be strong or nonexistent in families. Make sure you know what you're getting yourself into before you join the family.

- What are your goals?

  Early in a relationship, goals are often pushed aside, only to reappear after the newness of the relationship wears off. Make sure you have similar goals.

- Are you a "glass half full" or a "glass half empty" person?

A "glass half empty" person is cautious and will always play it safe. A "glass half full" person is optimistic and will take risks. Opposites do attract, and from an eternal perspective, it makes perfect sense. A cautious person needs an optimistic person to help them grow, and an optimistic person needs a cautious person to keep them under control. Add the two together and you meet in the middle, but that will create conflict.

- Where do you want to live?
  Your spouse will want to live somewhere. Make sure you also want to live there.

- What are your favorite sports and teams?
  One key to a successful marriage is finding time to spend together. What you like and what they like isn't as important as you being together. This will require you to be willing to do things you'd rather not do so you can be together.

- Do you believe in God? Do you belong to a religion?
  Religion will play a big part in the way you raise your kids, and it will affect their perspective on life. Religions and perspectives don't usually end a marriage, but they determine your happiness in marriage.

- How do you feel about debt? How do you feel about credit cards?
  Money can be a blessing if it's handled correctly, and it can be a curse if it's not. The correct answers could be, "I don't like debt, and I only use my credit card in an emergency."

- Do you like to play games? Which games?
  Games tell you about their personality. If they like board games, they might be a "glass half empty" person. If they like fast-action, high-graphic computer games, they might have a "glass half full" personality. Friends often like to play the same type of games.

- What is your favorite and least favorite season?

Older couples often travel to different climates during the year. If you love the snow and the cold, don't marry someone who looks forward to spending every winter in Arizona.

- How do you plan on supporting your family? (Question to guys.)
  Money problems are a major cause of divorce. Money will also determine whether your wife works, how many kids you can have, the home and neighborhood you'll live in, the schools your kids can attend, and the cars you will drive. All things money must be considered before you give your heart away.

- Who will manage the money? Is it yours, mine, or ours?
  Ask every question you can think of that relates to money. After you get the answers, work out a compromise that's acceptable to both of you before you get too serious. Also decide who will do the bookkeeping before you marry.

- Should we rent or buy a home? What size, when, and where?
  Homes will be your largest purchase. Make a plan before you marry. You can also use this question to open up a discussion about your budget.

- How many children do you want, and when do you want to have them?
  You must ask this question before you give your heart away, but it's not a question you would ask on your first few dates.

- How do you feel about new cars, clothes, shoes, jewelry, guns, electronics, food storage, and any other essential and nonessential purchases?
  These questions should be asked before you set your date to marry. They'll help you avoid a lot of hurt feelings on anniversaries and birthdays.

$$\pi$$

QUESTIONS TO ASK WHILE DATING

HERE IS A list of other important questions:

- How should we plan for the future?
- Should we have a retirement account?
- How much should we save each month?
- Do you want to make charitable and political donations?
- Do you pay your tithing on the gross or net?
- How will we discipline our kids?
- Do you favor physical discipline?
- Is our kids' schooling important to you?
- Will our kids attend private or public school, or will they be homeschooled?
- How can we teach our kids to respect their parents and grandparents?
- Is it important to spend time with extended family?
- Should we visit family once, twice, or three times every week?
- Should we vacation with family?
- Should we give family financial help?
- Should we ever let our parents live with us?

The list of questions you could ask is long, so use your imagination. Try to imagine situations that could arise in marriage that could create conflict. Most topics can and should be discussed during the early stages of dating. Why? You want to know the answers before you get too serious. The answers you get will help you make a well-informed choice.

Is every answer a game changer? Should you discontinue the relationship if every answer doesn't match how you feel? I can't answer those questions because I'm not you, but I can tell you that any committed couple can find room for compromise on almost any issue if they'll both keep an open mind during the discussion. Find the point of compromise before you marry.

You and only you should decide whom you will marry. If you want to make a good choice, use this one simple rule to guide you: Before you decide to keep them, make sure you can live with them. If you'll follow that rule, everything should work out fine—if you never take your eye off the prize.

TED PECK HAS taught seminary for The Church of Jesus Christ of Latter-day Saints for over ten years and has served as bishop of his home ward and a college campus singles ward, working with many young people. He's watched his three children and thirteen grandchildren grow and face their own life choices. Being married to his childhood sweetheart for forty-four years has taught him things he never imagined he would learn, and today the two of them are serving as a senior missionary couple for the Church.

0 26575 16379 7